D0818203

dirt candy

A COOKBOOK

dirt
candy
A COOKBOOK

flavor-forward food from the upstart
new york city **vegetarian** restaurant

AMANDA COHEN & RYAN DUNLAVEY
with grady hendrix

Clarkson Potter/Publishers
New York

Copyright © 2012 by Amanda Cohen
Artwork copyright © 2012 by Ryan Dunlavey

All rights reserved.
Published in the United States by Clarkson Potter/Publishers, an imprint of the
Crown Publishing Group, a division of Random House, Inc., New York.
www.crownpublishing.com
www.clarksonpotter.com

CLARKSON POTTER is a trademark and POTTER with colophon is a registered
trademark of Random House, Inc.

Library of Congress Cataloging-in-Publication Data
Cohen, Amanda.
Dirt Candy: a cookbook/Amanda Cohen and Ryan Dunlavey with Grady Hendrix.
     p. cm.
  Includes index.
  1. Vegetarian cooking. 2. Vegan cooking. 3. Dirt Candy (Restaurant) I. Dunlavey,
Ryan. II. Hendrix, Grady. III. Title.
 TX837.C543 2012
 641.5'636—dc23   2011047331

ISBN 978-0-307-95217-2
eISBN 978-0-307-95218-9

Printed in the United States of America

Book and cover design by Ashley Tucker
Book and cover illustrations by Ryan Dunlavey

10 9 8 7 6

First Edition

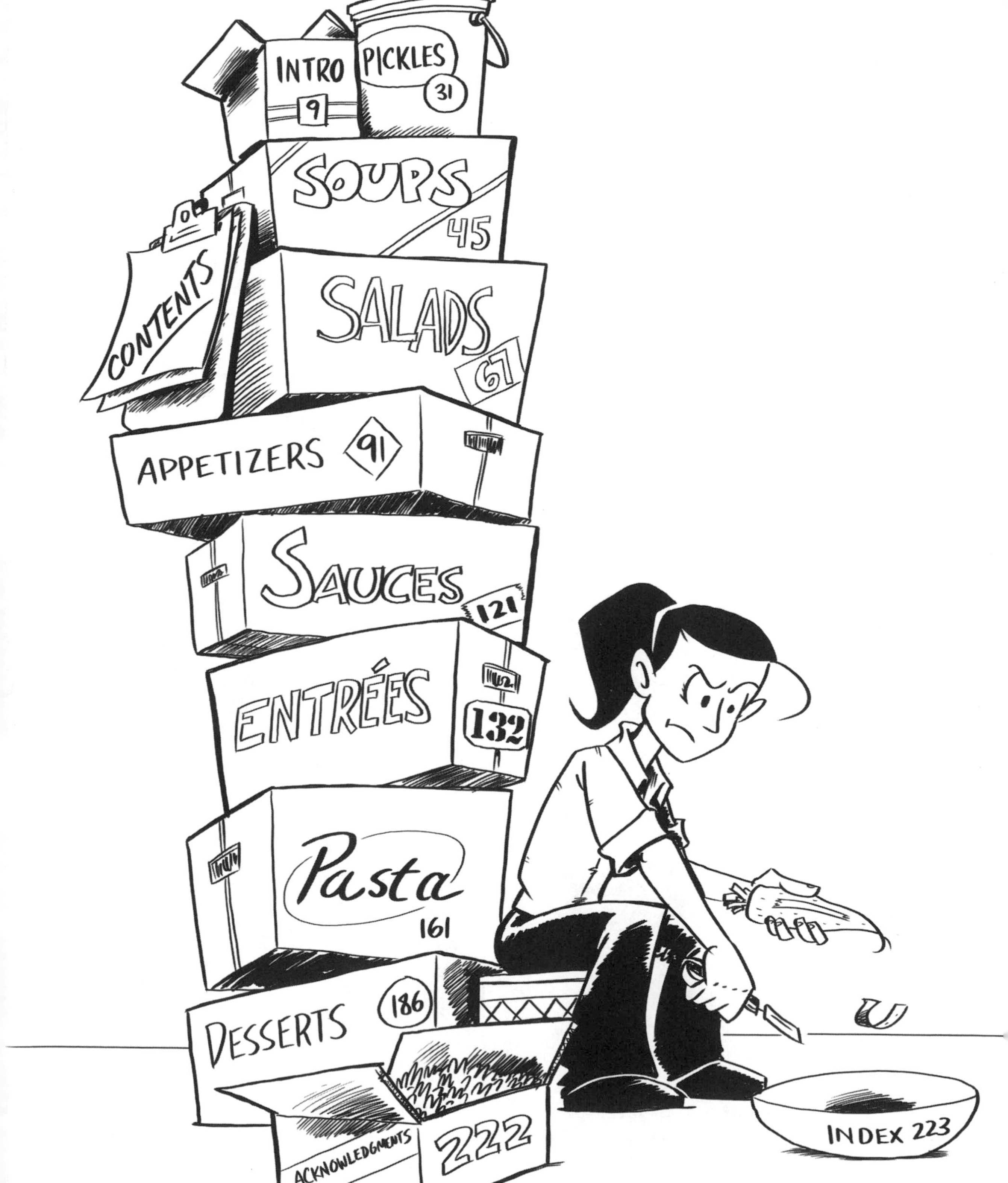

CONTENTS
INTRO
9
PICKLES
31
SOUPS
45
SALADS
67
APPETIZERS
91
SAUCES
121
ENTRÉES
132
Pasta
161
DESSERTS
186
ACKNOWLEDGMENTS
222
INDEX 223

I'M AMANDA AND I OWN DIRT CANDY.

IT'S AN ALL-VEGETABLE RESTAURANT IN NEW YORK CITY'S EAST VILLAGE. I WANTED PEOPLE TO THINK OF VEGETABLES AS A *TREAT*, AS SOMETHING *FUN*. LIKE CANDY FROM THE DIRT.

I ALSO WANTED A NAME PEOPLE WOULD *REMEMBER*.

SNAP!

It only has nine tables and my staff is *tiny*: two waiters (Diana and Kristen), one sous chef (Jesus), one dishwasher (William), and one prep chef (Danielle).

IT'S GOTTEN WAY MORE ATTENTION THAN A RESTAURANT WITH ONLY 18 SEATS SHOULD: AWARDS, GREAT PRESS, A LOT OF REGULARS. SO PEOPLE THINK I'M SOME KIND OF HIGH ROLLING CELEBRITY CHEF.

BUT IT'S A *TON* OF WORK. I'M ON THE LINE EVERY NIGHT, I WAIT ON TABLES WITH MY SERVER, I UNCLOG THE TOILETS.

MY 5-YEAR OLD SELF WOULD BE DISAPPOINTED. SHE THOUGHT I'D BE A PRINCESS BY NOW.

YOU'RE *NOT* A PRINCESS?

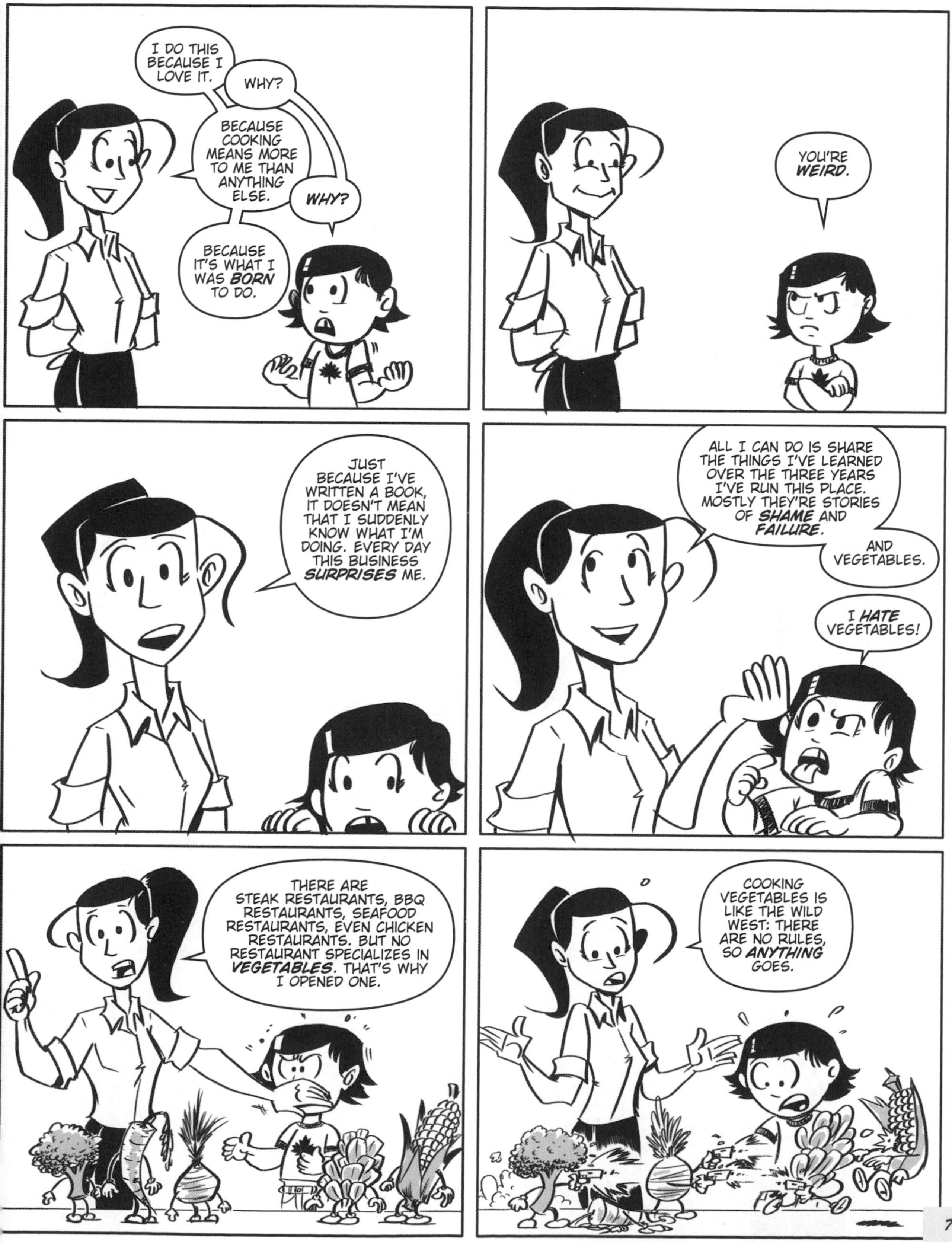
I DO THIS BECAUSE I LOVE IT.
WHY?
BECAUSE COOKING MEANS MORE TO ME THAN ANYTHING ELSE.
WHY?
BECAUSE IT'S WHAT I WAS BORN TO DO.
YOU'RE WEIRD.
JUST BECAUSE I'VE WRITTEN A BOOK, IT DOESN'T MEAN THAT I SUDDENLY KNOW WHAT I'M DOING. EVERY DAY THIS BUSINESS SURPRISES ME.
ALL I CAN DO IS SHARE THE THINGS I'VE LEARNED OVER THE THREE YEARS I'VE RUN THIS PLACE. MOSTLY THEY'RE STORIES OF SHAME AND FAILURE.
AND VEGETABLES.
I HATE VEGETABLES!
THERE ARE STEAK RESTAURANTS, BBQ RESTAURANTS, SEAFOOD RESTAURANTS, EVEN CHICKEN RESTAURANTS. BUT NO RESTAURANT SPECIALIZES IN VEGETABLES. THAT'S WHY I OPENED ONE.
COOKING VEGETABLES IS LIKE THE WILD WEST: THERE ARE NO RULES, SO ANYTHING GOES.

VEGETABLES WILL MESS WITH YOUR HEAD. ONCE I STARTED MAKING THEM THE CENTER OF MEALS I BEGAN TO REALIZE HOW *LITTLE* I KNEW.

AFTER TEN YEARS OF COOKING VEGETABLES I'VE HAD TO LEARN HOW TO CONTROL THEM BETTER. HOW TO KEEP THEM *BRIGHT* AND *CRISP*, RATHER THAN GOING ALL *GRAY* AND *SOGGY*.

FOCUSING ON VEGETABLES CHANGED THE WAY I THOUGHT ABOUT FOOD, AND THAT'S WHAT THIS BOOK IS: WHAT I'VE LEARNED FROM YEARS OF RUNNING A RESTAURANT AND COOKING VEGETABLES.

I SAID I *HATE* VEGETABLES!!!

MAYBE THE BOOK WILL EXPLAIN HOW WE ENDED UP HERE?!

YOU SHOULD HAVE BEEN A *PRINCESS* INSTEAD.

THIS BOOK BETTER HAVE SOME *MONKEYS* IN IT. OR SOME COOL *MONSTERS*.

AMANDA
Executive Chef/Owner

SKILL LEVEL: HIGH
RELIABILITY: GOOD
COMMUNICATION SKILLS: HIGH
GOAL: TO GET IT RIGHT. JUST ONCE.
SPECIAL ATTACK: UNPREDICTABLE RAGE
POWER-UP: BLOODY MARY
WEAKNESS: CRIPPLING SELF-DOUBT
STRESS LEVELS: 500%

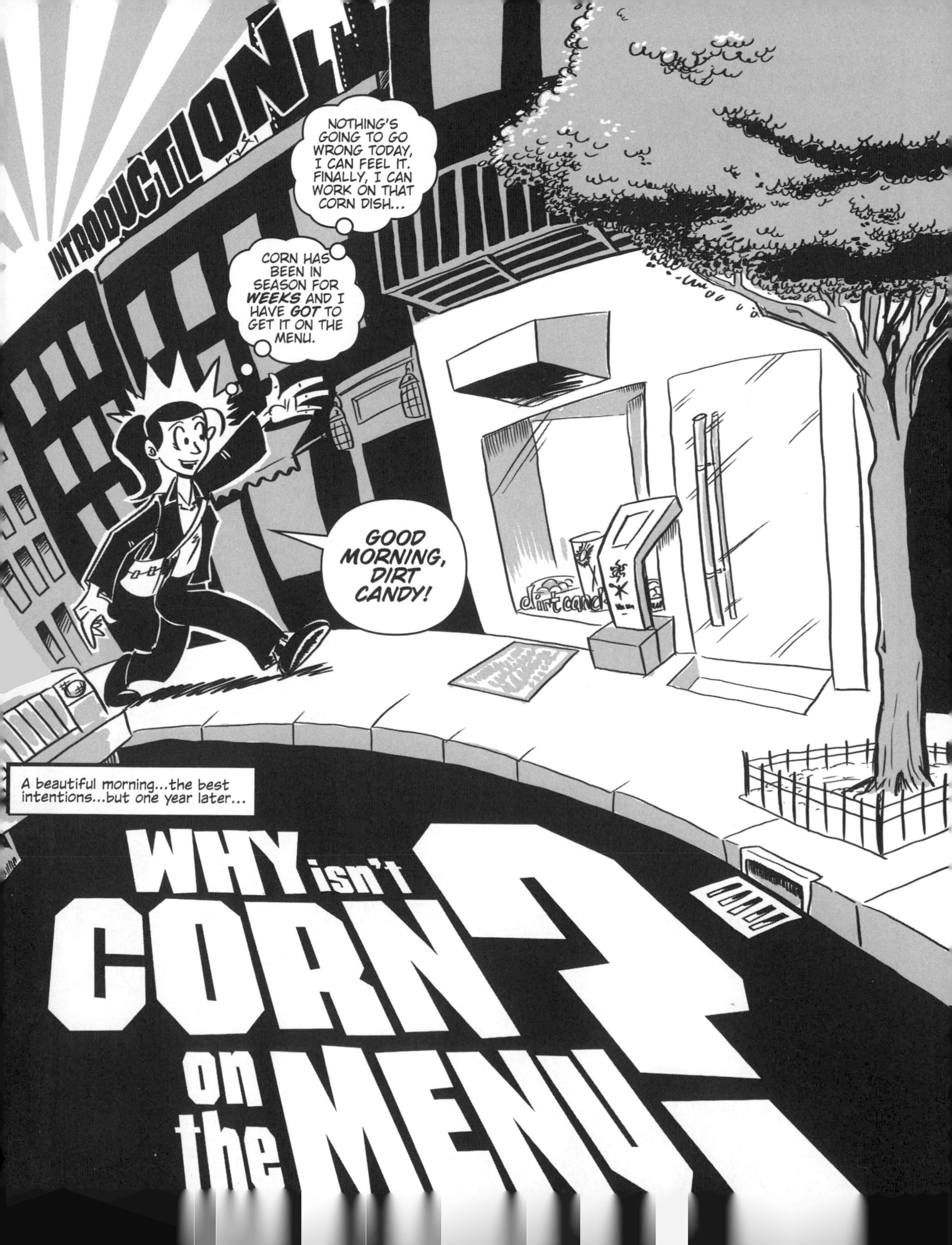
INTRODUCTION
NOTHING'S GOING TO GO WRONG TODAY, I CAN FEEL IT. FINALLY, I CAN WORK ON THAT CORN DISH...
CORN HAS BEEN IN SEASON FOR WEEKS AND I HAVE GOT TO GET IT ON THE MENU.
GOOD MORNING, DIRT CANDY!
dirt candy
A beautiful morning...the best intentions...but one year later...
WHY isn't CORN on the MENU?

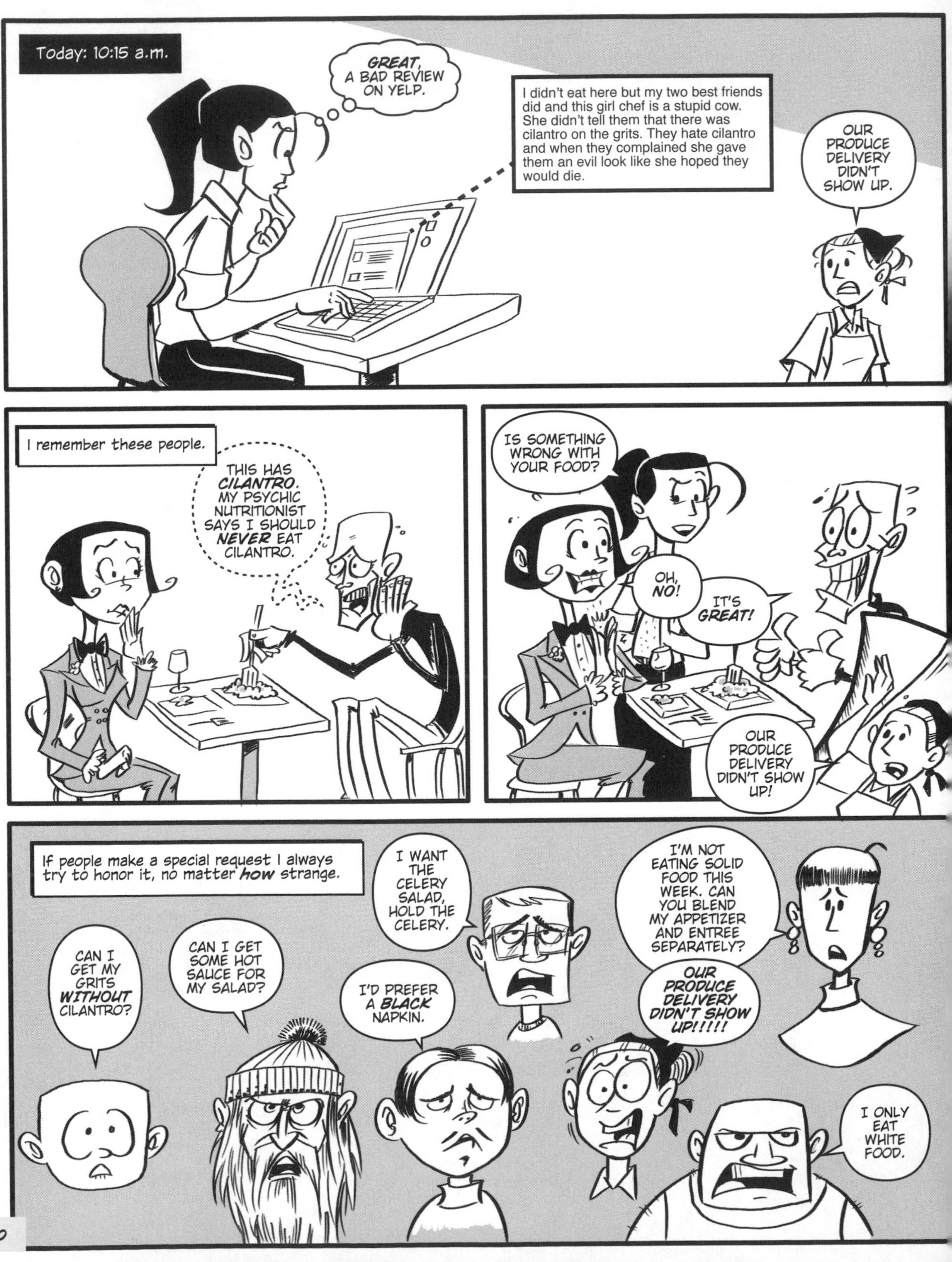
Today: 10:15 a.m.
GREAT, A BAD REVIEW ON YELP.
I didn't eat here but my two best friends did and this girl chef is a stupid cow. She didn't tell them that there was cilantro on the grits. They hate cilantro and when they complained she gave them an evil look like she hoped they would die.
OUR PRODUCE DELIVERY DIDN'T SHOW UP.
I remember these people.
THIS HAS CILANTRO. MY PSYCHIC NUTRITIONIST SAYS I SHOULD NEVER EAT CILANTRO.
IS SOMETHING WRONG WITH YOUR FOOD?
OH, NO!
IT'S GREAT!
OUR PRODUCE DELIVERY DIDN'T SHOW UP!
If people make a special request I always try to honor it, no matter how strange.
CAN I GET MY GRITS WITHOUT CILANTRO?
CAN I GET SOME HOT SAUCE FOR MY SALAD?
I WANT THE CELERY SALAD, HOLD THE CELERY.
I'D PREFER A BLACK NAPKIN.
I'M NOT EATING SOLID FOOD THIS WEEK. CAN YOU BLEND MY APPETIZER AND ENTREE SEPARATELY?
OUR PRODUCE DELIVERY DIDN'T SHOW UP!!!!!
I ONLY EAT WHITE FOOD.

DANIELLE
Prep Chef

SKILL LEVEL: HIGH
COMMUNICATION SKILLS: TOO GOOD
GOAL: NOT TO BE YELLED AT
SPECIAL ATTACK: OBSESSIVE COUNTING
POWER-UP: REAL HOUSEWIVES OF WHEREVER
WEAKNESS: TIME MANAGEMENT
STRESS LEVELS: 68%

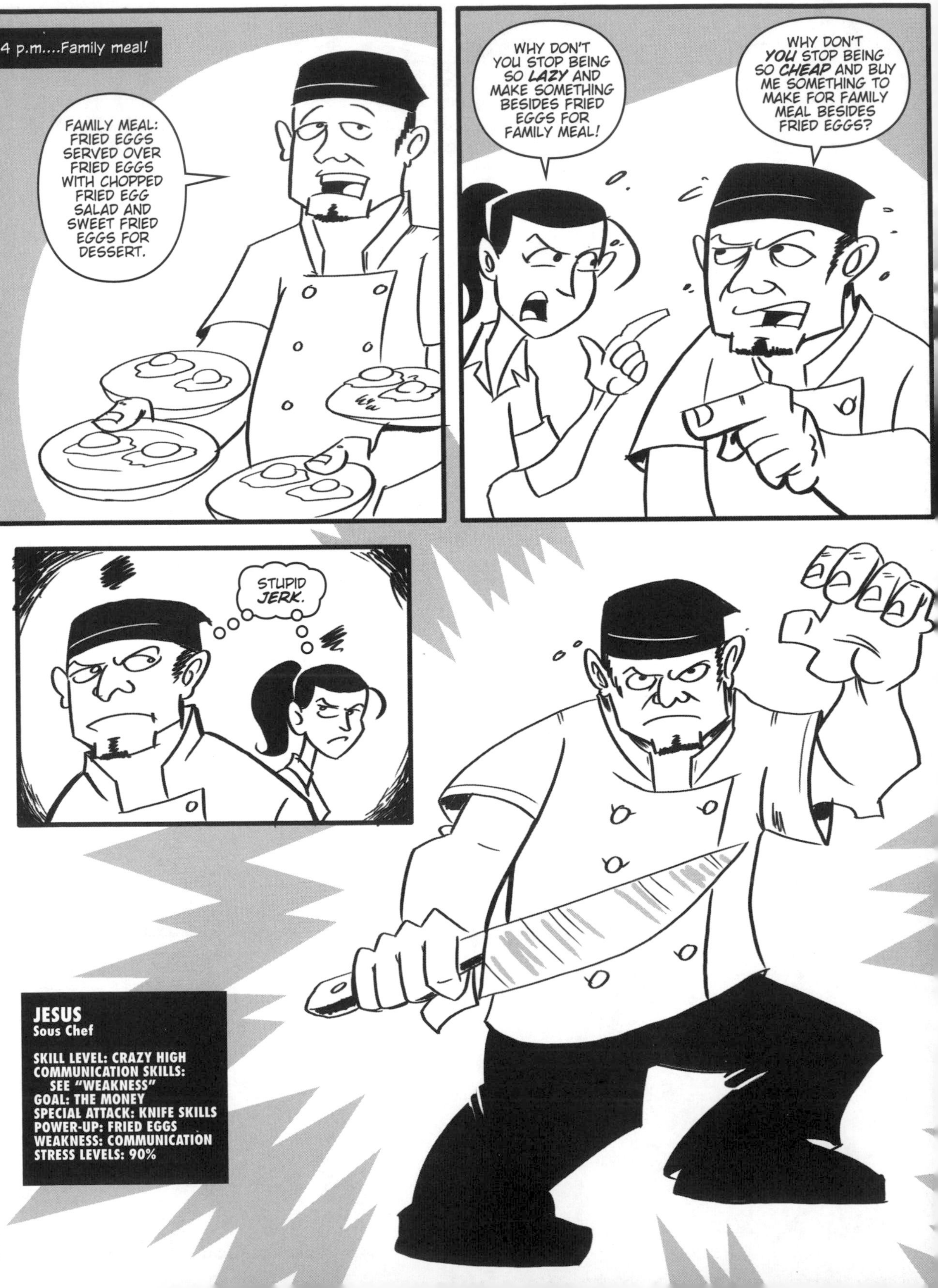

4 p.m....Family meal!
FAMILY MEAL: FRIED EGGS SERVED OVER FRIED EGGS WITH CHOPPED FRIED EGG SALAD AND SWEET FRIED EGGS FOR DESSERT.
WHY DON'T YOU STOP BEING SO LAZY AND MAKE SOMETHING BESIDES FRIED EGGS FOR FAMILY MEAL!
WHY DON'T YOU STOP BEING SO CHEAP AND BUY ME SOMETHING TO MAKE FOR FAMILY MEAL BESIDES FRIED EGGS?
STUPID JERK.
JESUS
Sous Chef
SKILL LEVEL: CRAZY HIGH
COMMUNICATION SKILLS: SEE "WEAKNESS"
GOAL: THE MONEY
SPECIAL ATTACK: KNIFE SKILLS
POWER-UP: FRIED EGGS
WEAKNESS: COMMUNICATION
STRESS LEVELS: 90%

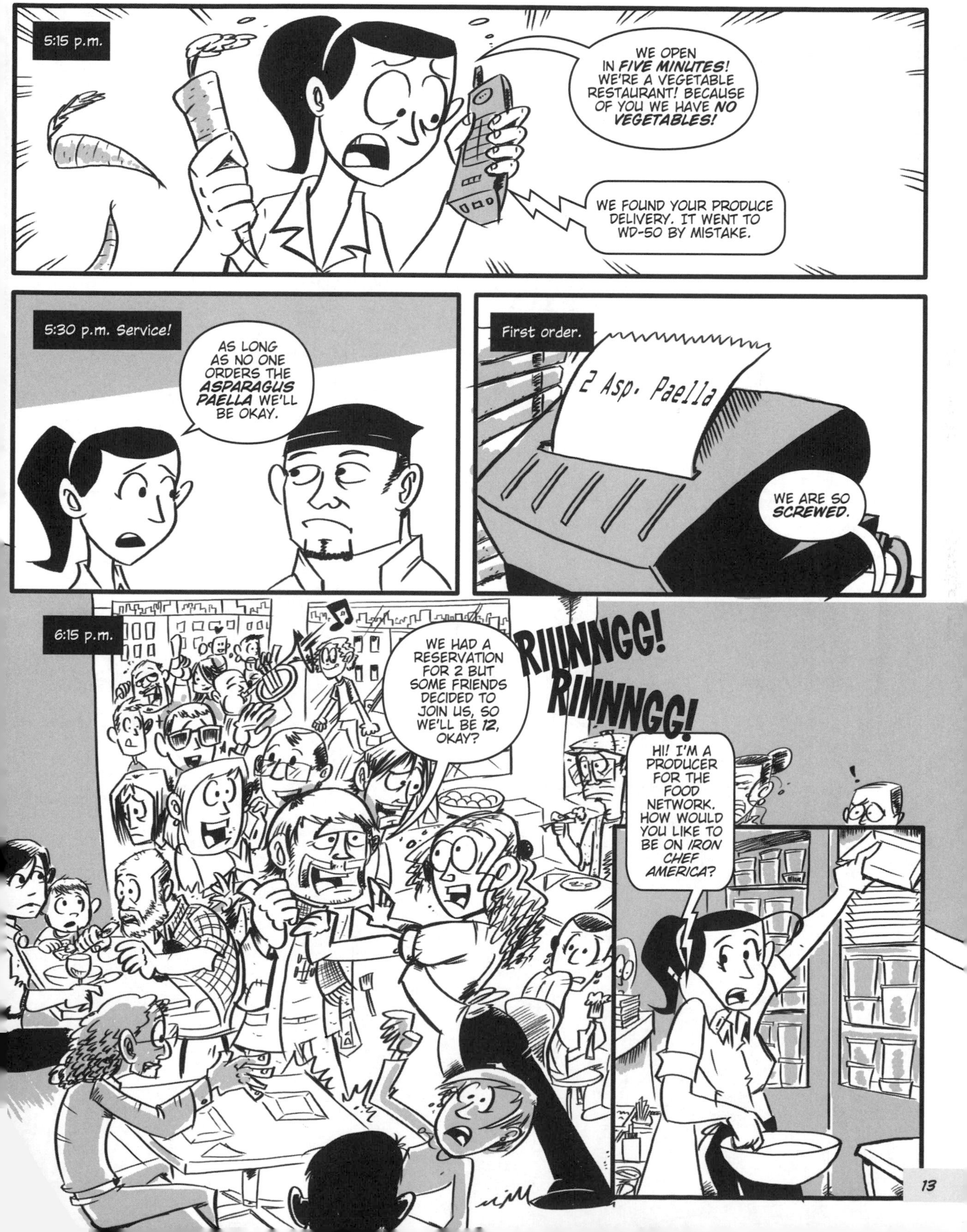

5:15 p.m.
WE OPEN IN FIVE MINUTES! WE'RE A VEGETABLE RESTAURANT! BECAUSE OF YOU WE HAVE NO VEGETABLES!
WE FOUND YOUR PRODUCE DELIVERY. IT WENT TO WD-50 BY MISTAKE.
5:30 p.m. Service!
AS LONG AS NO ONE ORDERS THE ASPARAGUS PAELLA WE'LL BE OKAY.
First order.
2 Asp. Paella
WE ARE SO SCREWED.
6:15 p.m.
WE HAD A RESERVATION FOR 2 BUT SOME FRIENDS DECIDED TO JOIN US, SO WE'LL BE 12, OKAY?
RIIINNGG! RIIINNGG!
HI! I'M A PRODUCER FOR THE FOOD NETWORK. HOW WOULD YOU LIKE TO BE ON IRON CHEF AMERICA?

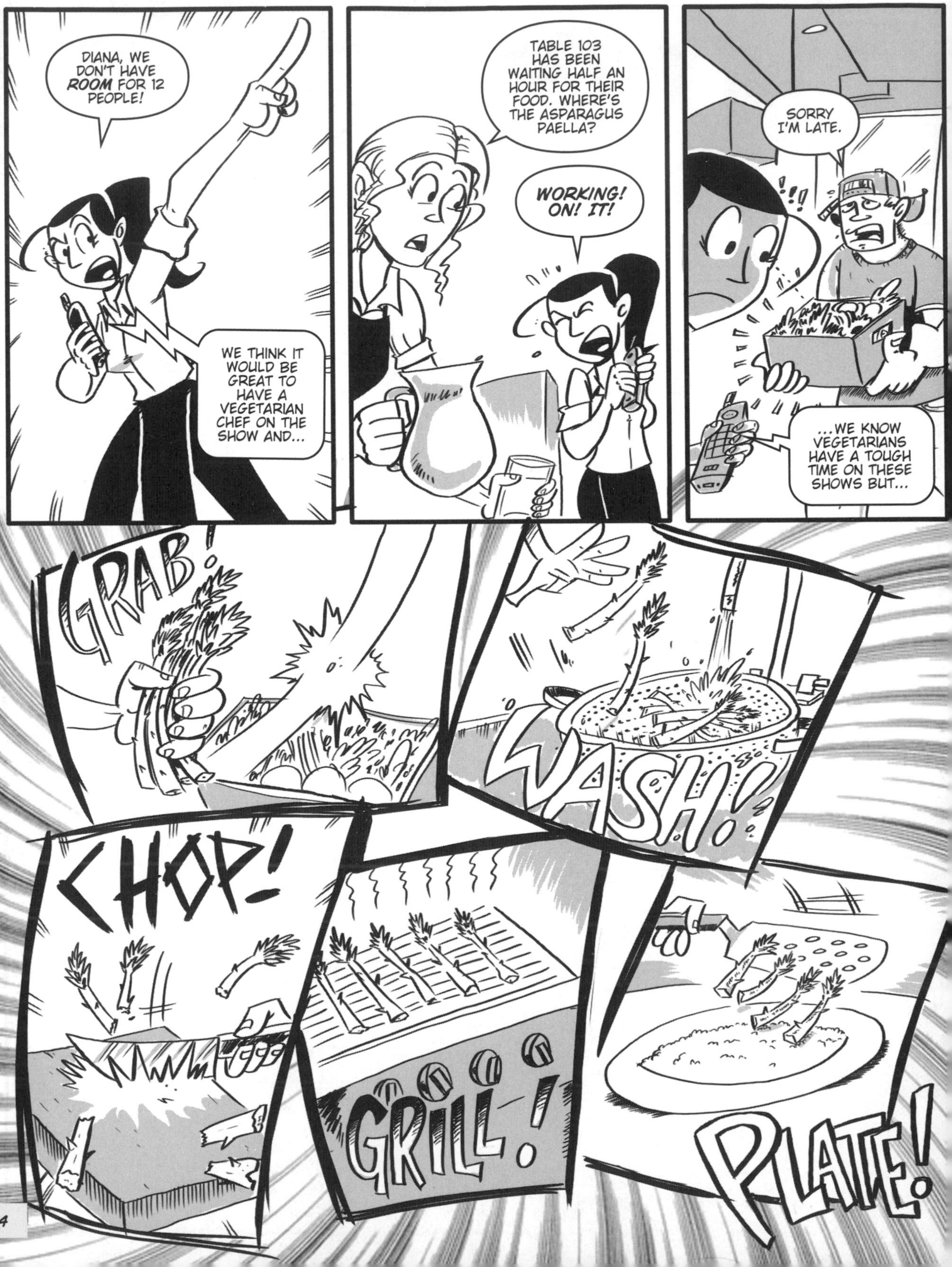

DIANA, WE DON'T HAVE ***ROOM*** FOR 12 PEOPLE!
WE THINK IT WOULD BE GREAT TO HAVE A VEGETARIAN CHEF ON THE SHOW AND...
TABLE 103 HAS BEEN WAITING HALF AN HOUR FOR THEIR FOOD. WHERE'S THE ASPARAGUS PAELLA?
WORKING! ON! IT!
SORRY I'M LATE.
...WE KNOW VEGETARIANS HAVE A TOUGH TIME ON THESE SHOWS BUT...
GRAB!
WASH!
CHOP!
GRILL!
PLATE!

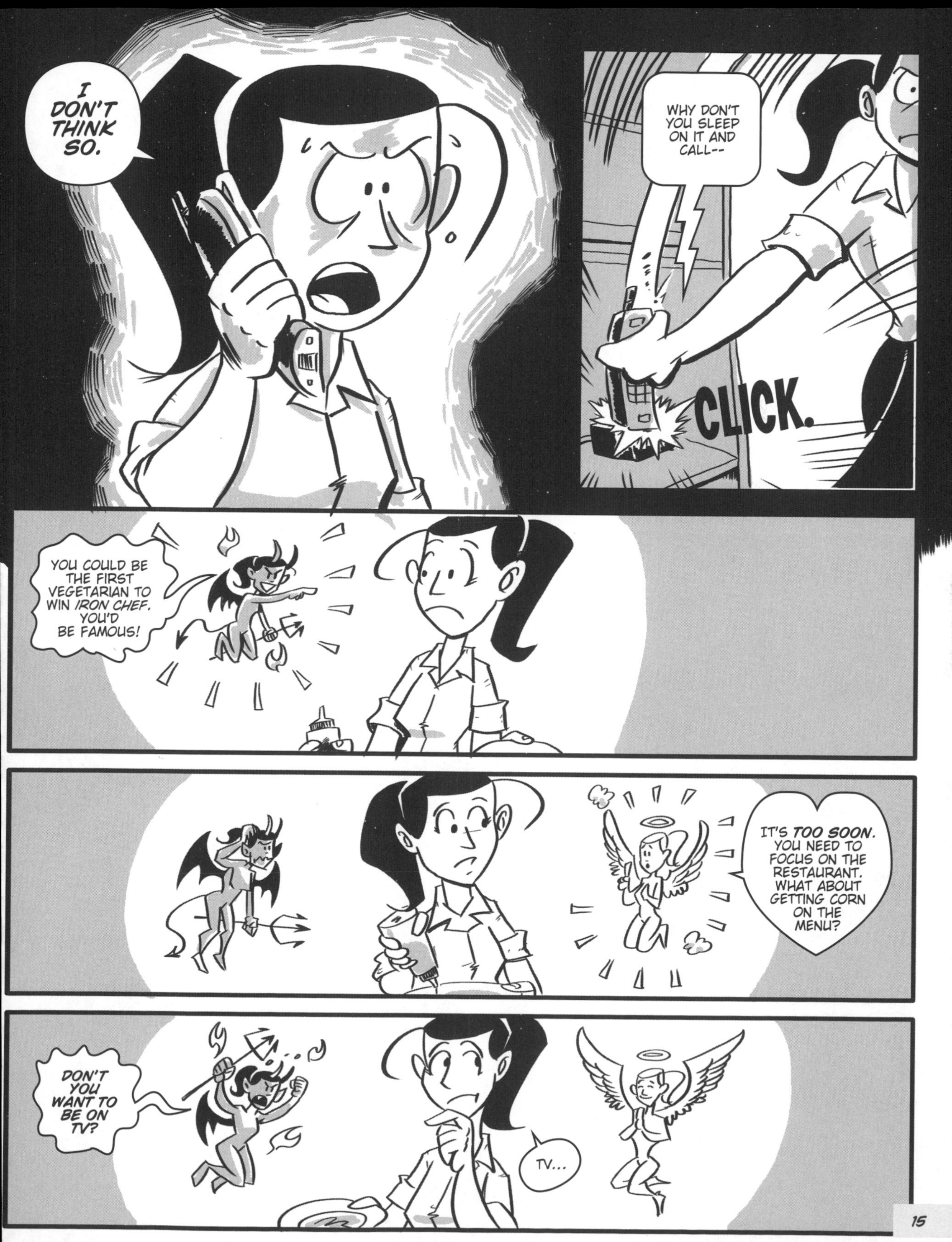
I DON'T THINK SO.
WHY DON'T YOU SLEEP ON IT AND CALL--
CLICK.
YOU COULD BE THE FIRST VEGETARIAN TO WIN IRON CHEF. YOU'D BE FAMOUS!
IT'S TOO SOON. YOU NEED TO FOCUS ON THE RESTAURANT. WHAT ABOUT GETTING CORN ON THE MENU?
DON'T YOU WANT TO BE ON TV?
TV...

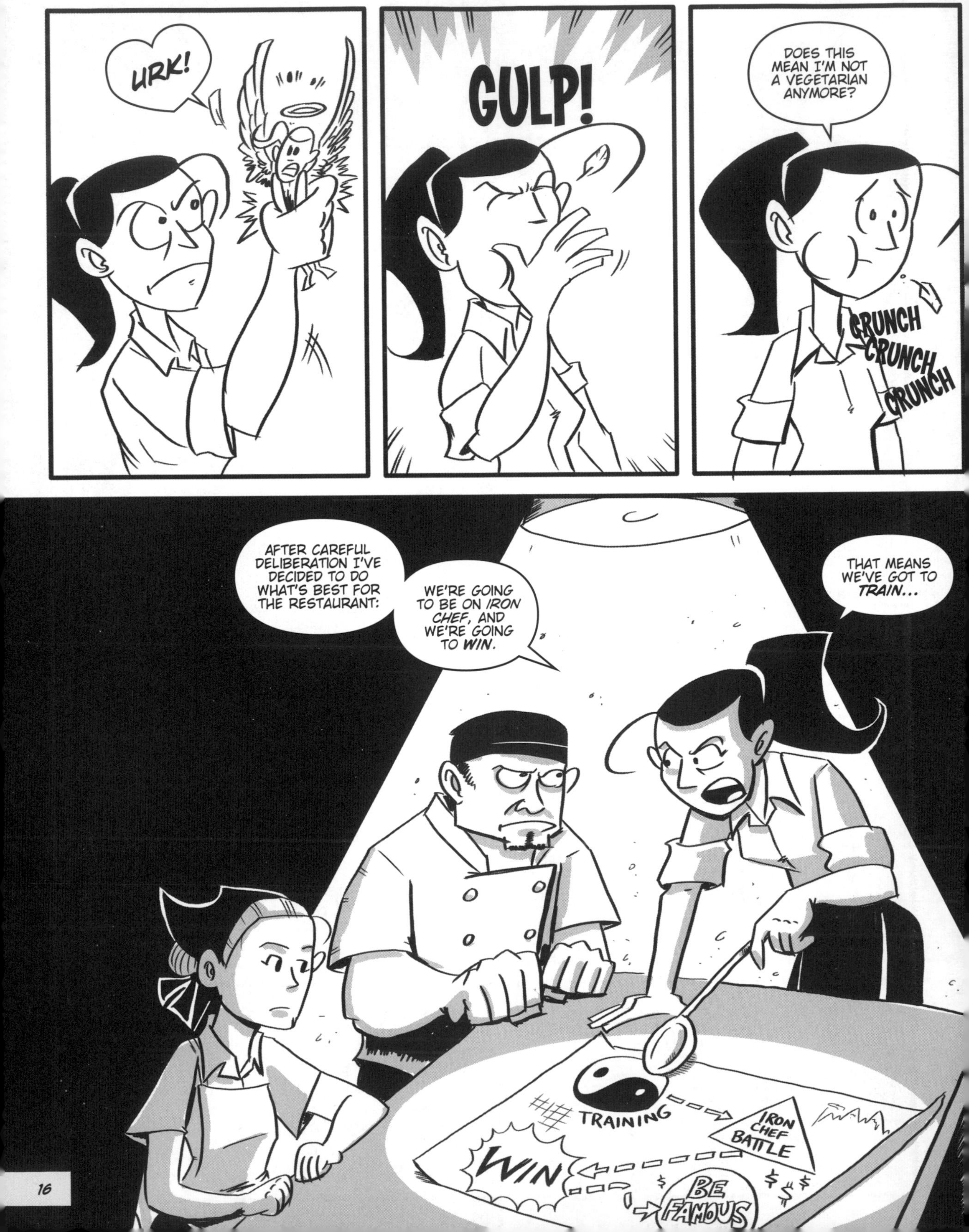
URK!
GULP!
DOES THIS MEAN I'M NOT A VEGETARIAN ANYMORE?
CRUNCH
CRUNCH
CRUNCH
AFTER CAREFUL DELIBERATION I'VE DECIDED TO DO WHAT'S BEST FOR THE RESTAURANT:
WE'RE GOING TO BE ON *IRON CHEF*, AND WE'RE GOING TO ***WIN***.
THAT MEANS WE'VE GOT TO ***TRAIN...***
TRAINING
IRON CHEF BATTLE
WIN
BE FAMOUS

...AND I'M TALKING HARDCORE *36 CHAMBERS-STYLE* TRAINING!

There are three ways to begin every recipe, each more complicated than the last: *starting a pan*, *sweating*, and *caramelizing*.

STARTING A PAN!

This is the first move in almost every recipe.

Put about 2 table-spoons of extra-virgin olive oil in a pan over low heat.

Drop in a single bit of diced onion and when it starts to *sizzle* the oil is ready.

Add the rest of your diced onions and stir them so they don't burn. Cook until translucent.

About 5 minutes.

Then add your aromatics--garlic, ginger, galangal, whatever the recipe calls for--and keep stirring. Make sure they don't brown!

What you're doing is flavoring the oil. The oil is going to saturate your dish and if it's not flavored, your food will taste of grease and failure.

About 3 minutes.

SWEATING!

Sweating cooks vegetables without adding fat. Start heating a dry pan over *VERY LOW* heat. If oil is called for, it's usually less than a tablespoon.

Add 1 cup of onions (or whatever vegetable is called for in the recipe) and 1/4 teaspoon of salt and stir to keep them from browning.

About 10 minutes.

Suddenly: the onions *RELEASE THEIR JUICES!* Now they will *COOK* in it! Keep stirring--don't let them brown!

Cook for 5 minutes.

CARAMELIZING!

Caramelizing takes *forever* because the goal is to cook the sugar in the onions. Warm 2 tablespoons of extra-virgin olive oil over very, very low heat.

Add your onions and stir and stir while your sugars caramelize. The dish is done when the onions are dark brown and smell *sweet*.

This might take 30 minutes, it might take 90 minutes. It all depends on the onions. *Patience!*

Caramelizing cruds up your pan. When you're done, dump in water and heat it over high flame. The gunk'll come right off the bottom.

BLANCH & SHOCK

Blanching and shocking cooks vegetables fast, but keeps their color and flavor.

Blanch! Bring water to a boil, plunge in the vegetables, then let the water come back up to a boil.

Whip them out of the water. (A basket works better than tongs.) Shake the hot water off and...

Shock! Submerge them in ice water. Leave the vegetables in until they're the same temperature as the water.

Your kitchen fu is probably too weak to use your bare hands.

IN GENERAL: BLANCH GREEN, ORANGE, YELLOW AND OTHER BRIGHTLY COLORED VEGETABLES. *NEVER* BLANCH MUSHROOMS, POTATOES, OR ONIONS.

NO BLANCH

BLANCH

Chop hard vegetables *BEFORE* blanching, but chop leafy vegetables *AFTER*.

BEFORE | AFTER

Make sure your pot is big enough. *Overcrowded* vegetables won't blanch properly.

BALSAMIC VINEGAR REDUCTION

INGREDIENTS: 4 cups balsamic vinegar

| Pour the balsamic vinegar into a pot over low heat. | Let it sit for 20 minutes, stirring occasionally. | After 20 minutes, pour it into a measuring cup to see how much you have left. | The goal is to reduce it to a 1/2 cup. If you have more, keep reducing. |

OVEN REDUCING!

Reduce Stance #2 is **Oven Reducing**! Put the vegetables in an ungreased baking pan and pour in stock.

Put the baking pan in the oven at 250°F and let it sit for 2 to 4 hours. This simultaneously dehydrates the vegetables and reduces the stock.

The big advantage is the crust that forms on top where the sugars caramelize. This adds a welcome *sweetness* to the reduction.

DEHYDRATING!

REDUCE STANCE #3 IS *DEHYDRATE*! EACH RECIPE TELLS HOW TO PREPARE FOOD FOR DEHYDRATING. YOU CAN USE A DEHYDRATOR, BUT ALL OUR RECIPES ARE FOR OVEN DEHYDRATING.

Use your chi to dehydrate if your kung fu is good enough.

A DEHYDRATOR SET AT 120°F TAKES *FOUR TIMES* LONGER TO DEHYDRATE THAN AN OVEN, SO MULTIPLY THE TIMES IN THIS BOOK BY *4* IF USING A DEHYDRATOR.

YOUR OVEN NEEDS TO BE ON ITS LOWEST SETTING. THAT'S 150°F OR BELOW. THE "WARM" SETTING ON MOST OVENS IS 150-200°F, SO TAKE YOUR OVEN'S TEMPERATURE FIRST!

IF YOUR OVEN DOESN'T GO TO 150°F OR BELOW, YOU CAN USE THE **"ON/OFF" STANCE.** PREHEAT TO 200°F, THEN TURN IT OFF AND PUT THE FOOD IN TO DEHYDRATE FOR AN HOUR. THEN REPEAT.

ON! OFF! ON!

MAKE LIFE EASIER AND BUY A FEW NONSTICK SILICON **SILPATS.** PUT THEM ON THE BAKING TRAYS TO MAKE DEHYDRATING EASIER AND LESS CRUD-CAKED.

RAW VEGETABLES SHOULD TAKE 1 TO 3 HOURS TO DEHYDRATE. THEY ARE MOSTLY WATER.

SAUTEED VEGETABLES, PARMESAN CHEESE, AND OTHER OILY FOODS REQUIRE 6 TO 12 HOURS. OIL IS ALMOST **IMPOSSIBLE** TO DEHYDRATE.

JUICING!

TO INTENSIFY FLAVORS, COOK VEGETABLES IN THEIR OWN JUICE, NOT IN WATER.

OUTSOURCE YOUR JUICING. MOST OF THE JUICES IN THESE RECIPES CAN BE BOUGHT ANYWHERE THAT MAKES FRESH JUICES.

THE **TONGS METHOD** IS THE BEST WAY TO JUICE CITRUS. JUST HOLD YOUR CITRUS LIKE THIS AND PRESS!!!

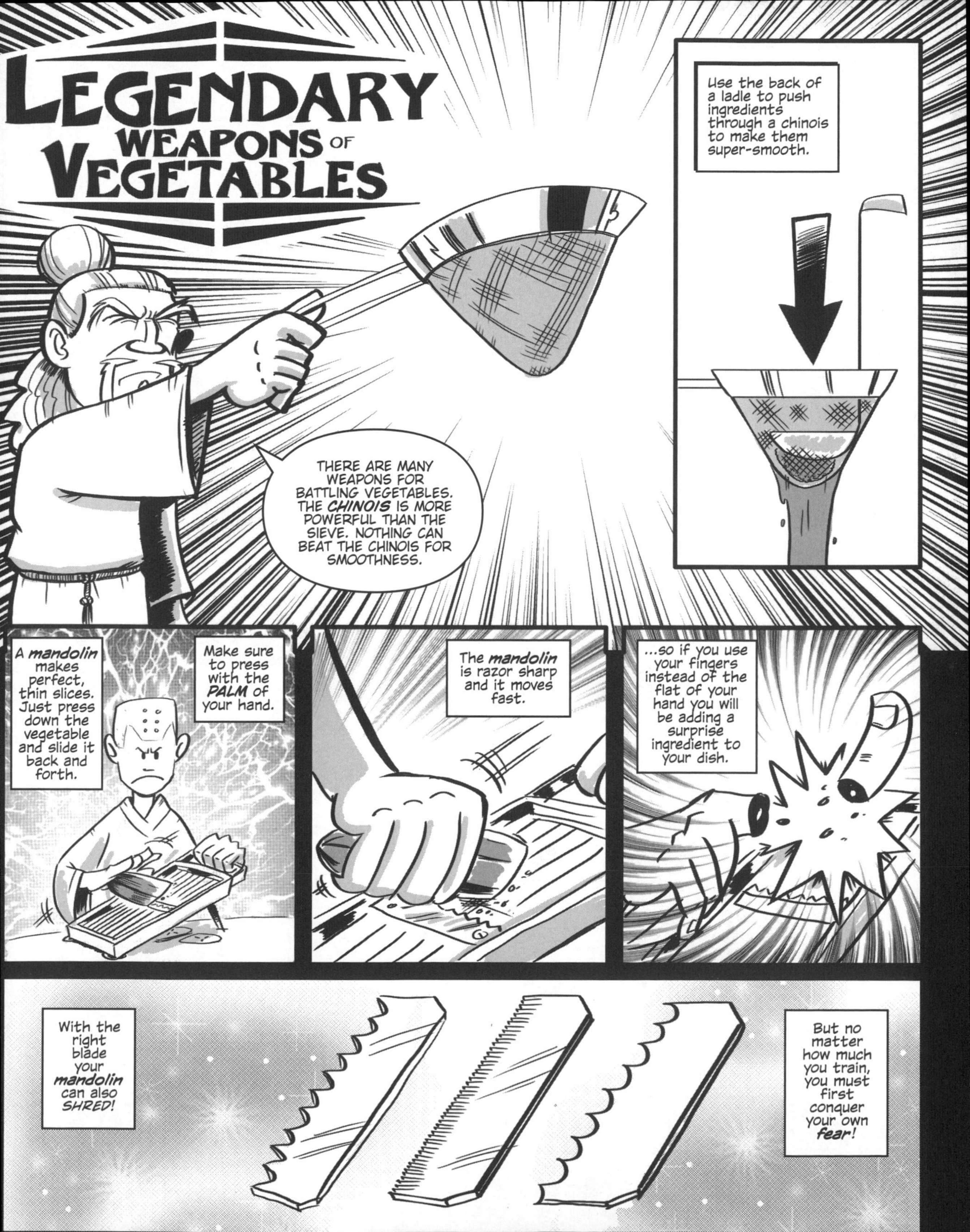
LEGENDARY WEAPONS OF VEGETABLES
Use the back of a ladle to push ingredients through a chinois to make them super-smooth.
THERE ARE MANY WEAPONS FOR BATTLING VEGETABLES. THE CHINOIS IS MORE POWERFUL THAN THE SIEVE. NOTHING CAN BEAT THE CHINOIS FOR SMOOTHNESS.
A mandolin makes perfect, thin slices. Just press down the vegetable and slide it back and forth.
Make sure to press with the PALM of your hand.
The mandolin is razor sharp and it moves fast.
...so if you use your fingers instead of the flat of your hand you will be adding a surprise ingredient to your dish.
With the right blade your mandolin can also SHRED!
But no matter how much you train, you must first conquer your own fear!

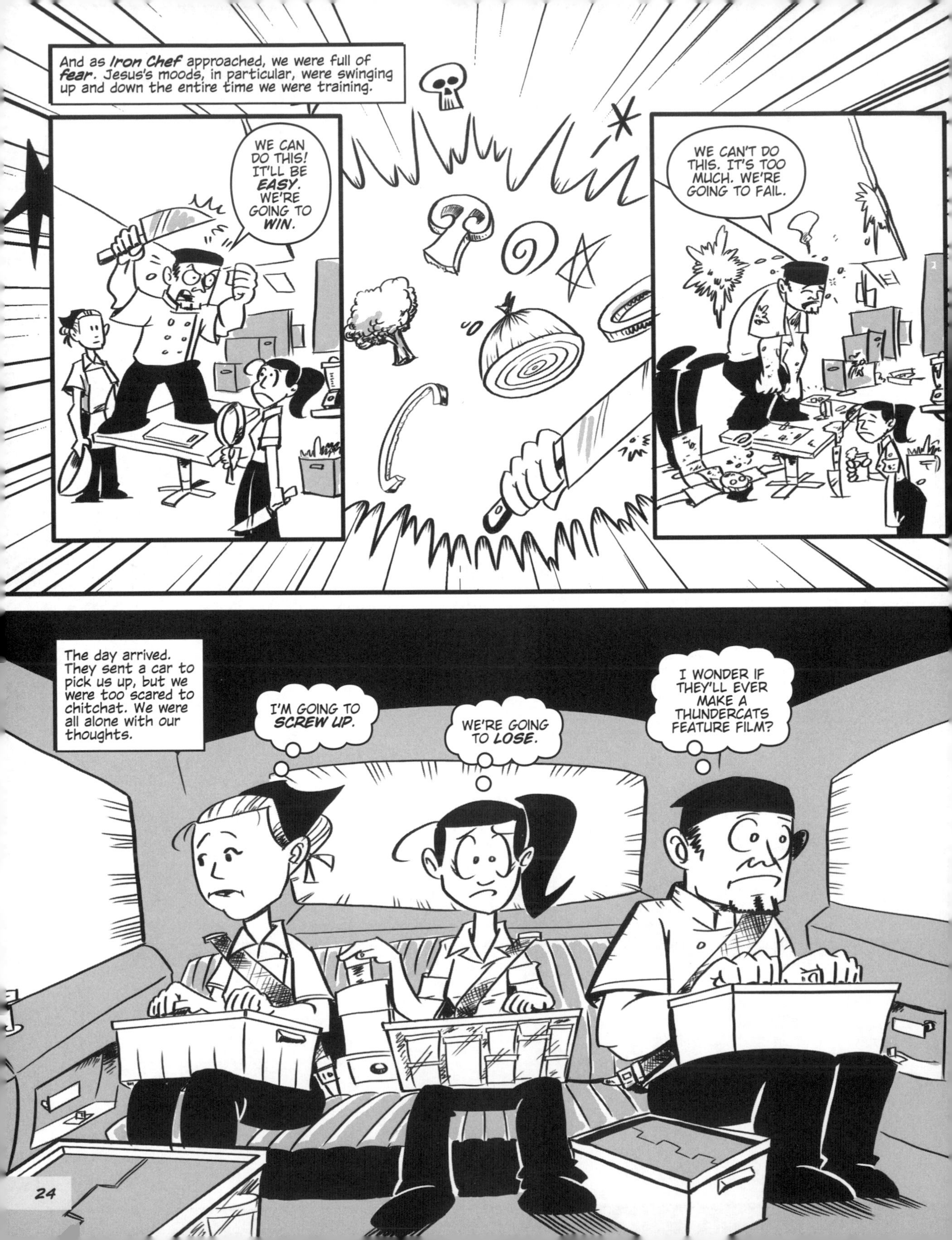

And as *Iron Chef* approached, we were full of **fear**. Jesus's moods, in particular, were swinging up and down the entire time we were training.
WE CAN DO THIS! IT'LL BE **EASY**. WE'RE GOING TO **WIN**.
WE CAN'T DO THIS. IT'S TOO MUCH. WE'RE GOING TO FAIL.
The day arrived. They sent a car to pick us up, but we were too scared to chitchat. We were all alone with our thoughts.
I'M GOING TO **SCREW UP**.
WE'RE GOING TO **LOSE**.
I WONDER IF THEY'LL EVER MAKE A THUNDERCATS FEATURE FILM?

Hair, make-up, and a lot of waiting later and then I was standing in front of Mark Dacascos, ready to battle.

CHEF COHEN, ARE YOU READY TO CHOOSE YOUR *IRON CHEF*?

YES. I HAVE THOUGHT ABOUT IT HARD AND I CHOOSE --

CUT. SOUND PROBLEM.

CHEF COHEN, ARE YOU READY TO CHOOSE YOUR *IRON CHEF*?

YES. I HAVE THOUGHT ABOUT IT HARD AND I CHOOSE --

CUT. I NEED YOU TO LOOK MORE TO HIS RIGHT. NO, NOT MY RIGHT. HIS RIGHT.

45 minutes later.

CHEF COHEN, ARE YOU READY TO CHOOSE YOUR *IRON CHEF*?

YES. I HAVE THOUGHT ABOUT IT HARD AND I CHOOSE --

CUT. I'M GETTING A LENS FLARE IN CAMERA 2.

It took six hours to shoot a one-hour show.

Most of that time we spent waiting. It was making us crazy.

...SO THEN WHEN WE RAISE THIS COVER I'LL SAY, "OKAY!" AND THAT'S WHEN THE CLOCK STARTS. IT'S ONLY ONE HOUR TO COOK SO YOU'VE GOT TO HUSTLE.

SO GUYS, LOWER THAT COVER. BRING IT DOWN. IS THAT WINCH STICKING?

WHEN HE SAYS *OKAY:* RUN. WHEN HE SAYS *OKAY:* RUN. WHEN HE SAYS *OKAY:* RUN.

MAYBE WE NEED TO BRING IT BACK UP? YEAH?

WHEN HE SAYS *OKAY:* RUN. WHEN HE SAYS *OKAY:* RUN. WHEN HE SAYS *OKAY:* RUN.

YEAH, RAISE IT JUST FOR A SECOND, JERRY.

OKAY.

HE SAID *OKAY!*

25

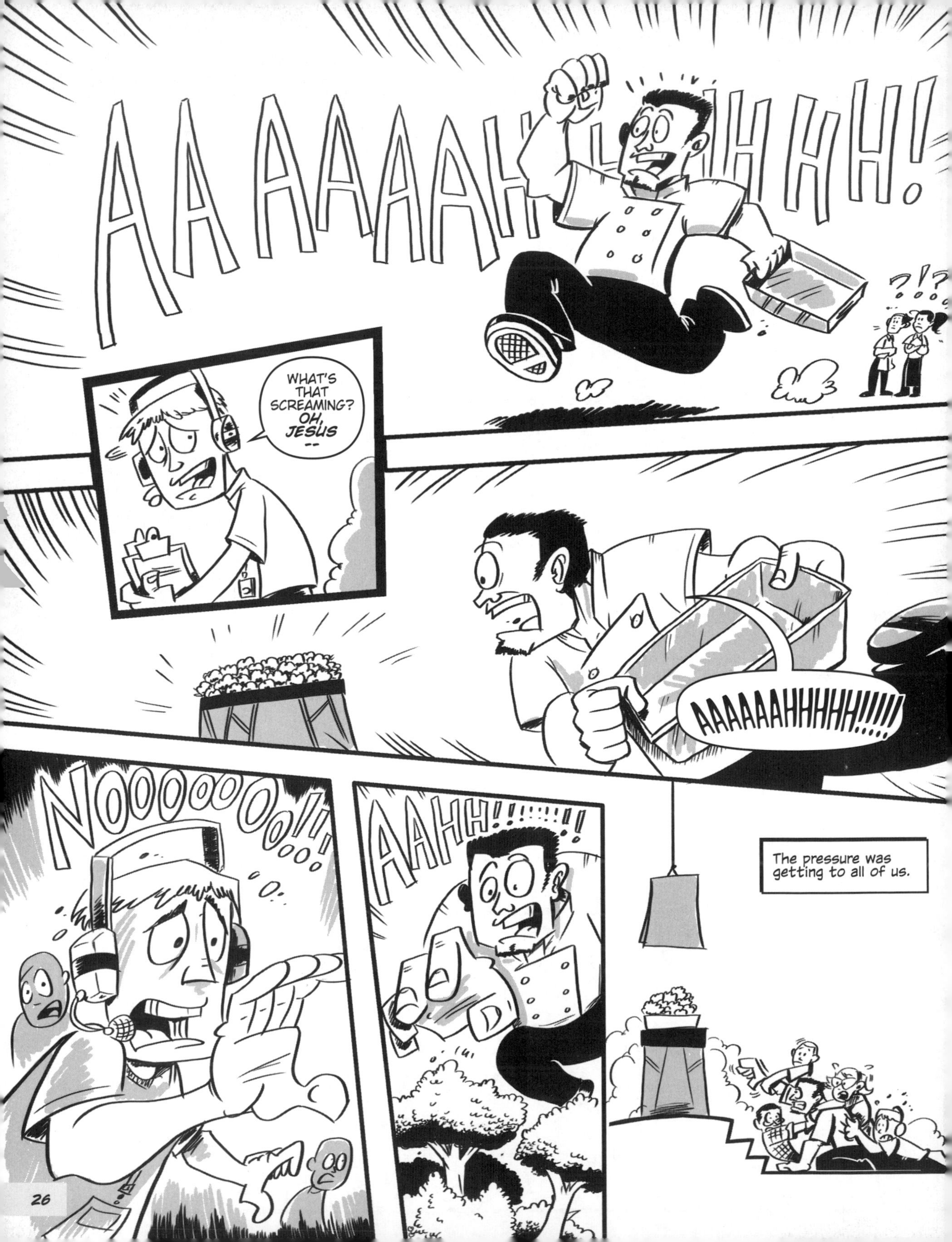
AAAAAAHHHHH!
?!?
WHAT'S THAT SCREAMING? OH, JESUS --
AAAAAAHHHHH!!!!!
NOOOOOOOo!!!
AAHH!!!!!!!
The pressure was getting to all of us.

I got to go up against *Iron Chef Morimoto*, which made me happy. He's the most hardcore of the bunch. But then I saw the judges and I knew we were in trouble.

I'M A *PURIST*. I LIKE MY BROCCOLI STEAMED LIGHTLY OR "NAKED."

Kelly Hu, actress.

I LOVE BROCCOLI.

Melanie Mannarino, food writer.

But I was excited that the toughest judge, Jeffrey Steingarten, was on the panel.

I HATE KITTENS.

Jeffrey Steingarten, curmudgeon.

The battle literally takes 60 minutes--no reshoots, no do-overs. It went by in a whirl, and then my problems really began...

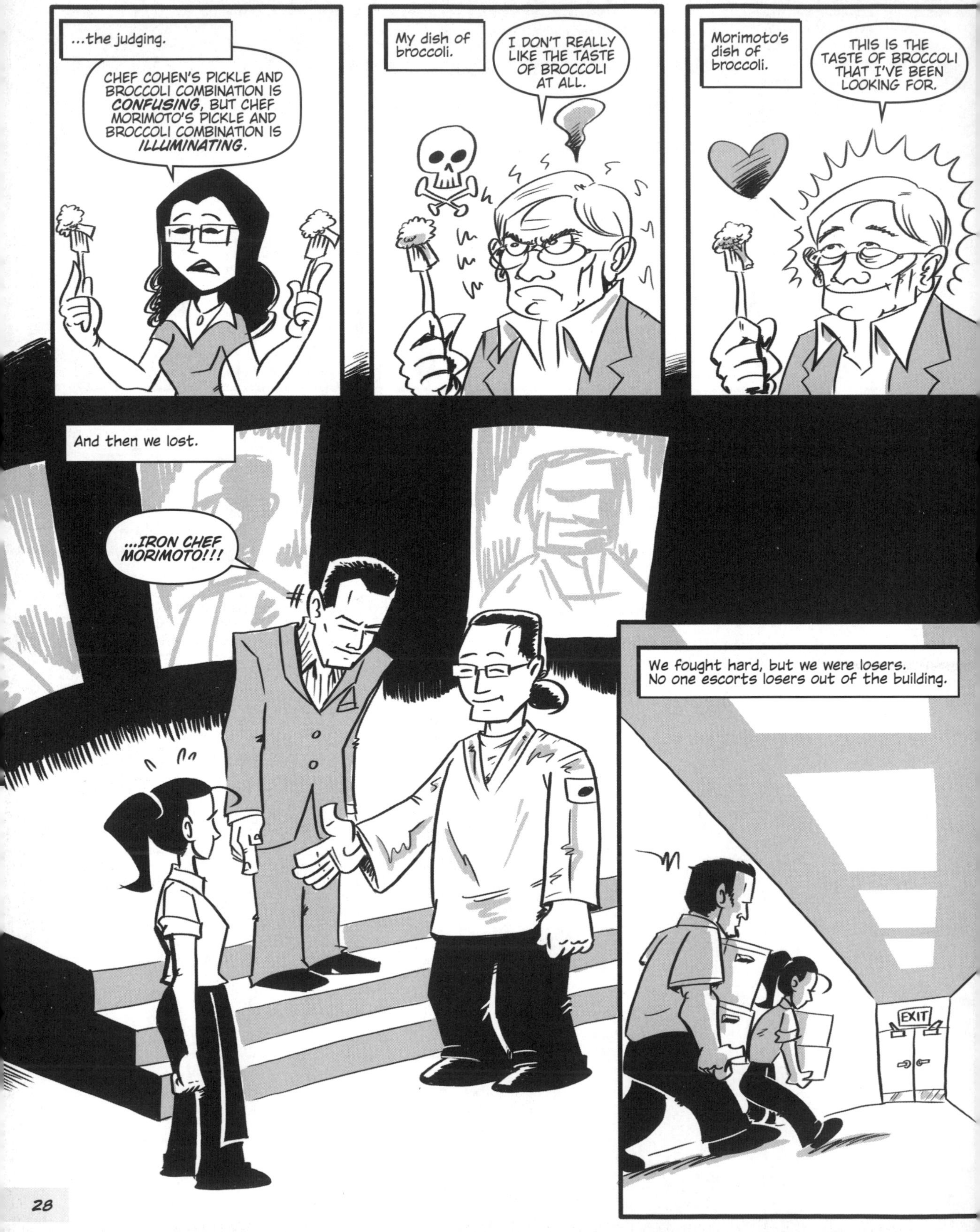
...the judging.
CHEF COHEN'S PICKLE AND BROCCOLI COMBINATION IS **CONFUSING**, BUT CHEF MORIMOTO'S PICKLE AND BROCCOLI COMBINATION IS **ILLUMINATING**.
My dish of broccoli.
I DON'T REALLY LIKE THE TASTE OF BROCCOLI AT ALL.
Morimoto's dish of broccoli.
THIS IS THE TASTE OF BROCCOLI THAT I'VE BEEN LOOKING FOR.
And then we lost.
...IRON CHEF MORIMOTO!!!
We fought hard, but we were losers.
No one escorts losers out of the building.
EXIT

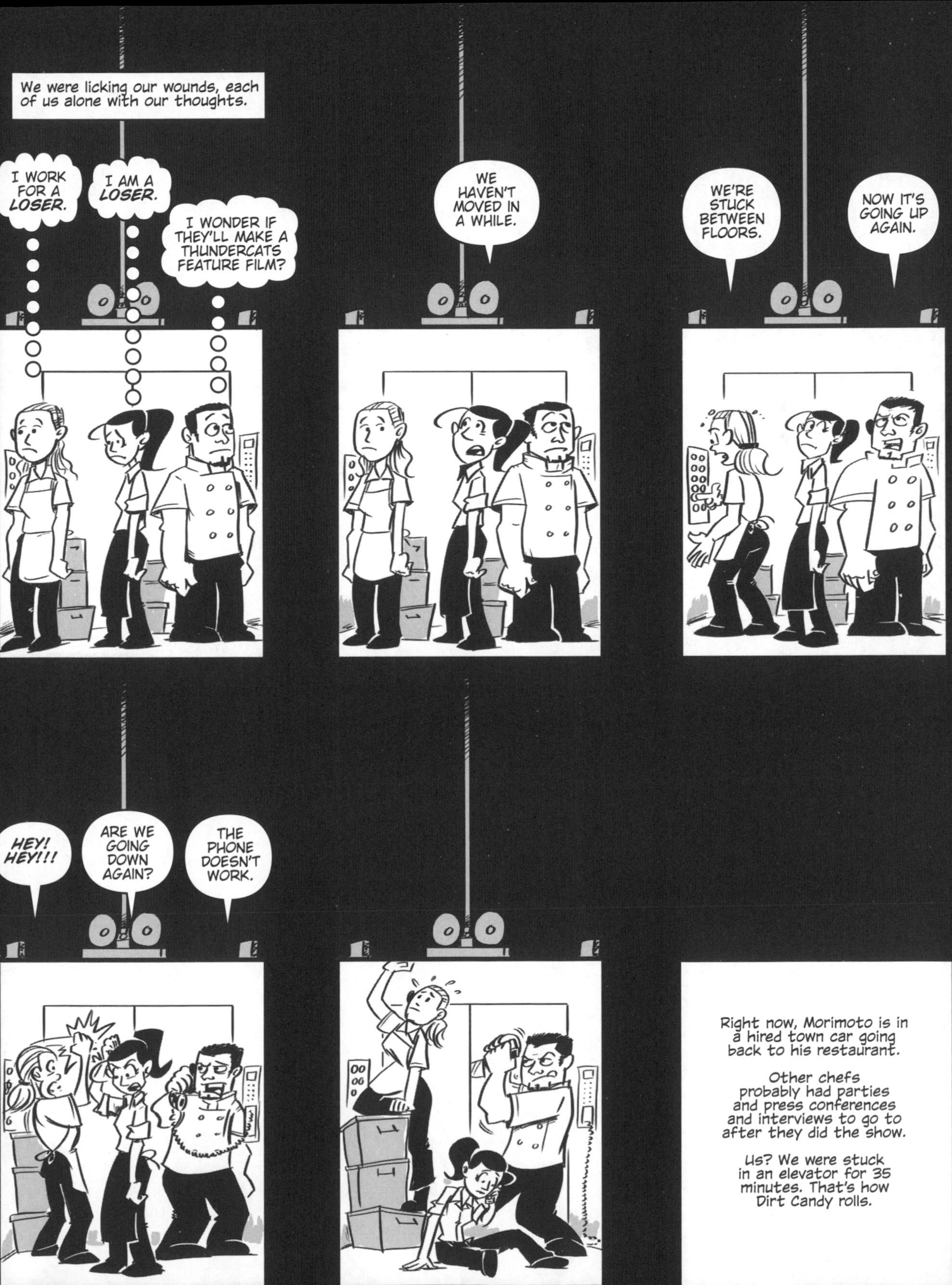
We were licking our wounds, each of us alone with our thoughts.
I WORK FOR A **LOSER**.
I AM A **LOSER**.
I WONDER IF THEY'LL MAKE A THUNDERCATS FEATURE FILM?
WE HAVEN'T MOVED IN A WHILE.
WE'RE STUCK BETWEEN FLOORS.
NOW IT'S GOING UP AGAIN.
HEY! HEY!!!
ARE WE GOING DOWN AGAIN?
THE PHONE DOESN'T WORK.
Right now, Morimoto is in a hired town car going back to his restaurant.
Other chefs probably had parties and press conferences and interviews to go to after they did the show.
Us? We were stuck in an elevator for 35 minutes. That's how Dirt Candy rolls.

ONE YEAR LATER...

THE *IRON* CHEF VIEWING PARTY

I CAN'T BELIEVE IT TOOK THEM A YEAR TO AIR MY EPISODE.

IRON CHEF AMERICA

I CAN'T BELIEVE THIS MANY OF MY CUSTOMERS CAME OUT TO *WATCH* IT!

WATCHING THIS IS LIKE GOING BACK IN TIME. I DIDN'T EVEN THINK I WAS GOING TO BE OPEN IN A YEAR BACK THEN. *UGH,* I LOOK SO *HELPLESS.*

NOW I'M THE REAL DEAL, ALL *CHEFY* AND--

HI, THIS IS MY FRIEND DAVID. I'VE BEEN TELLING HIM HE HAS TO COME TRY DIRT CANDY.

THANKS FOR COMING OUT TO WATCH!

IT WAS GREAT, BUT I'VE GOT ONE QUESTION...

...ARE YOU EVER GOING TO PUT *CORN ON THE MENU?*

YOU FORGOT? *YOU FORGOT?* WORK HARDER! STOP SLACKING! YOU ARE SHAME CHEF! FAILURE CHEF! LAZY CHEF!

MONKEY!

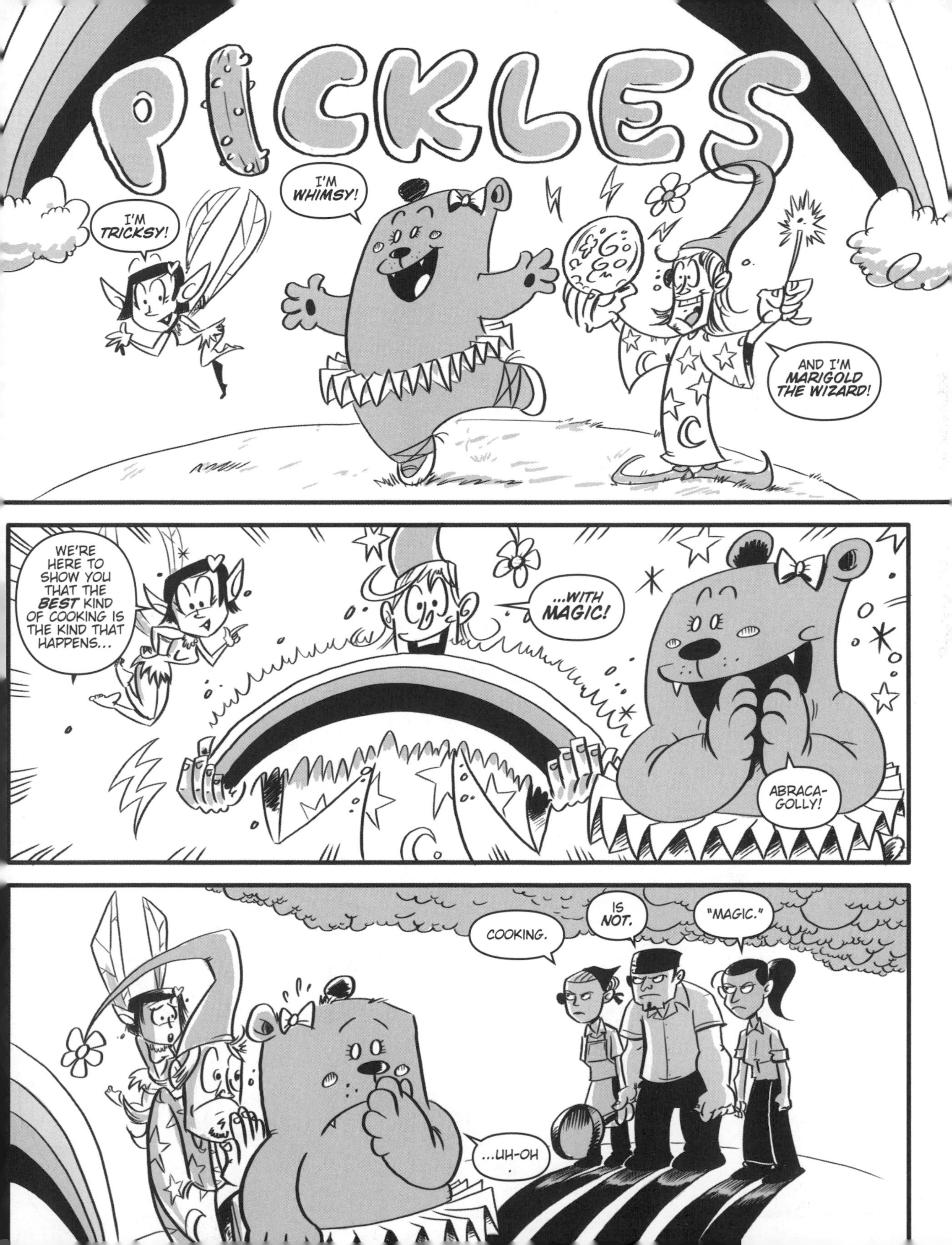
PICKLES
I'M TRICKSY!
I'M WHIMSY!
AND I'M MARIGOLD THE WIZARD!
WE'RE HERE TO SHOW YOU THAT THE BEST KIND OF COOKING IS THE KIND THAT HAPPENS...
...WITH MAGIC!
ABRACA-GOLLY!
COOKING.
IS NOT.
"MAGIC."
...UH-OH.

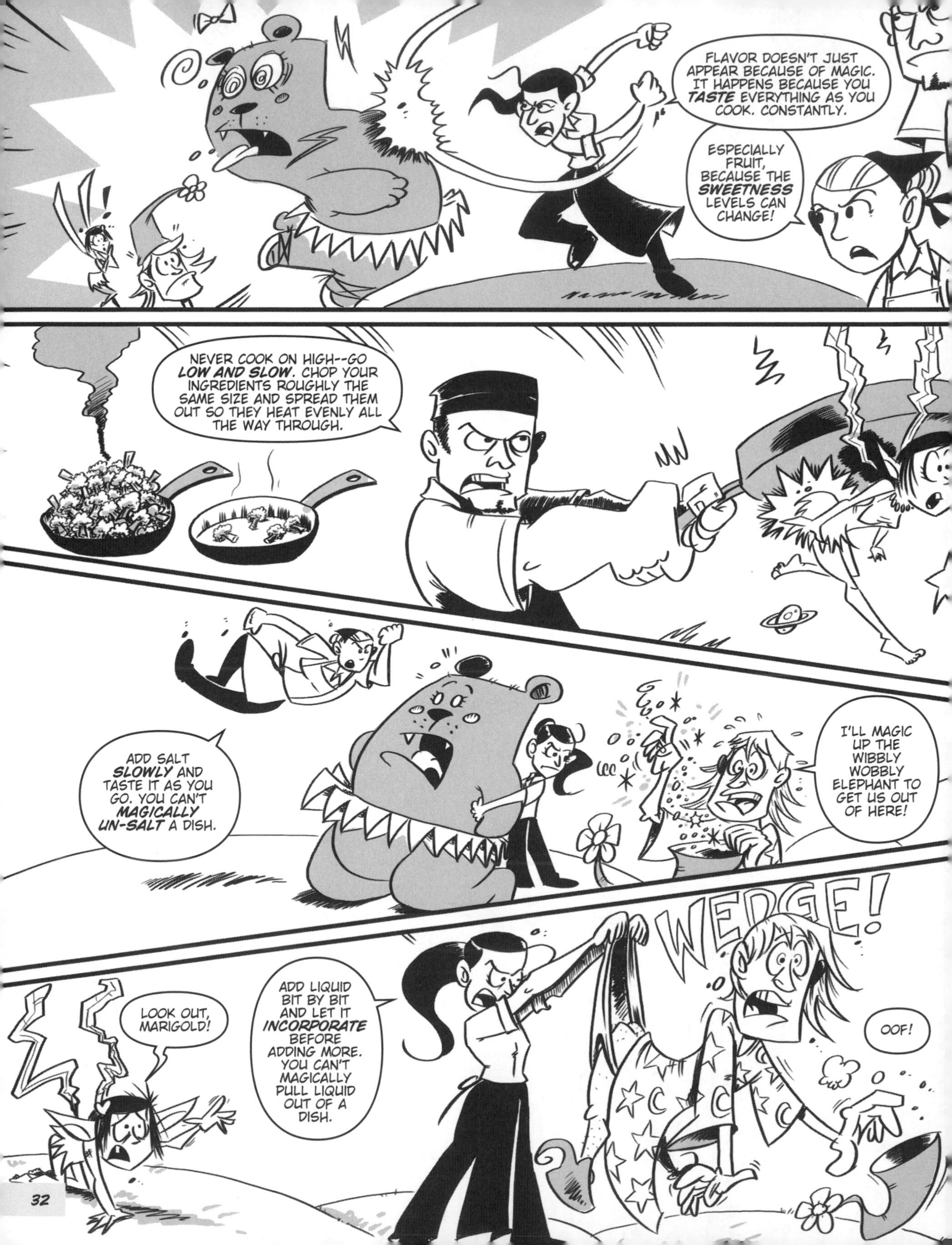
FLAVOR DOESN'T JUST APPEAR BECAUSE OF MAGIC. IT HAPPENS BECAUSE YOU TASTE EVERYTHING AS YOU COOK. CONSTANTLY.
ESPECIALLY FRUIT, BECAUSE THE SWEETNESS LEVELS CAN CHANGE!
NEVER COOK ON HIGH--GO LOW AND SLOW. CHOP YOUR INGREDIENTS ROUGHLY THE SAME SIZE AND SPREAD THEM OUT SO THEY HEAT EVENLY ALL THE WAY THROUGH.
ADD SALT SLOWLY AND TASTE IT AS YOU GO. YOU CAN'T MAGICALLY UN-SALT A DISH.
I'LL MAGIC UP THE WIBBLY WOBBLY ELEPHANT TO GET US OUT OF HERE!
LOOK OUT, MARIGOLD!
ADD LIQUID BIT BY BIT AND LET IT INCORPORATE BEFORE ADDING MORE. YOU CAN'T MAGICALLY PULL LIQUID OUT OF A DISH.
WEDGE!
OOF!

TO A LOT OF PEOPLE THAT MIDDLE STEP MIGHT AS WELL BE MAGIC, BUT IT'S **COOKING**. AND COOKING IS A SKILL: ONCE YOU LEARN HOW, YOU CAN DO IT AGAIN AND AGAIN.

The recipes at Dirt Candy look intimidating but they're not hard. Each dish is a lot of little recipes.

...that all **combine**...

...into one mighty, mega-recipe!

You're cooking for you, so if you don't like one part of a recipe, **leave it out**. No one's judging, and they'll still work.

33

THE RECIPE IS NOT YOUR MASTER!

YOU ARE NOT ITS SLAVE!

BUT *ALWAYS* OBEY BAKING INSTRUCTIONS EXACTLY. YOU CAN'T IGNORE THE MEASUREMENTS IN BAKING AND HOPE IT'LL MAGICALLY WORK OUT.

AND IF YOU'RE VEGAN, *DION THE DAIRY-FREE COW* WILL BE SHOWING YOU HOW TO TWEAK RECIPES TO MAKE THEM VEGAN.

I'LL BE THERE FOR YOU!

BUT PICKLES *ARE* MAGICAL! PICKLING IS COOKING VEGETABLES WITHOUT HEAT.

UH-OH.

PICKLED RED ONION

MAKES ½ CUP

1 red onion, very thinly sliced

5 tablespoons salt, plus more as needed

1 cup fresh lime juice, or as needed

This is the simplest pickle of all. Onion is rubbed with salt to draw out the moisture, then the lime juice "cooks" it. Use in Greek Salad (page 85) and Mint and Tarragon Fettuccine (page 176).

1. Put the onion in a bowl and add 1 tablespoon salt. Massage the salt into the onion until the onion weeps. Squeeze to remove any excess liquid and rinse.

2. Repeat step 1.

3. Put the onion in a bowl with 1 tablespoon salt and ¼ cup lime juice. Let sit for 20 minutes. Squeeze the excess liquid from the onion. Rinse and drain and return to the bowl.

4. Repeat step 3 until the onion turns bright pink (probably 2 more times).

5. Pour over any remaining lime juice and sprinkle lightly with salt. Use right away, or cover and refrigerate for up to 4 weeks.

PICKLED SHIITAKES

MAKES 1 CUP

- 5 cups fresh shiitakes, stemmed and sliced
- 2 teaspoons pickling spice
- ⅔ cup red wine vinegar
- ⅔ cup sugar
- 2 teaspoons salt
- 8 garlic cloves, sliced
- ½ cup sliced yellow onion
- 2 tablespoons thinly sliced jalapeños

Shiitake mushrooms have a high water content, so sweat them before submerging them in the vinegar solution. Pair them with grits (page 153) or add them to any vegetable soup.

1. In a dry pan over low heat, sweat the shiitakes (page 18) until all their liquid has cooked off, about 30 minutes. Remove from the heat and let cool.

2. Wrap the pickling spice in a cheesecloth and tie it closed. In a pot, bring the vinegar to a boil over high heat, and then add the sugar, salt, and pickling spice pouch. Reduce the heat to medium low and simmer until the sugar and salt dissolve, 4 to 5 minutes. Remove from the heat and let cool.

3. Put the shiitakes, garlic, onion, and jalapeño in a container. Pour in the pickling liquid, cover with a lid, and shake to mix the ingredients. Store in the fridge overnight before using, or for up to 4 weeks.

PICKLED SQUASH BLOSSOMS

MAKES 6 PICKLED SQUASH BLOSSOMS

- ¾ cup rice vinegar
- ½ cup sugar
- ½ teaspoon salt
- 6 large squash blossoms (about ½ pound)

There's a really short season for squash blossoms, so this is a way to make them last longer. This recipe plays a key part in Mint and Tarragon Fettuccine (page 176), and once diced, adds a summery bite to any pasta.

1. Heat the vinegar, sugar, and salt in a saucepan over high heat until the mixture reaches a low boil and the sugar has dissolved, about 10 minutes. Remove from the heat and let cool to room temperature.

2. Place the squash blossoms in a lidded container. Pour the vinegar over the blossoms, and let sit at room temperature until the blossoms soften, about 30 minutes.

3. Cover and refrigerate overnight before using, or for up to 3 weeks.

PICKLED POTATOES

MAKES 4 CUPS

- ½ pound whole baby potatoes
- ½ cup cilantro sprigs
- 2 tablespoons sliced peeled fresh ginger
- 2 tablespoons sliced garlic
- 4 strips of lime peel, removed with a peeler
- 1 jalapeño, seeded and sliced
- 1½ cups rice wine vinegar
- ¾ cup sugar
- ¼ cup salt

These add savory intensity to an omelet, or you can use them in Pea Soup (page 65) or throw a handful in potato salad to give it some pep.

1. Drop the potatoes in a pot of cold water and bring to a boil over high heat. Cook until potatoes are barely fork-tender. Drain. Let cool, then refrigerate until cold; this makes them easier to slice.

2. Peel the potatoes and slice them into ⅛-inch-thick rounds. Put them in a container with the cilantro, ginger, garlic, lime peel, and jalapeño.

3. Warm the vinegar, sugar, and salt in a pot over high heat until the sugar dissolves. Remove from the heat and let cool until lukewarm.

4. Pour the vinegar over the potatoes. Cover and refrigerate overnight before using, or for up to about 3 weeks.

PICKLED BABY EGGPLANT

MAKES 2 CUPS

- ½ pound baby Italian eggplant
- ¼ cup salt
- 1 tablespoon white wine vinegar
- ½ tablespoon reduced balsamic vinegar (page 20) or plain balsamic vinegar
- 3 garlic cloves, smashed and chopped
- ½ teaspoon crushed red pepper flakes
- 6 sprigs fresh thyme
- 1¼ cups extra-virgin olive oil, or as needed

1. Cut the eggplant into ½-inch-thick slices. Toss with the salt and let sit until soft, about 35 minutes. Rinse off the salt and drain.

2. Bring a pot of water to a boil, add the eggplant, and simmer the slices until pliable, about 5 minutes. Drain and set aside.

3. In a large bowl, mix the white wine vinegar, balsamic vinegar, garlic, crushed red pepper flakes, and thyme. Add the eggplant slices and toss.

4. Pack the eggplant slices into a lidded container and add enough olive oil to cover them. Cover and refrigerate overnight before using, or for up to 2 weeks.

CUCUMBER PICKLES

MAKES 2 CUPS

- 2 cups white vinegar
- 8 garlic cloves, smashed
- ¼ cup chopped peeled fresh ginger
- 4 bird's-eye chiles, chopped
- 2 tablespoons salt
- 2 cups julienned hothouse cucumbers (use a mandolin)

A quick pickle, good for sandwiches; fried, they can be used with Coconut-Poached Tofu (page 148).

1. Bring all ingredients *except the cucumbers* to a boil in a small saucepan over high heat. Remove from the heat and let cool until lukewarm.

2. Carefully put the cucumbers in containers. They're very delicate, so try not to break them. Pour the warm liquid over the cucumbers, cover, and refrigerate overnight before using, or for up to a week.

VARIATION

FRIED PICKLES

To make fried pickles (frickles!), make your cucumber pickles above, drain, and blot them dry. Toss the cucumbers in ½ cup cornstarch, or as much as you need to completely coat them, and deep-fry (page 76) for 30 seconds to 1 minute, until they hold their shape.

PICKLED CAULIFLOWER

MAKES 4 CUPS

- 4 cups cauliflower florets
- ¾ cup white vinegar
- 6 tablespoons white wine vinegar
- 4 sprigs fresh rosemary
- 4 sprigs fresh thyme
- 1 tablespoon sugar
- 1½ tablespoons salt

As the X-Men movies taught us, mutants are hated and feared by society. But mutants (like cauliflower, a big knob of mutated floral stem cells) are also delicious when pickled and served with beer.

1. Steam the cauliflower until crisp-tender, 2 to 3 minutes, let cool to room temperature, then put it in a lidded container.

2. In a pot, bring all ingredients except the cauliflower to a boil over high heat, stirring to dissolve the sugar and salt. Remove from the heat and let cool to lukewarm.

3. Pour the contents of the pot over the cauliflower, then cover, and refrigerate overnight before using, or for up to 3 weeks.

SOUR RED CABBAGE

MAKES 1½ CUPS

- 1 teaspoon caraway seeds
- 2 cups very thinly sliced red cabbage
- 2 tablespoons salt
- ½ cup red wine vinegar
- ¼ cup sugar

This is actually a quick version of sauerkraut. Quick pickling is a cheat: by pouring hot vinegar over the vegetable you get all the flavor without the fermentation.

1. In a dry pan over medium heat, toast the caraway seeds until fragrant, about 5 minutes. Set aside.

2. Put the cabbage and salt in a medium bowl. Massage the salt into the cabbage until it weeps. Rinse the cabbage under running water and drain. Shake the excess water off the cabbage and put it in a lidded container. Add the caraway seeds.

3. In a small pot over high heat, simmer the vinegar and sugar until the sugar melts, about 2 minutes. Let cool, then pour over the cabbage. Cover and refrigerate overnight before using, or for up to 4 weeks.

PRESERVED ZUCCHINI

MAKES 2 CUPS

- 2 pounds zucchini, thickly sliced
- ¼ cup salt
- 10 garlic cloves
- 2 cups extra-virgin olive oil
- 2 tablespoons apple cider vinegar
- 1 tablespoon sugar
- 1 cup lightly packed tarragon sprigs
- 1 cup lightly packed mint sprigs

I serve these with Mint and Tarragon Fettuccine (page 176) but use them to add kick to any Middle Eastern dish, such as falafel or hummus, or grilled and chopped in salads.

1. In a large bowl, toss the zucchini with the salt. Let it sit for one hour, and then rinse and drain.

2. Meanwhile, blend the garlic and olive oil in a blender then pour into a saucepan. *Slowly* bring to a boil over low heat.

3. Add the vinegar and sugar and *slowly* return to a boil. Remove from the heat and let cool to room temperature.

4. Pack the zucchini, tarragon, and mint into a container and pour in the oil mixture until they're covered. Cover and refrigerate overnight before using, or for up to 2 weeks.

KIMCHI

MAKES 6 CUPS

- ½ cup kosher salt
- 1¼ pounds watermelon radish, julienned
- ¼ pound carrots, julienned
- ¼ pound Jerusalem artichokes, julienned
- ¼ pound kohlrabi, julienned
- ¾ pound daikon radish, julienned
- ¾ pound red radish, julienned
- 2 tablespoons minced garlic
- 2 tablespoons minced peeled fresh ginger
- 2 tablespoons grated fresh horseradish (page 131)
- 2 tablespoons minced bird's-eye chiles

Besides Preserved Lemons (opposite), this is the only other fermented pickle in this book. I use it in Kimchi Doughnuts (page 108), but it tastes good on pretty much anything you can fit in your mouth.

1. In a large container, mix the salt with 2 cups water.

2. Add the watermelon radish, carrots, Jerusalem artichokes, kohlrabi, daikon radish, and red radish to the salt water. Weigh them down to completely submerge the vegetables.

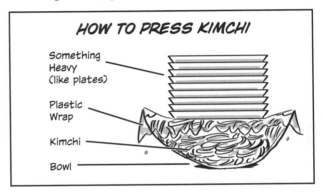

HOW TO PRESS KIMCHI

Something Heavy (like plates)

Plastic Wrap

Kimchi

Bowl

3. Let stand, covered, at room temperature for 24 hours to soften the vegetables so they are better able to absorb the aromatics.

4. Drain the vegetables, but reserve the soaking brine. Taste a vegetable; it should be just on the verge of "too salty." If it tastes inedibly salty, rinse the vegetables. If it is not salty at all, massage a tablespoon of salt into the vegetables.

5. In a food processor, pulse the aromatics—garlic, ginger, horseradish, and chiles—into a rough paste.

6. In a large bowl, mix the veggies with the paste. Pack them into as small a container as possible. Add the reserved brine to cover the vegetables, then weigh them down again and cover with plastic wrap.

7. Let them sit in a cool, dark place for at least 1 week and up to 3 weeks. The longer they ferment, the better they become. After the first 48 hours, check to ensure tiny bubbles are forming. This is proof of fermentation. Store covered in the fridge for up to 3 weeks.

PRESERVED LEMONS

MAKES 5½ CUPS

- 1 teaspoon coriander seeds
- 10 lemons
  Kosher salt, as needed
- 2 teaspoons saffron
- ¾ cup fresh lemon juice, or as needed

This classic Moroccan pickle is one of only two recipes in this book that actually needs to ferment, so use a glass jar instead of plastic because it reacts less with food over the long haul. Dice it fine and add it to sautéed vegetables, or use it in Jicama Slaw (page 89) and Preserved Lemon Mayonnaise (page 127).

1. In a dry pan on medium heat, toast the coriander seeds until fragrant, about 5 minutes. Set aside.

2. Rinse the lemons, and then cut a deep X in one end of each lemon.

3. Pack the X with as much salt as possible, about 2 tablespoons per lemon.

4. Stuff the lemons in a glass jar and add the coriander seeds, saffron, and ¼ cup salt. Pack tightly and press down so the lemons release their juice. Add enough lemon juice to cover.

5. Let sit in a cool place for at least 2 weeks before using, turning over the jar every 3 days.

PEAR AND FENNEL COMPOTE

MAKES 1¾ CUPS

- ¼ cup dried sour cherries
- 2 tablespoons chopped crystallized ginger
- ½ cup diced fennel
- 2 cups diced peeled pears
- 1 tablespoon agave nectar
- 1 tablespoon apple cider vinegar
- ½ tablespoon ground fennel seeds
- ½ tablespoon ground ginger
  Pinch of salt

Make sure the fennel and pears are diced the same size and substitute peach for pear when in season.

1. Soak the cherries and crystallized ginger in 1 cup hot water until soft, about 30 minutes. Drain and finely chop.

2. In a dry saucepan over very low heat, sweat the fennel (page 18) until soft, 10 to 15 minutes. Add the pears and cook until partially soft, about 10 minutes.

3. Add the remaining ingredients and cook for at least 10 minutes, stirring constantly, until everything is soft and well mixed. Let cool and serve.

EGGPLANT JAM

MAKES 2 CUPS

1¼ pounds Japanese eggplant

This...   ...not this.

4 tablespoons extra-virgin olive oil
1 teaspoon minced garlic
1 tablespoon sugar
2 tablespoons chopped flat-leaf parsley
2 teaspoons fresh lemon juice
Salt

Designed for Olive Fettuccine (page 173), this tastes like a sweeter version of baba ganoush and goes well with all kinds of pasta, and even works as a dip.

1. Trim and peel the eggplants. Cut them in half lengthwise and coat them with 2½ tablespoons of the olive oil. Save the peels if you are making Eggplant Ribbons (page 175).

2. Grill the eggplant halves (page 77) until they're charred on all sides. Alternatively, roast over an open flame on the stove for a few minutes to char.

3. Put the eggplant in a food processor and process for up to 1 minute to make a chunky paste.

4. Start a pan with the remaining 1½ tablespoons olive oil and the garlic (page 17). Add the eggplant paste and cook on low heat until there's no liquid left, about 15 minutes.

5. Add the sugar, parsley, and lemon juice and cook, stirring, until the excess liquid has cooked away, about 3 minutes. Salt to taste and remove from the heat. Let cool. Store covered in the fridge for up to 1 week.

RED PEPPER JAM

MAKES 1 CUP

1 pound red bell peppers
½ cup sugar

I use this in my Red Pepper Velvet Cake (page 207), and it also makes a killer cream-cheese-and–Red Pepper Jam sandwich. You'll need a candy thermometer for this recipe.

1. Seed and dice ½ pound of the peppers and put them in a medium pot.

2. Use a juicer (page 22) to juice the remaining ½ pound peppers and add the juice to the pot.

3. Add the sugar to the pot and cook over medium-low heat until the mixture reaches 220°F. Pour into a bowl and let cool.

4. Blend the mixture in a blender until smooth. Cover and refrigerate until ready to use, for up to 1 month.

LEMON CONFIT

MAKES ¼ CUP

2 lemons

3 tablespoons sugar

This adds sweet-and-sour notes to any soup, and is especially good with Spinach Soup (page 58). Any citrus fruit can be made into a confit with this recipe.

1. Use a zester to remove the zest from the lemons. Squeeze the lemons to get 3 tablespoons juice and set aside.

2. In a pot over high heat, bring 2 cups water to a boil. Add the lemon zest and return the water to a boil. Boil for 3 minutes. Drain the zest. Repeat twice more, using fresh water each time (this makes the zest less bitter).

3. In a very small pot, bring the lemon juice and sugar to a boil over low heat and cook until the sugar is totally dissolved.

4. Add the zest to the lemon juice. If the zest is not covered by the juice, add water until covered. Turn the heat to low and cook until the zest is almost translucent and the lemon juice is thick and syrupy, about 20 minutes. Cool before serving. Store covered in the fridge for up to 1 month.

HOW TO PREPARE FRUIT RIND FOR COOKING

PEEL to add flavor to a liquid.

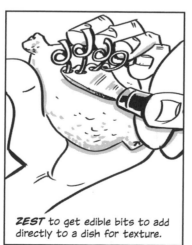

ZEST to get edible bits to add directly to a dish for texture.

RASP to get very fine bits to add taste but not texture.

KUMQUAT-PINK PEPPERCORN MARMALADE

MAKES 2 CUPS

- 2 cups sliced and seeded kumquats
- 1 cup fresh orange juice
- 3 tablespoons sugar
- 2 tablespoons whole pink peppercorns, cracked
- 1 tablespoon ginger juice (squeezed from 3 tablespoons grated peeled fresh ginger)

Jam, like the ones that have come before, includes pieces of fruit, but no skin or rind. Marmalade, on the other hand, is fruit cooked with its rind in sugar. This marmalade, made with kumquats, is used in Onion Soup (page 60). The two that follow are prepared the same way but produce very different results.

1. Bring 3 cups water to a boil and blanch the kumquat in the water for about 2 minutes (see page 19); this will remove some of the bitterness from the peel. Drain and let dry.

2. In a pan over low heat, simmer the orange juice and sugar until the sugar has dissolved. Add the kumquats, peppercorns, and ginger juice. Simmer, stirring occasionally, until the mixture becomes a thick, syrupy paste, 30 to 40 minutes.

3. Remove from the heat and let cool. Store covered in the fridge for up to 1 month.

VARIATIONS

LEMON–BLACK PEPPER MARMALADE

Blanch 2 cups diced and seeded lemon (with peel) as in step 1 of Kumquat–Pink Peppercorn Marmalade. In a pan over low heat, simmer 1/4 cup fresh lemon juice and 1/4 cup sugar until the sugar has dissolved. Add 2 tablespoons grated lemon zest and 2 tablespoons cracked black peppercorns and proceed as in step 2 of Kumquat–Pink Peppercorn Marmalade.

GRAPEFRUIT-CORIANDER MARMALADE

In a dry pan on medium heat, toast 2 tablespoons coriander seeds until fragrant, about 5 minutes. Set aside. Blanch 2 cups diced and seeded grapefruit, with peels, as in step 1 of Kumquat–Pink Peppercorn Marmalade. In a pan over low heat, simmer 1 cup fresh grapefruit juice and 1/4 cup sugar until the sugar has dissolved. Add 2 tablespoons grated grapefruit zest and proceed as in step 2 of Kumquat–Pink Peppercorn Marmalade.

This is my contractor, B▮▮▮▮▮▮▮.* I hired him to build Dirt Candy.

*My lawyer says I can't use real names. It makes me want to go all Charles Bronson that they stole my money and I have to worry about *them* suing *me*.

I was willing to overlook the warning signs.

YOU TOLD ME THAT THIS FLOORING COST $1200. BUT THE INVOICE SAYS $2600.

ARE YOU SAYING I'M *LYING*? ARE YOU CALLING ME A LIAR?

MOM? SHE JUST CALLED ME A *LIAR*! AM I A LIAR, MOM?

MY MOM SAYS I'M *NOT* A LIAR!

A *lot* of warning signs.

Carl, B████'s foreman.

B█████ ISN'T HERE. HE HAD A **NERVOUS BREAKDOWN** AND IS IN THE HOSPITAL. BUT HE WAS RIPPING YOU OFF. PAY ME $50,000...

...AND *I'LL* FINISH THE JOB FOR YOU.

Two days later.

HOSPITAL? I WASN'T IN THE HOSPITAL. I WAS ON ANOTHER JOB. I'M FINE.

I NEVER SAID HE HAD A BREAKDOWN. B████'S DOING A **GREAT** JOB!

Why did I think this disturbed person could build my restaurant? Why didn't I immediately grasp that he was *hopelessly* insane? Obviously I was deluding myself.

But everyone who opens a restaurant lives in a state of constant delusion. We all dream of **SUCCESS** and **CELEBRITIES** and **FABULOSITY**.

SALMAN? WOULD YOUR GUESTS BE MORE COMFORTABLE IN MY PRIVATE ROOM?

(HOW DOES SHE GET HER ROLLS SO *YEASTY?*)

TABLE 104 WANTS YOU TO KNOW THAT YOUR FOOD *SUCKS*.

Sudden Reality Onset Syndrome is the reason *half* of all restaurants go *bust*.

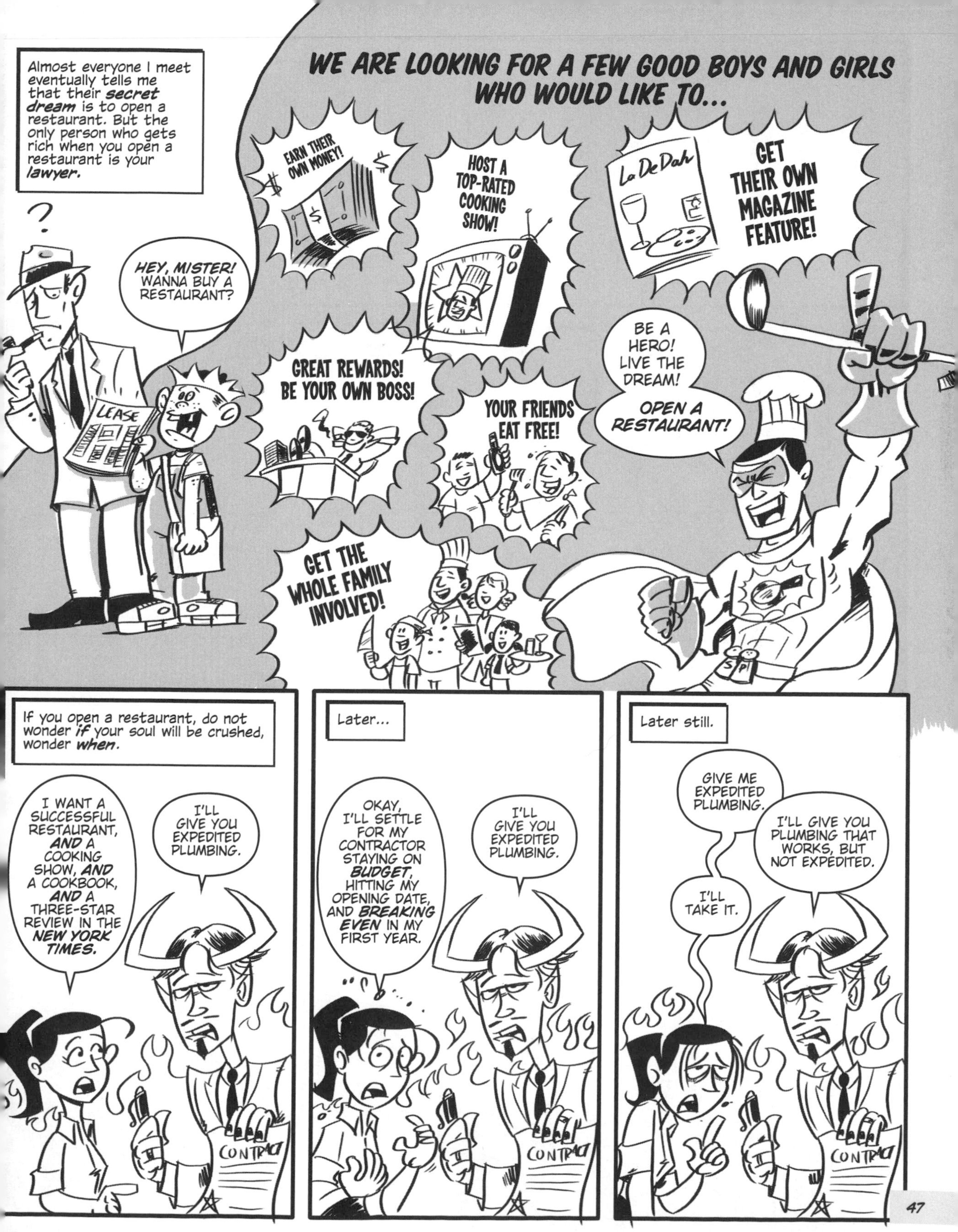

Almost everyone I meet eventually tells me that their **secret dream** is to open a restaurant. But the only person who gets rich when you open a restaurant is your **lawyer.**
WE ARE LOOKING FOR A FEW GOOD BOYS AND GIRLS WHO WOULD LIKE TO...
EARN THEIR OWN MONEY!
HOST A TOP-RATED COOKING SHOW!
La De Dah
GET THEIR OWN MAGAZINE FEATURE!
LEASE
HEY, MISTER! WANNA BUY A RESTAURANT?
GREAT REWARDS! BE YOUR OWN BOSS!
YOUR FRIENDS EAT FREE!
BE A HERO! LIVE THE DREAM!
OPEN A RESTAURANT!
GET THE WHOLE FAMILY INVOLVED!
If you open a restaurant, do not wonder *if* your soul will be crushed, wonder *when*.
I WANT A SUCCESSFUL RESTAURANT, **AND** A COOKING SHOW, **AND** A COOKBOOK, **AND** A THREE-STAR REVIEW IN THE ***NEW YORK TIMES.***
I'LL GIVE YOU EXPEDITED PLUMBING.
CONTRACT
Later...
OKAY, I'LL SETTLE FOR MY CONTRACTOR STAYING ON **BUDGET**, HITTING MY OPENING DATE, AND **BREAKING EVEN** IN MY FIRST YEAR.
I'LL GIVE YOU EXPEDITED PLUMBING.
CONTRACT
Later still.
GIVE ME EXPEDITED PLUMBING.
I'LL GIVE YOU PLUMBING THAT WORKS, BUT NOT EXPEDITED.
I'LL TAKE IT.
CONTRACT

BUY A LEASE

- buy an existing restaurant
- pay current owner key money ($75,000 - $300,000)
- take over liquor license
- take over lease
- take over old problems

BUILD-OUT

- build a restaurant from scratch
- negotiate a new lease
- apply for a new liquor license
- hire a contractor and an architect
- develop new problems

There are two ways to wind up with a restaurant. You can either buy a lease (used), or do a build-out (new).

At first I tried to buy a lease, but that didn't go very well.

I WANT $200,000 IN KEY MONEY. *CASH.*

LIKE A *CASHIER'S* CHECK?

LIKE IN A BAG. A NICE BAG.

I WANT TO KEEP THE BAG.

Then I found a tiny space on Ninth Street that had low rent.

IT NEEDS NEW WIRING, PLUMBING, WALLS, A NEW CEILING, THE FLOOR IS ROTTEN, IT DOESN'T HAVE A HOOD.

I *LOVE* IT! I'LL *TAKE* IT! IT'S *MINE!*

Clearly deluded.

I hired Craig as my architect, and he was as blind-sided by what happened next as I was. We planned for everything: budget overruns, scheduling problems, materials issues. But opening Dirt Candy was like getting run over by a *truck*.

...WELL, THAT WAS WORSE THAN I EXPECTED.

DID YOU ANGER AN OLD WITCH IN A PREVIOUS LIFE? BECAUSE YOU ARE CLEARLY *CURSED.*

First we chose our contractor, which is like picking your mugger.
You know it's going to hurt, but you want someone who might leave you with cab money.

I expected any contractor would **steal** a bit, shaving off money over here, and inflating a quote over there. B▓▓▓'s problem was that he stole too much.

$4500

The job cost **way** more than his quote, but by the time he figured that out he'd already taken $110,000 to do $25,000 worth of work. How was he going to steal enough of my money to finish?

CHANGE ORDER $85000

A change order! For $85,000. He dropped it on us in May, the month we were supposed to open. Dirt Candy was still a gutted shell and suddenly we magically owed him $85,000 more.

IT'S A LEGIT CHANGE ORDER! FOR THE FIRE SUPPRESSION SYSTEM!

THAT'S IN THE ORIGINAL PLANS!

IS NOT!

IT'S RIGHT **THERE!**

I'M GOING TO CALL MY DAD!

HE CAN'T FINISH THE JOB BECAUSE HE'S ALREADY SPENT THE MONEY. WE NEED TO PAY HIM MORE MONEY OR FIRE HIM.

I WOULDN'T BE SURPRISED IF HE *DISAPPEARED.*

Which is exactly what he did. But not before stealing **ALL** the materials I'd paid for.

....CRAP....

I *ransomed* them back from B█████'s dad for $6,000, but it took four weeks and the handover didn't go so smoothly.

I WANT $5,000 MORE!

GIVE ME MY WOOD!

A GIRL CAN'T MAKE ME DO ANYTHING!

I WILL RIP OUT YOUR HEART!

DON'T YOU DISRESPECT ME!

Craig hired M███ to be my new contractor. It was June, we'd missed two opening dates. I'd spent $110,000 and I didn't have a restaurant. And M███ wasn't listening to me because...I was a girl!? I still don't know.

I NEED YOU TO CALL AND SCHEDULE THE GAS INSPECTION.

SURE.

SURE.

THERE'S A THREE-MONTH WAITING LIST FOR INSPECTIONS, AND THEY WON'T TURN MY GAS ON UNTIL I'M INSPECTED.

SO YOU'RE GOING TO CALL THEM TOMORROW?

SURE.

Then there was Joey, B█████'s plumber. I kept him on because he was putting in the gas and it already looked like I might not get it turned on in time. My nightmare was to open without gas.

YOU *WILL* HAVE GAS. TRUST ME. YOU *MUST* HAVE GAS TO OPEN. OF COURSE!

Unfortunately, I had given Joey and M███ a gift: someone else to blame.

HE'S IN CHARGE OF A/C!

HE IS THE ONE DOING THE A/C!

PLUMBER DOES A/C!

ELECTRICIAN HANDLES A/C!

PLUMBER!

ELECTRICIAN!

It was October. I'd blown *three* opening dates. Staff was on the clock. I'd spent $320,000 and still: no restaurant. And then...

I CALLED TO SCHEDULE THE GAS INSPECTION TODAY.

...THEY SAID THEY'LL DO IT IN *JANUARY*.

51

YEAH, THE JOB'S FINISHED, TOO. I'M NOT DOING ANY MORE.

GET JOEY TO FINISH IT FOR YOU.

Then Joey took some more of my money and *HE* disappeared, too. And still, no one had scheduled the gas inspection. For the first five months we cooked on electric mini-appliances from Bed Bath & Beyond.

THIS MIGHTY TOASTER OVEN IS *PERFECT* FOR BAKING! THIS COUNTERTOP DEEP-FAT FRYER WILL FRY *MOUNTAINS* OF HUSH PUPPIES! THIS TEENY GRILL WILL BE A *VOLCANO* OF HEAT AND POWER!

I'M ALREADY LOOKING FOR ANOTHER JOB.

And, after all that work, the walls still weren't level.

@#$!

3"

My little restaurant is 650 square feet and I've spent over *$400,000* to get it up and running.

I knew it would be hard, but I was deluding myself about just *how* hard it would be. But maybe we need our delusions. Maybe they're what gets us through the tough times.

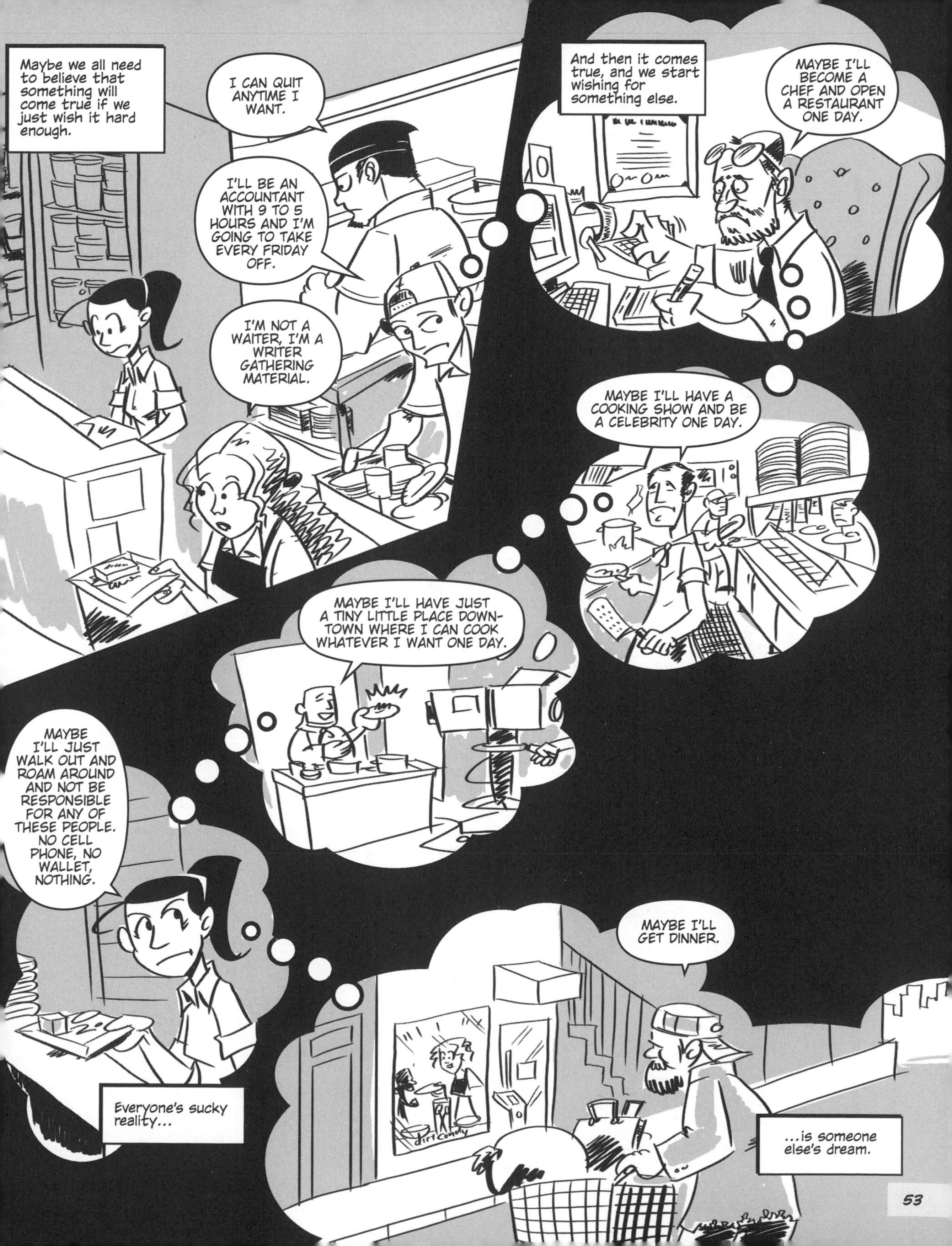

Maybe we all need to believe that something will come true if we just wish it hard enough.
I CAN QUIT ANYTIME I WANT.
I'LL BE AN ACCOUNTANT WITH 9 TO 5 HOURS AND I'M GOING TO TAKE EVERY FRIDAY OFF.
I'M NOT A WAITER, I'M A WRITER GATHERING MATERIAL.
And then it comes true, and we start wishing for something else.
MAYBE I'LL BECOME A CHEF AND OPEN A RESTAURANT ONE DAY.
MAYBE I'LL HAVE A COOKING SHOW AND BE A CELEBRITY ONE DAY.
MAYBE I'LL HAVE JUST A TINY LITTLE PLACE DOWN-TOWN WHERE I CAN COOK WHATEVER I WANT ONE DAY.
MAYBE I'LL JUST WALK OUT AND ROAM AROUND AND NOT BE RESPONSIBLE FOR ANY OF THESE PEOPLE. NO CELL PHONE, NO WALLET, NOTHING.
MAYBE I'LL GET DINNER.
Everyone's sucky reality...
dirt candy
...is someone else's dream.

BASIC STOCK

MAKES 6 CUPS

- 1 cup chopped yellow onion
- ½ cup chopped carrot
- ½ cup chopped celery
- ¼ cup chopped fresh shiitakes
- 3-inch piece of lemongrass, bruised and sliced
- 4 garlic cloves, smashed
- 8 sprigs flat-leaf parsley
- 4 sprigs fresh cilantro

Dirt Candy's basic stock is the basis for most of the dishes in this cookbook. All the ingredients should be chopped the same size and shape, as much as is possible, so they cook at the same speed.

1. Put all of the ingredients in a large pot with 8 cups water. Bring to a boil over medium heat, reduce the heat, and simmer until the vegetables are soft, about 30 minutes.

2. Strain and let cool. Freeze for up to 3 months, or store in the fridge for up to 1 week.

Peel off the outer leaves of the lemongrass.

Hit the piece with the back of a knife several times to break fibers and release oils.

Scrape back and forth with the knife. Then slice it.

VARIATIONS

CORN STOCK

To make a corn stock, include 4 corncobs (with or without kernels) when making the Basic Stock recipe. I use this in grits (page 153).

ASPARAGUS STOCK

Add 2 cups diced asparagus stems and peelings to the Basic Stock recipe. This stock is used to make Asparagus Paella (page 150).

RADISH STOCK

Add 2 cups chopped radishes to the Basic Stock recipe, and use only 2 garlic cloves instead of 4. I use this in Lemon Corn Sauce (page 127).

CARROT STOCK

MAKES 6 CUPS

- 4 cups sliced carrots
- 1 cup roughly chopped yellow onion
- 3 garlic cloves, chopped
- 1 cup sliced celery

1. Put all of the ingredients in a large pot with 8 cups water. Bring to a boil over medium heat, reduce the heat, and simmer for 30 minutes.

2. Strain and let cool. Freeze for up to 3 months, or store in the fridge for up to 1 week.

ROASTED POTATO SOUP

WITH CRISPY VINEGAR POTATOES AND TOMATO PEARLS

ROASTED
POTATO SOUP

+

TOMATO PEARLS
(OPTIONAL)
page 57

+

VINEGAR POTATOES
(OPTIONAL)
page 100

SERVES 4 TO 6

⅓ cup plus ¼ cup extra-virgin
    olive oil

1 cup chopped white onion

10 garlic cloves, smashed

1 teaspoon grated lemon zest
    (page 43)

6 to 8 cups Basic Stock (opposite)

6 russet (Idaho) potatoes
    Salt

⅓ cup crème fraîche (optional)

The trouble with potato soup: how to keep it from getting gluey. I do this by roasting the potatoes first, to break down their starches, then using a food mill instead of a blender, which keeps them from becoming overprocessed and gummy.

1. Start a pot over medium heat with ⅓ cup of the olive oil, the onion, and the garlic (page 17).

2. Add the lemon zest, then pour in 6 cups of the stock. Bring to a boil, and let boil for 15 minutes, stirring occasionally. Remove from the heat and let cool to room temperature. Puree in a blender until silky.

3. Preheat the oven to its lowest temperature (150° to 200°F). Poke holes in the potatoes with a fork and wrap them in foil.

4. Roast the potatoes for 3 hours, until tender. Unwrap the potatoes and peel them. The skins should slide right off. Smash them onto a baking sheet in a layer about ½ inch thick, completely breaking them apart in the process. Pour the remaining ¼ cup oil over the potatoes and sprinkle them with 1 teaspoon salt.

RECIPE CONTINUES ➡

Roasting like this is actually baking. In the oven, you've dried the potatoes by evaporating their water.

Now you're giving the potatoes more flavor by pouring in the soup base...

...and letting capillary action suck it into the desiccated potatoes. This rehydrates them with delicious stock instead of flavorless water.

5. Return the potatoes to the oven. Roast until they're golden brown and have a crunchy crust, about 30 minutes.

6. Remove the potatoes from the oven, put them in a pot, and pour in 6 cups of the soup base. Cook over low heat, stirring occasionally, until the potatoes are very soft, 20 to 30 minutes. Remove from heat and let cool to room temperature.

7. Puree the potatoes in a food mill (**not** a food processor or blender) and push through a chinois (page 23) to remove lumps. Put the pureed potatoes in a pot.

8. Add additional soup base or Basic Stock (up to 2 cups) to thin the soup until it has a thick and creamy texture, if needed. Every potato is different—some are bigger, some are starchier, some are just plain weird—so adjust accordingly. Salt to taste.

9. *To serve:*

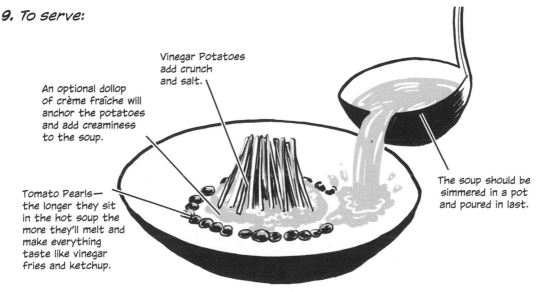

Vinegar Potatoes add crunch and salt.

An optional dollop of crème fraîche will anchor the potatoes and add creaminess to the soup.

Tomato Pearls— the longer they sit in the hot soup the more they'll melt and make everything taste like vinegar fries and ketchup.

The soup should be simmered in a pot and poured in last.

TOMATO PEARLS

MAKES ½ CUP

2.5 grams sodium alginate
50 milliliters ketchup
2.5 grams calcium gluconate

Molecular cooking is hard, but there's a mad-scientist rush when you pull off this recipe. Think of it as ketchup caviar, because what goes better with potatoes than ketchup? All ingredient measurements are given in metric for super-science accuracy, and one of the best online sources for molecular gear is Le Sanctuaire.

1. Blend 500 milliliters water with the sodium alginate in a blender. Pour into a bowl and cover with plastic wrap.

2. Thoroughly rinse the blender. **This is very important:** alginate cannot even **touch** the gluconate. Blend the ketchup and 50 milliliters water with the calcium gluconate in the blender. Transfer to a bowl and cover with plastic wrap.

3. Keeping the mixtures separate, let them settle overnight in the fridge.

4.

Drop a small strainer into the sodium alginate mixture.

Fill another bowl with cold water.

Using a dropper or syringe, slowly dribble the gluconate mixture into the alginate solution. Stop pressing the dropper before any two droplets touch.

Let the balls settle, give a little shake, then lift out of the mixture.

Gently slide the balls into the bowl of clean water. Repeat until the gluconate solution is finished.

5. Rinse the tomato balls gently under running water and then throw out any broken ones. Store in the fridge for up to 2 days.

SPINACH SOUP

WITH SMOKED CORN DUMPLINGS AND LEMON CONFIT

SPINACH
SOUP

+

SMOKED CORN DUMPLINGS
(OPTIONAL)
opposite

+

LEMON CONFIT
(OPTIONAL)
page 43

SERVES 4 TO 6

- 6 tablespoons extra-virgin olive oil
- ½ cup diced yellow onion
- 1½ tablespoons minced garlic
- 1½ tablespoons minced peeled fresh ginger
- ½ tablespoon grated lime zest (page 43)
- ½ tablespoon diced seeded jalapeño
- ¼ cup diced peeled potato
- 3 cups Basic Stock (page 54)
- 4 cups tightly packed spinach leaves
- 1½ cups roughly chopped flat-leaf parsley
- 1 cup roughly chopped fresh cilantro
- Salt

This is my simplest soup; it's just an easy puree. Heat makes vegetables bright, but you only get one chance to bring out the color of a green vegetable. That's why I don't cook the spinach until the very last minute.

1. Start a pot over medium heat with the olive oil and the onion (page 17), then add the garlic, ginger, lime zest, and jalapeño and cook until very soft, about 6 minutes.

2. Add the potato and stir once or twice. Pour in the stock, bring to a simmer, and cook until the potatoes are soft, about 10 minutes. Remove from heat and let cool for 15 minutes in an ice bath.

3.

Blend Stock

Strain

Chill until ice cold

4.

Add:
-Raw
 Spinach
-Cilantro
-Parsley
...then
blend
again.

Strain
Should
look
almost
black!

Strain again

Smooth
as silk!

5. Heat the soup over medium heat. This is when it should turn bright green. Add salt to taste and serve immediately, topping each portion with Smoked Corn Dumplings and Lemon Confit, if you like.

SMOKED CORN DUMPLINGS

MAKES 32 DUMPLINGS

- 2 cups fresh or frozen corn kernels
- 3 tablespoons finely diced peeled jicama
- 1½ teaspoons finely chopped scallion
- 1½ teaspoons finely chopped fresh mint
- ¼ teaspoon salt
- 2 teaspoons potato starch
- ¾ teaspoon rice wine vinegar
- ¼ teaspoon sesame oil
- 1 (14-ounce) package of store-bought eggless wonton wrappers (see Note)

1. Smoke the corn kernels (page 78) until they're light caramel colored, about 2 cycles in the smoker.

2. In a bowl, mix all of the ingredients except the wonton wrappers. This is the filling.

3. Cut, fill, and form the dumplings (see below).

4. Bring a deep pot of water to a boil. Drop the dumplings into the pot in batches and let them boil for 2 to 3 minutes. The dumplings will float to the surface when they're done, but there are a million reasons why they might not, so let them boil for at least 2 minutes before scooping them out with a slotted spoon.

Wonton wrappers are your secret weapon. You can always use them as an easy wrapper for any dumpling.

HOW TO MAKE DUMPLINGS

Lay the wrappers on the work surface and punch out the center with a round 2-inch cookie cutter. The round shape is easier to fold than square.

Place a heaping tablespoon of filling in the middle of the wrapper.

1 TBSP

...and fold into a half-moon.

Wet the edges of the wrapper with water...

Pinch the edges of the dumpling together.

ONION SOUP

WITH KUMQUAT-PINK PEPPERCORN MARMALADE AND GRILLED CHEESE CROUTONS

ONION
SOUP

+

GRILLED CHEESE
CROUTONS
page 84

+

KUMQUAT-PINK
PEPPERCORN MARMALADE
(OPTIONAL) page 44

+

PEARL ONION
FLOWERS (OPTIONAL)
opposite

SERVES 4

12 cups thinly sliced white onions
6 tablespoons extra-virgin olive oil
4 cups Basic Stock (page 54)
   Salt

This is where flavors start getting layered and soup starts getting complicated. It'll take you two days to make this soup, but it can be frozen for future generations to enjoy once you're done.

1. In a pan over low heat, caramelize the onions in the olive oil (page 18), stirring continuously until they turn very dark and sweet, about 1 hour. Lay the onions on paper towels and blot them to absorb all the oil; the onions must be completely dry.

2. Spread the onions across a baking sheet. Turn the oven to dehydrating temperature (page 21) and dehydrate the onions for about 10 hours, until they are dry, like hard onion candy; once they darken, peek in every 30 minutes or so to make sure they're not burning. Remove and let cool.

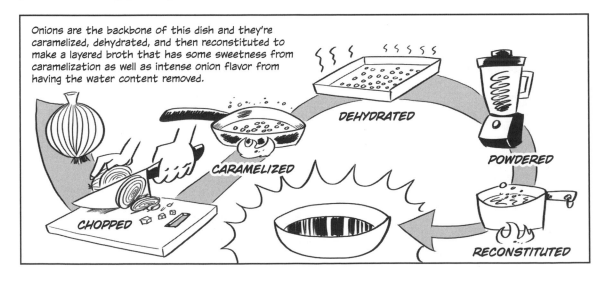

Onions are the backbone of this dish and they're caramelized, dehydrated, and then reconstituted to make a layered broth that has some sweetness from caramelization as well as intense onion flavor from having the water content removed.

DEHYDRATED

POWDERED

CARAMELIZED

CHOPPED

RECONSTITUTED

3. Pulse the onions in a blender until they form a powder. Add the stock and blend for 2 to 3 minutes, until smooth. Push through a chinois (page 23) to remove all the onion pieces. The final result should be a broth that's the color of weak coffee, with a super-strong onion taste.

4. To serve:

Pearl Onion Flowers

Just enough Kumquat-Pink Peppercorn Marmalade on top of each crouton to anchor the Pearl Onion Flowers.

Grilled Cheese Crouton

Bring soup to a simmer in a pot and pour it in last— gently so you don't knock over your pretty crouton stack!

PEARL ONION FLOWERS

MAKES 8 ONION FLOWERS

8 **pearl onions (not pickled cocktail onions)**
Oil for deep-frying (page 76)
¼ **cup cornstarch**
2 **cups Beer Batter (page 100)**

There's no such thing as having too many onions in onion soup. The garnish should always reinforce the main vegetable, just altering its texture or taste.

1. Peel the onions and cut off the top third. On the flat side of the onion, cut an *X* that goes about halfway through. Prepare a large bowl of ice water and soak the onions for 30 minutes.

2. Drain the onions. Shake off the excess water and blot with paper towels until the onions are completely dry.

3. Prepare a large pot of oil for deep-frying (page 76).

4. Roll the onions in cornstarch, and then dip in batter and immediately lower them into the hot oil. Use a slotted spoon to lift them from the oil the second they turn golden; you don't want them to get brown. Serve warm.

BUTTERNUT SQUASH SOUP

WITH BUTTERNUT SQUASH DUMPLINGS

BUTTERNUT
SQUASH SOUP

+

BUTTERNUT SQUASH
DUMPLINGS
opposite

+

COCONUT CREAM
(OPTIONAL)
see note, page 64

SERVES 4

- 1½ teaspoons coriander seeds
- ½ cup pumpkin seeds
- 3 tablespoons extra-virgin olive oil
- 2 cups chopped yellow onions
- 2 tablespoons chopped garlic
- 3 tablespoons chopped peeled fresh ginger
- 2 teaspoons ground sambar or curry powder
- ½ jalapeño, seeded and chopped
- 1 stalk lemongrass, chopped (page 54)
- 1 lemon, peel only, removed with a peeler
- 1 tablespoon salt
- 4 cups diced peeled butternut squash, with seeds
- 2 tablespoons sugar (optional)

At the restaurant, I roast spaghetti squash and add a little pile of it to the bottom of each bowl. I also make the soup creamier by adding a dollop of coconut cream on top.

1. Preheat the oven to 350°F.

2. In a dry pan over medium heat, toast the coriander seeds until fragrant, 5 minutes. Set aside.

3. Toast the pumpkin seeds on a baking sheet in the oven until they turn golden brown and you hear them pop, about 15 minutes. Let cool, then grind them into a powder.

4. Start a pot over medium heat with the olive oil, onions, and garlic (page 17). Add 8 cups water and all of the remaining ingredients except for the butternut squash, sugar, and coconut cream. Bring to a boil over medium heat, then reduce the heat to low, and simmer for 30 minutes.

5. Add the squash and cook until fork-tender, about 20 minutes. Taste, and if it's slightly bitter, add the sugar a teaspoon at a time (up to 2 tablespoons). How much you need to add depends on the sugar content of the squash.

6. Pour the contents of the pot into a baking dish and roast in the oven until it reduces and a crust starts to form, about 1 hour.

7. Remove from the oven and strain, then push through a chinois (page 23). Let cool to room temperature. Skim the oil off the top. Line a chinois with cheesecloth and push through again to make sure all the chunks are removed.

8. To serve:

1 tablespoon of Coconut Cream. Fat carries flavor. Adding butter or a cream at the last minute rounds out the edges in a dish and unifes the flavors.

The dumpling wrappers slowly melt and dissolve in the soup, adding extra squash flavor.

Heat soup to a low simmer in a pot and pour it in gently.

BUTTERNUT SQUASH DUMPLINGS

MAKES 20 DUMPLINGS

- 1 **butternut squash, halved, seeds removed**
- ¼ **cup extra-virgin olive oil**
- 2 **teaspoons minced garlic**
- 2 **teaspoons minced peeled ginger**
- 1 **cup diced sunchokes**
- ¼ **cup fresh lemon juice**
- 2 **teaspoons sugar**
- 2 **teaspoons Urfa biber pepper flakes**
- 1 **cup pumpkin seeds**
- 2 **tablespoons chopped fresh cilantro**
  Salt

Urfa biber is a dried Turkish pepper available at Middle Eastern grocery stores. If you can't find it, substitute your favorite chile powder.

1. Preheat the oven to 350°F.

2. Put the butternut squash flat side down on a baking sheet and bake until fork-tender, about 45 minutes. Let cool, then scoop out the flesh, reserve 1 cup for the filling, and puree the rest in a blender until smooth.

3. Reduce the oven temperature to dehydrate (page 21). Line 2 baking sheets with Silpat liners.

4. Spread the puree very thinly on the Silpats. Dehydrate the puree in the oven until the sheets are the texture of a fruit roll-up, about 4 hours; rotate the baking sheets every hour to ensure even dehydrating. Remove from the oven and let the wrappers cool. The wrappers can be stored for up to 1 week wrapped in plastic in a cool, dry place.

RECIPE CONTINUES ➡

LEAVE A 13.5-OUNCE CAN OF COCONUT MILK IN THE FRIDGE FOR AT LEAST 2 HOURS. STRAIN OFF THE LIQUID AND WHAT YOU'RE LEFT WITH IS SEMI-SOLID **COCONUT CREAM.**

5. While the wrappers are cooling, prepare the filling. Start a pan over medium heat with the oil, garlic, and ginger (page 17). Add the sunchokes and cook until they are almost translucent and smell very nutty, 3 minutes.

6. Stir the lemon juice and sugar into the pan and cook until the liquid has evaporated. Stir in the Urfa biber and reserved 1 cup butternut squash and cook for 5 minutes.

7. Stir in the pumpkin seeds, cilantro, and salt and cook for 5 minutes. Remove from the heat and let cool. Filling can be kept in the fridge for up to 1 week.

8.

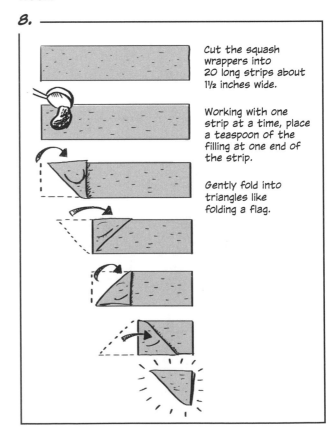

Cut the squash wrappers into 20 long strips about 1½ inches wide.

Working with one strip at a time, place a teaspoon of the filling at one end of the strip.

Gently fold into triangles like folding a flag.

PEA SOUP

WITH SPRING PEA FLAN AND PICKLED POTATOES

PEA SOUP

+

SPRING PEA FLAN
page 102

+

PICKLED POTATOES
(OPTIONAL) page 37

+

WASABI PEA LEAVES
(OPTIONAL) page 104

SERVES 4

- ½ tablespoon extra-virgin olive oil
- ¼ cup diced yellow onion
- ½ tablespoon chopped garlic
- ½ tablespoon chopped peeled fresh ginger
- 1 celery stalk, chopped
- 1 lemongrass stalk, chopped (page 54)
- 1 kaffir lime leaf
- 4 cups fresh or frozen peas
- 2 tablespoons chopped fresh mint
- 2 tablespoons chopped flat-leaf parsley
- 2 tablespoons chopped fresh cilantro
- Salt
- ¼ cup fresh peas, blanched and shocked (page 19)

Normally, pea soup is a thick glop full of ham that makes you want to hibernate. I created a pea soup that wakes you and gets you out of your winter cave. Vinegary Pickled Potatoes give it extra pop and Wasabi Pea Leaves add heat.

TO MAKE IT VEGAN

Use Vegan Spring Pea Flan (page 103).

1. In a large pot over low heat, add the oil and sweat the onions, garlic, and ginger (page 18). Add the celery, lemongrass, and kaffir lime leaf and cook, stirring, until the celery softens. Add about 4½ cups water, turn up the heat to bring to a boil, and then reduce the heat to a simmer.

2. Add the peas, mint, parsley, and cilantro. As soon as the peas turn bright green, 3 to 5 minutes, *immediately* remove the pot from the heat. Use a slotted spoon or a ricer to mash the peas so that they release their bright green, cooked liquid.

3. Pour through a strainer to remove large pieces, and then push through a chinois (page 23) to remove any remaining pieces. Let cool, then skim the oil off the surface.

4. Line a chinois with cheesecloth and push through again to remove all chunks. Return to the saucepan and simmer over medium heat before serving. Salt to taste.

5. To serve:

1 Wasabi Pea Leaf in each bowl adds spiciness.

The Spring Pea Flan will melt in the broth and thicken it.

Each bowl gets 1 tablespoon of blanched and shocked peas to add the taste of fresh peas to the dish.

Heat the soup to a light simmer and pour it in last.

4-5 pieces of Pickled Potato per bowl to give some bite.

WHY IS THERE ALWAYS BREAD AT A RESTAURANT?

A: RESTAURANTS WANT YOU TO GO HOME FULL AND BREAD IS A CHEAPER WAY TO FILL YOUR STOMACH THAN THIMBLES OF CAVIAR.

WHAT'S UP WITH THE PAPER DOILIES UNDER MY BOWL OF SOUP?

A: IT KEEPS THE BOWL FROM SLIDING OFF YOUR PLATE WHEN IT'S SET DOWN ON THE TABLE.

WHY ARE SO MANY RESTAURANTS RED?

A: THERE'S A LEGEND FLOATING AROUND THE RESTAURANT BUSINESS THAT RED MAKES PEOPLE HUNGRY.

WHO BUILT THE PYRAMIDS?

A: TEN-FOOT-TALL, SHAPE-SHIFTING LIZARDS FROM THE ALPHA DRACONIS SYSTEM.

WHAT IS THE CHUPACABRA?

A: THERE IS NO CHUPACABRA. IT IS A CONFUSED LEPRECHAUN LOST IN MEXICO.

WHO PAINTS RESTAURANT ART?

A: A ROBOT IN TUSCANY TAKES THE B&W PHOTOS, ANOTHER ROBOT IN CHINA DOES THE PAINTINGS.

THE WORLD IS FULL OF MYSTERIES. SOME WILL SURVIVE TO TROUBLE THE SLEEP OF FUTURE GENERATIONS. BUT TONIGHT WE ARE HERE TO SOLVE...ALMOST COMPLETELY UNSOLVABLE MYSTERIES.

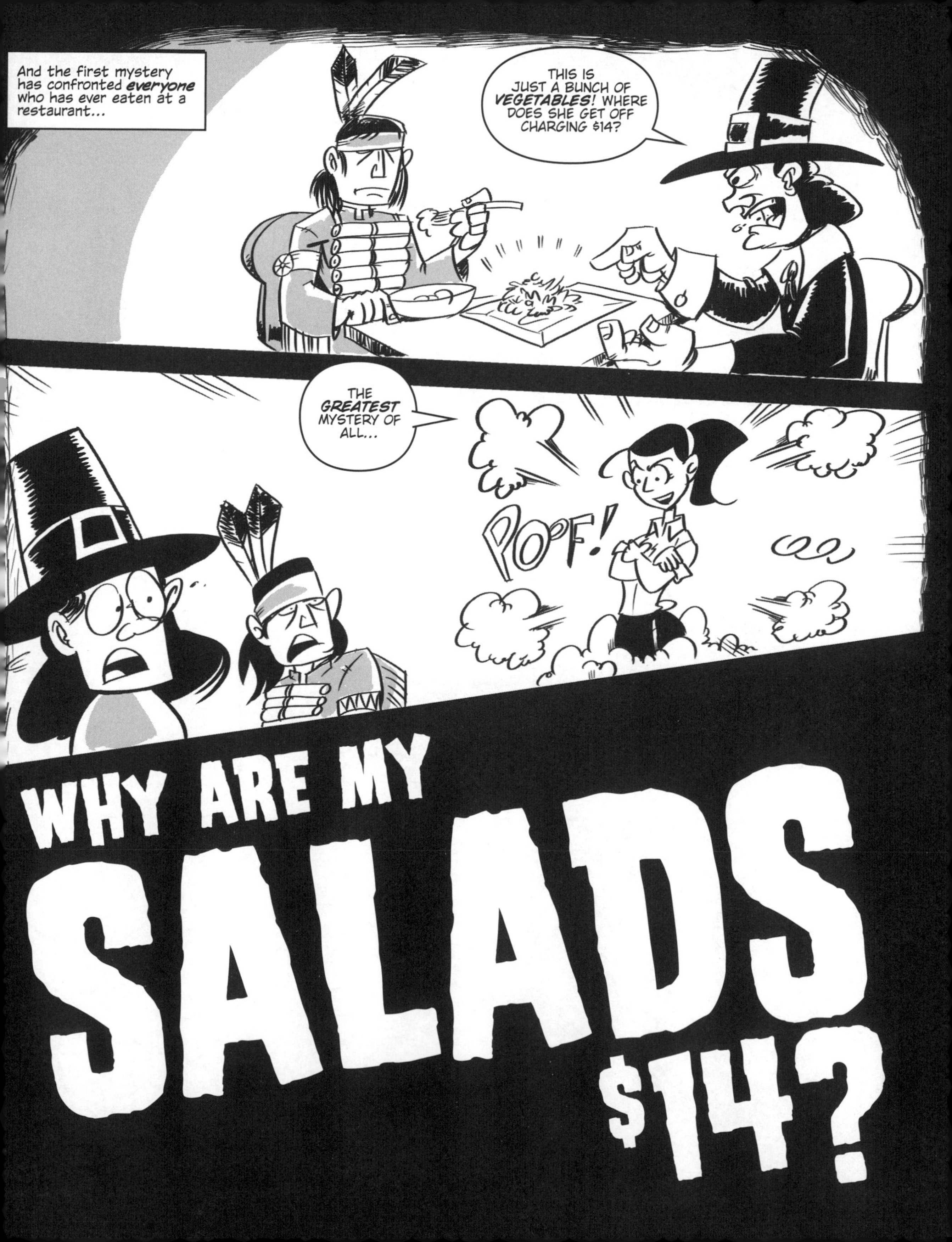

And the first mystery has confronted **everyone** who has ever eaten at a restaurant...
THIS IS JUST A BUNCH OF **VEGETABLES!** WHERE DOES SHE GET OFF CHARGING $14?
THE **GREATEST** MYSTERY OF ALL...
POOF!
WHY ARE MY SALADS $14?

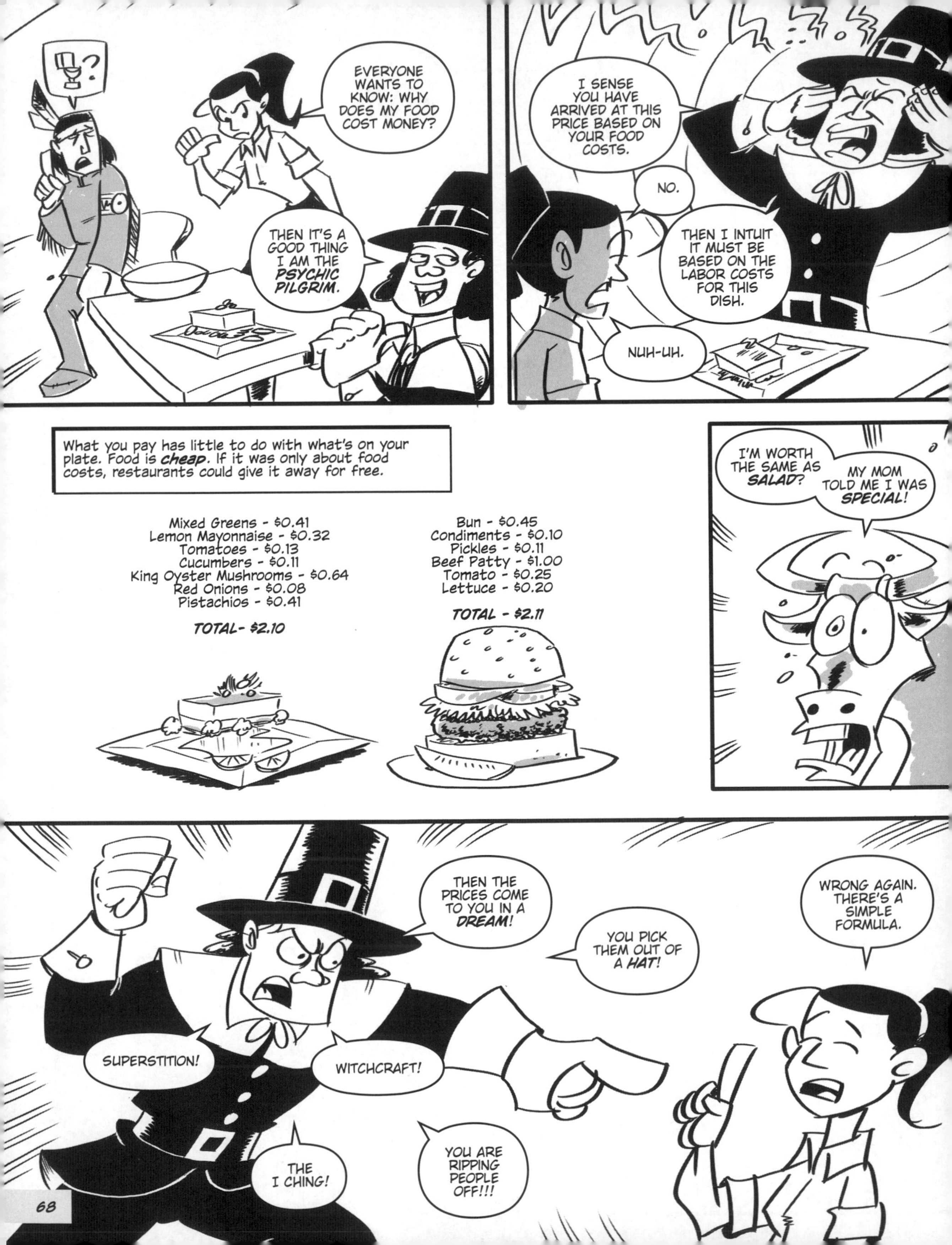
EVERYONE WANTS TO KNOW: WHY DOES MY FOOD COST MONEY?
THEN IT'S A GOOD THING I AM THE ***PSYCHIC PILGRIM***.
I SENSE YOU HAVE ARRIVED AT THIS PRICE BASED ON YOUR FOOD COSTS.
NO.
THEN I INTUIT IT MUST BE BASED ON THE LABOR COSTS FOR THIS DISH.
NUH-UH.
What you pay has little to do with what's on your plate. Food is ***cheap***. If it was only about food costs, restaurants could give it away for free.
Mixed Greens - $0.41
Lemon Mayonnaise - $0.32
Tomatoes - $0.13
Cucumbers - $0.11
King Oyster Mushrooms - $0.64
Red Onions - $0.08
Pistachios - $0.41
TOTAL- $2.10
Bun - $0.45
Condiments - $0.10
Pickles - $0.11
Beef Patty - $1.00
Tomato - $0.25
Lettuce - $0.20
TOTAL - $2.11
I'M WORTH THE SAME AS ***SALAD***?
MY MOM TOLD ME I WAS ***SPECIAL***!
THEN THE PRICES COME TO YOU IN A ***DREAM***!
YOU PICK THEM OUT OF A ***HAT***!
SUPERSTITION!
WITCHCRAFT!
THE I CHING!
YOU ARE RIPPING PEOPLE OFF!!!
WRONG AGAIN. THERE'S A SIMPLE FORMULA.

FORMULA FOR PRICING A DISH

What I Need to Make Each Night to Stay Open

DIVIDED BY

Number of Customers I Can Serve Per Night

Then I take that number and spread it across the menu. So when you eat the salad you're not just paying for the salad, you're paying for...

Jesus's paycheck!

Paper towels!

Unemployment insurance!

Cutlery!

My rent!

When you buy a dish, you're not paying for the food, you're *renting* the table, like renting an apartment, only for a shorter period of time, and you're not allowed to walk around in your *underwear*.

I CAN WEAR WHATEVER I WANT. I RENTED THIS TABLE.

Food costs are usually 25% of a restaurant's budget. To get a rough food cost you can divide by four, so a $30 steak costs the restaurant about $8.

- ☐ Salaries - 25%
- Food Costs - 23%
- ||| Wine Costs - 20%
- ■ Operating Expenses (utilities, trash removal, exterminator) - 14%
- ■ Rent - 8%
- Credit Card and Open Table charges - 7%
- Insurance - 3%

LYING WENCH! YOU CUT YOUR COSTS BY HIRING ILLEGAL IMMIGRANTS TO DO YOUR DIRTY WORK!!!

Actual illegal immigrant who actually worked illegally in Hong Kong.

Note: Don't assume every dishwasher is illegal! Some are just straight-up immigrants.

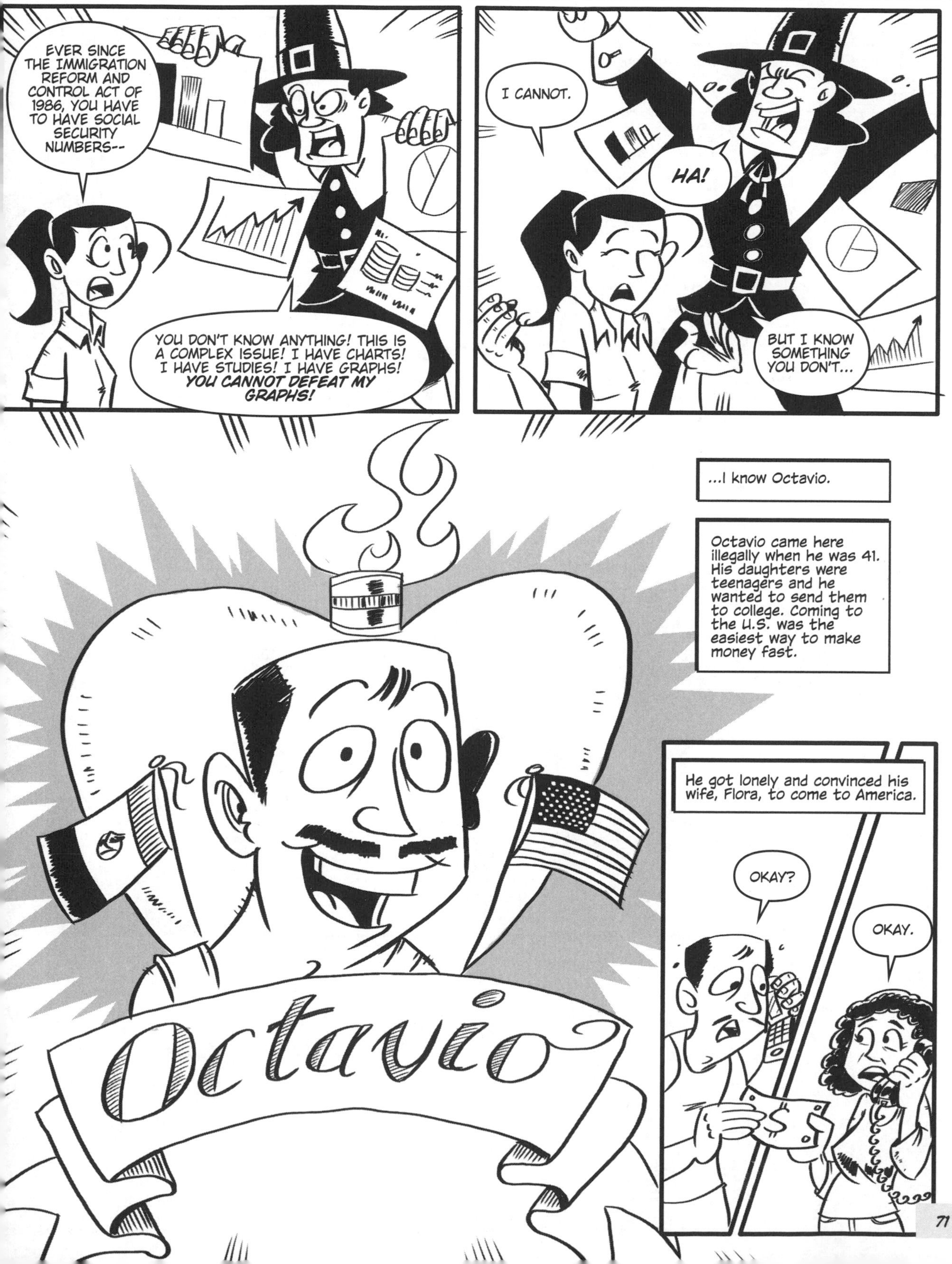
EVER SINCE THE IMMIGRATION REFORM AND CONTROL ACT OF 1986, YOU HAVE TO HAVE SOCIAL SECURITY NUMBERS--
YOU DON'T KNOW ANYTHING! THIS IS A COMPLEX ISSUE! I HAVE CHARTS! I HAVE STUDIES! I HAVE GRAPHS! ***YOU CANNOT DEFEAT MY GRAPHS!***
I CANNOT.
HA!
BUT I KNOW SOMETHING YOU DON'T...
...I know Octavio.
Octavio
Octavio came here illegally when he was 41. His daughters were teenagers and he wanted to send them to college. Coming to the U.S. was the easiest way to make money fast.
He got lonely and convinced his wife, Flora, to come to America.
OKAY?
OKAY.

She got busted coming over the border and Immigration warned her that if they caught her again she'd go to prison.

Octavio convinced her to try one more time.

OKAY?

...OKAY.

Flora came over with her 11-year-old nephew. His parents were in Illinois and they wanted their son with them, so they agreed to pay half her costs. They traveled in the back of a moving truck.

Because she had to travel light, Flora didn't bring anything with her. Only the clothes on her back.

I WILL BUY ALL MY WIFE'S FAVORITE CLOTHES, SO WHEN SHE ARRIVES IN NEW YORK THERE WILL BE A WHOLE NEW WARDROBE WAITING FOR HER!

The trip took forever, but then the van finally reached North Carolina, and...

...the driver was pulled over for speeding. His license was expired and that was all it took for them to open up the back.

Flora sat in detention in North Carolina for 3 months until they had enough illegals to ship back to Mexico.

It **destroyed** Octavio.

NO...
NO...
NO...
NO...
NO...

Octavio wanted to go see her. He fought us to let him go. We told him that if he went they'd arrest him too, and he'd lose everything he had worked for.

WE KEPT HIM FROM GOING BUT HE WASN'T THE SAME AFTER THAT.

THERE ARE A LOT OF CHARTS AND GRAPHS AND STATISTICS ABOUT ILLEGALS COMING TO AMERICA. BUT FOR ME, WHEN I THINK ABOUT IMMIGRATION ...

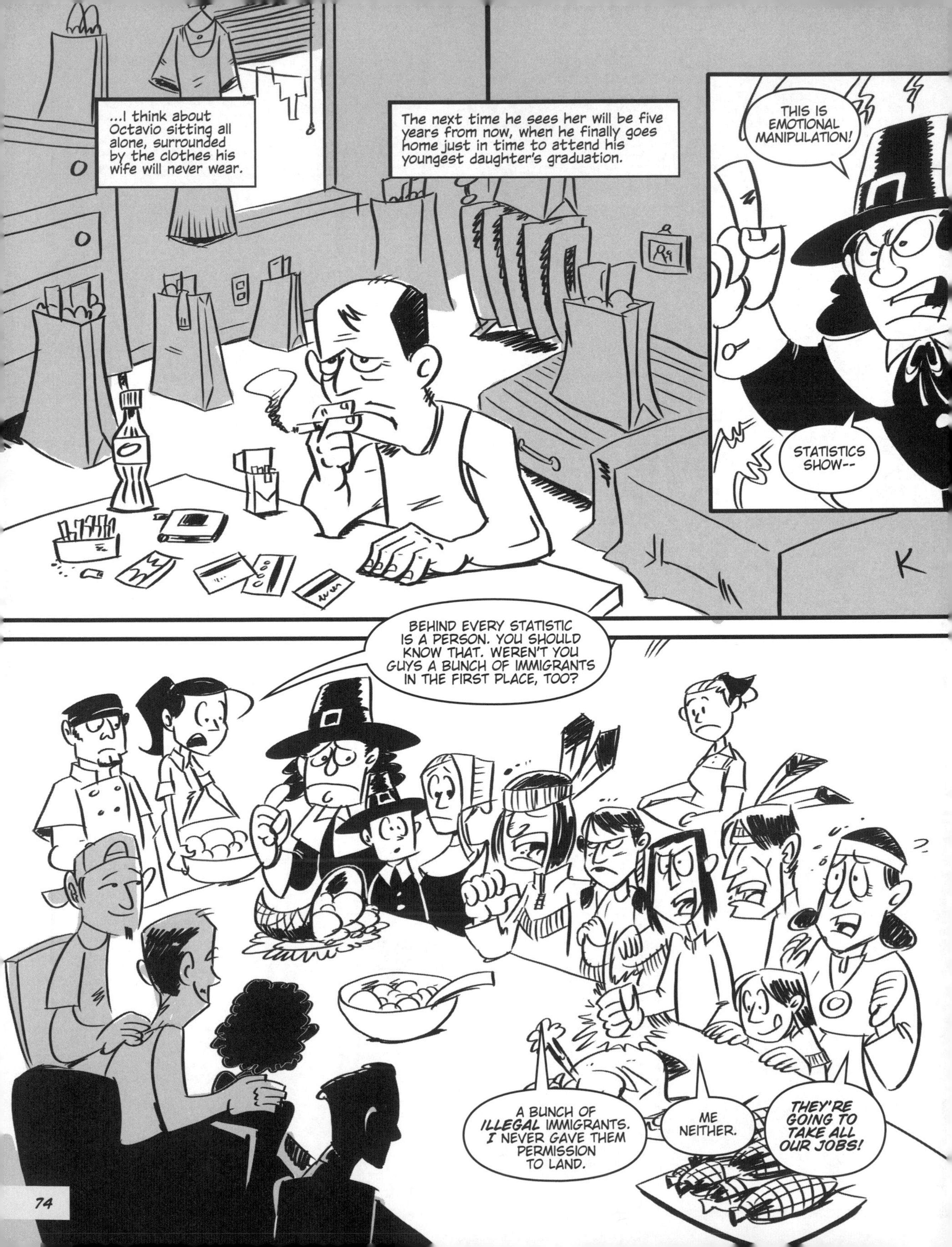
...I think about Octavio sitting all alone, surrounded by the clothes his wife will never wear.
The next time he sees her will be five years from now, when he finally goes home just in time to attend his youngest daughter's graduation.
THIS IS EMOTIONAL MANIPULATION!
STATISTICS SHOW--
BEHIND EVERY STATISTIC IS A PERSON. YOU SHOULD KNOW THAT. WEREN'T YOU GUYS A BUNCH OF IMMIGRANTS IN THE FIRST PLACE, TOO?
A BUNCH OF *ILLEGAL* IMMIGRANTS. *I* NEVER GAVE THEM PERMISSION TO LAND.
ME NEITHER.
THEY'RE GOING TO TAKE ALL OUR JOBS!

There are **OTHER** mysteries as well. Such as: If it's **SO GOOD** for us....

Why Is SALAD So BORING?

≳ SIGH ≲

What am I doing **WRONG**?

SMASH

SALAD, YOU DON'T HAVE TO BE BORING!!!

...I **...DON'T?**

...But I'm **SUPPOSED** to be boring...

NEVER! There are **EASY** ways to make you more attractive to diners.

We want to **WAKE UP** people's taste buds. We'll give you a strong dressing: very **SOUR**, or very **ACIDIC**, or very **BITTER**.

You need to have **DIFFERENT TEXTURES** in every bite. Every forkful of you should be full of surprises.

We'll use lots of different techniques to make sure you're **PACKED** with textures. First up...

DEEP-FAT FRYING

AAAAAH!!!! RUN!!!!!!!

IT'S GOING TO MAKE US FAT!

NO!!! MY SKIN!!!!!

WHAT'S EVERYONE RUNNING FOR?

I'M JUST OIL.

EVERYONE HAS BEEN TAUGHT TO BE AFRAID OF ME, BUT IF YOU TREAT ME RIGHT I'M NOT BAD AT ALL.

ALWAYS PUT ME IN A HEAVY-BOTTOMED POT THAT'S DEEP ENOUGH FOR THE FOOD TO BE **COMPLETELY** SUBMERGED.

AND IT'S IMPORTANT TO USE A CANDY OR "DEEP-FRY" THERMOMETER.

NOTE: Always use enough oil to completely submerge your food.

TOO COLD AND I'LL MAKE YOUR FOOD *GREASY*, TOO HOT AND I'LL BURN IT. *325-375°F* IS BEST. AND MAKE SURE I'M ALREADY AT THE RIGHT TEMPERATURE BEFORE PUTTING FOOD IN ME.

WHEN YOU PULL FOOD OUT OF ME, PUT IT ON *PAPER TOWELS* THAT'LL WICK AWAY THE EXTRA GREASE.

AND MAKE SURE YOU CHANGE ME WHEN I START TO GET DARK. THAT'S WHEN I'VE BEEN USED TOO MANY TIMES.

MY NAME IS CANOLA OIL. I'M FROM CANADA, AND I JUST WANT YOU TO STOP BEING SCARED OF ME.

RIBBON FRYING

Ribbon frying is another easy technique.

Peel off a strip of carrot or zucchini or whatever vegetable you're using.

Roll it in 1/2 cup of cornstarch to seal it, then fry it at 325°F in 8 cups of canola oil. Pull it out VERY quickly--it'll take less than 25 seconds to get crisp.

300°-350°

GRILLING

Another way to add layers of texture and flavor to salads is grilling. But be careful: overgrilling can swamp the delicate flavor of the vegetables with the strong taste of char.

First, coat the vegetables with extra-virgin olive oil, either by tossing or, for more delicate vegetables and tofu, brushing the oil on.

Make sure your grill is super-hot before your vegetables touch it! That way it chars the outside quickly but the inside retains some crunch.

Charred and with grill marks.

Still crisp!

SMOKING

SURGEON GENERAL'S WARNING: Smoking causes delicious tastiness, extreme flavor, and may make your entire house smell edible.

There are two ways to smoke food.

Either buy a little smoker, or you can make one yourself, MacGyver-style.

LINE A SAUCEPAN WITH TIN FOIL SO YOU DON'T RUIN IT. THEN TAKE A STEAMER RACK, WRAP IT IN FOIL AND POKE HOLES IN IT. YOU WANT SMOKE TO GO THROUGH IT, BUT YOU DON'T WANT YOUR FOOD TO FALL THROUGH.

GET SOME WOOD CHIPS. SOAK THEM IN WATER FOR AT *LEAST* AN HOUR. YOU CAN'T OVER-SOAK THEM.

STRAIN THE CHIPS AND POUR INTO THE SAUCEPAN, PLACE THE RACK ON TOP OF THEM. THEN: THE LID.

FIRST, THE PRE-SMOKE. NO FOOD. TURN HEAT ON HIGH AND LET COME TO A FULL SMOKE.

THEN PUT IN THE FOOD AND...

...LET SMOKE FOR *5 MINUTES*.

TURN OFF THE HEAT, AND LET IT SIT IN ITS SMOKE FOR *5 MINUTES*.

THEN KEEP REPEATING THIS CYCLE (HEAT ON FOR 5, HEAT OFF FOR 5), UNTIL...

...YOUR FOOD LOOKS LIKE IT'S BEEN TO THE TANNING PARLOR.

ENTER

EXIT

Grilling, frying, and smoking are all ways to get more *texture* and *excitement* into your salad.

I'M GLAD HE'S HAPPY, BUT I WISH HE'D PAY ATTENTION TO ME BELOW THE NECK.

FENNEL SALAD

WITH CANDIED GRAPEFRUIT POPS AND GRILLED CHEESE CROUTONS

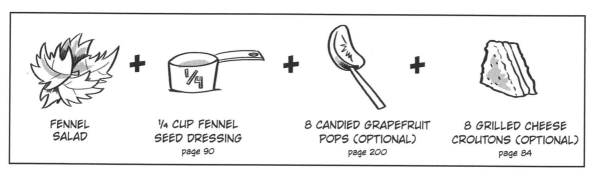

FENNEL
SALAD

+

¼ CUP FENNEL
SEED DRESSING
page 90

+

8 CANDIED GRAPEFRUIT
POPS (OPTIONAL)
page 200

+

8 GRILLED CHEESE
CROUTONS (OPTIONAL)
page 84

SERVES 4

- 3 tablespoons sliced almonds
- 4 cups mixed greens
- 1 cup sliced fennel
  Salt
- ¼ cup diced ripe avocado

1. Preheat the oven to 350°F.

2. Toast the almonds on a baking sheet until golden brown, about 5 to 10 minutes, stirring once. Let cool.

3. In a large bowl, mix the greens and fennel with the salad dressing. Salt to taste, and divide among 4 plates.

4. To serve:

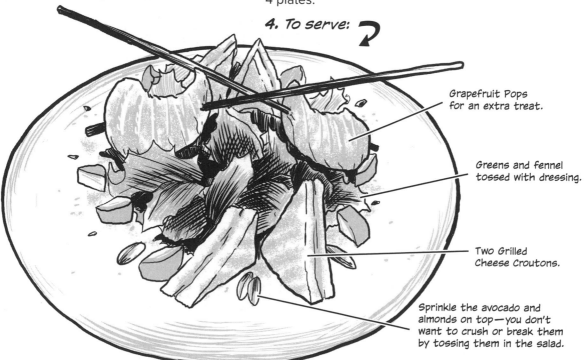

Grapefruit Pops
for an extra treat.

Greens and fennel
tossed with dressing.

Two Grilled
Cheese Croutons.

Sprinkle the avocado and
almonds on top—you don't
want to crush or break them
by tossing them in the salad.

CELERY SALAD
WITH GRILLED KING OYSTER MUSHROOMS AND CELERY PESTO

 +  **+**  **+**

CELERY
SALAD

CELERY
PESTO
opposite

4 TABLESPOONS CELERY
SEED DRESSING
page 90

FRIED CHEESE
CURDS (OPTIONAL)
page 105

SERVES 4

- 6 large King Oyster mushrooms
- ¼ cup plus 2 tablespoons extra-virgin olive oil
- Salt
- 2 cups seedless grapes (red or green)
- 4 cups mixed greens
- 1½ cups very thinly sliced celery
- 2 tablespoons very thinly sliced Chinese celery

1. Peel and slice the mushroom stems (page 101). Gently toss them with ¼ cup olive oil and sprinkle with 1 teaspoon salt. Toss the grapes with 2 tablespoons olive oil.

2. Grill the mushrooms until they have grill lines, turning once (page 77). Put them in a large bowl.

3. Grill the grapes until their skins start to pucker and acquire char marks. The grapes will collapse after cooking. Don't panic; it's natural. Cut them in half and add them to the bowl with the mushrooms.

4.

Use three separate bowls.

Mix the pesto with the mushrooms and grapes. Salt to taste.

①

Toss the mixed greens with 2 tablespoons of the dressing.

②

Mix the regular sliced celery with the remaining 2 tablespoons dressing.

③

HOW TO SLICE CELERY

Remove the strings from the celery with a knife.

Slice the celery as thinly as possible, and on an angle.

DO NOT use a mandolin for this.

5. To serve:

Then the dressed celery (bowl 3).

Mushrooms, grapes, and pesto go last (bowl 1).

Dressed mixed greens go down first (bowl 2).

Scatter some diced Chinese celery around for extra crunch.

Use a ring mold (page 83) to make plating easier.

Fried Cheese Curds

CELERY PESTO

MAKES ½ CUP

- ½ cup sliced almonds
- 1 garlic clove, minced
- 1½ tablespoons extra-virgin olive oil
- 2 cups Chinese celery leaves, blanched and shocked (page 19)
- Salt

1. Preheat the oven to 350°F.

2. Toast the almonds on a baking sheet until golden brown, about 5 to 10 minutes, stirring once. Let cool.

3. Put the almonds and garlic in a food processor and pulse until all the almonds are broken. Add the olive oil and pulse once more.

4. Chop the blanched celery leaves and add them to the food processor. Process until the mixture forms a chunky paste. Salt to taste. Use immediately or cover and refrigerate for up to a week.

ROASTED SQUASH SALAD

WITH PEPITA CLUSTERS AND BLUE CHEESE CROUTONS

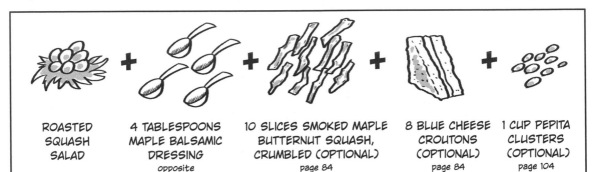

| ROASTED SQUASH SALAD | 4 TABLESPOONS MAPLE BALSAMIC DRESSING opposite | 10 SLICES SMOKED MAPLE BUTTERNUT SQUASH, CRUMBLED (OPTIONAL) page 84 | 8 BLUE CHEESE CROUTONS (OPTIONAL) page 84 | 1 CUP PEPITA CLUSTERS (OPTIONAL) page 104 |

SERVES 4

- ¼ cup extra-virgin olive oil
- ¼ cup lightly packed fresh sage leaves
- 1 cup medium dice of peeled and seeded delicata squash
- 1 cup medium dice of peeled and seeded acorn squash
- 1 cup medium dice of peeled and seeded butternut squash
- 1 cup medium dice of peeled and seeded Kabocha Squash
- Salt
- 4 cups mesclun mix
- ½ cup diced Asian pear

This is a winter salad that incorporates the best version of vegetarian bacon I've ever come across. You can simplify it by making it a mono-squash (or bi-squash) salad rather than using four different varieties of squash like I do (insanely) at Dirt Candy.

1. Preheat the oven to 350°F.

2. Put the olive oil and sage in a blender and blend until fully incorporated.

3. Put the squashes in a large roasting pan and toss with the oil mixture and 1 teaspoon salt. Roast until fork-tender, about 20 minutes. Remove from the oven and let cool slightly.

4. In a bowl, mix the lettuce and 2 tablespoons of the dressing. Salt to taste and divide among 4 plates.

5. In the same bowl, gently mix the roasted squash, smoked squash, and Asian pear with the remaining 2 tablespoons dressing. Salt to taste and divide among the 4 plates.

6. To serve:

Restaurant Trick #142: Impress your friends! Use a ring mold to plate salads. Just put it on the plate and...

...layer in the squash and pear second...

...after you've layered the mesclun mix on the bottom.

Layering with a ring mold works on any salad!

Smoked Maple Butternut Squash, crumbled.

Scatter Pepita Clusters for extra texture.

Blue Cheese Crouton

Mesclun mix

Roasted squash and Asian pear

MAPLE BALSAMIC DRESSING

MAKES APPROXIMATELY ¾ CUP

- 3 tablespoons extra-virgin olive oil
- ¼ cup chopped peeled fresh ginger
- 1 garlic clove, minced
- 6 tablespoons balsamic vinegar
- 2 tablespoons maple syrup
- 1 teaspoon Dijon mustard
- 1 teaspoon diced shallot
- 3 tablespoons fresh lemon juice
  Salt

1. Start a pan on medium heat with the olive oil, ginger, and garlic (page 17). Remove from the heat and strain. Set aside the oil.

2. Put the ginger and garlic in a blender with all the remaining ingredients except the oil. Blend until smooth, and then slowly stream in the reserved oil. Store covered in fridge for up to 1 week.

SMOKED MAPLE BUTTERNUT SQUASH

MAKES 48 SLICES

2 cups thinly sliced peeled butternut squash

½ cup sugar

Most vegetarian bacon is nice and salty, but full of chemicals. Here's a vegetarian bacon with just two ingredients: butternut squash and sugar. The flavor is all in the preparation.

1. Smoke the butternut squash **at least** twice (page 78). Between each smoke/rest cycle, release steam out of the lid of the smoker. Releasing the steam keeps the squash from getting soft.

2. Preheat the oven to 375°F. Line 2 baking sheets with Silpat liners.

3. In a blender, pulse the sugar for 2 minutes. This breaks the crystals so the sugar will melt quickly. Pat the butternut squash dry, and then toss it in the sugar until it's coated.

4. Arrange the squash in a single layer on the lined baking sheets. Bake for 4 minutes, and then flip the slices over and bake until crispy and light orange-brown, about 4 more minutes.

5. The smoked squash can be stored in a cool, dry place for up to a week.

YOU'LL NEED 1 QUART MAPLE CHIPS, FOR SMOKING.

GRILLED CHEESE CROUTONS

MAKES 8 CROUTONS

Grilled Cheese Croutons are superior to regular croutons in every way. Use regular cheese for the croutons in the Fennel Salad (page 79) and blue cheese for the Roasted Squash Salad (page 82). You're making one grilled cheese sandwich any way you like—white bread, Velveeta, soy cheese, go wild!

1. Hearty, rustic breads work best. Brush both sides of a slice of bread with olive oil (or melted butter). Put cheese in the middle.

2. Grill it on a grill, in a pan, or in a panini press.

3. When it's done, cut off the crusts, cut it into quarters, then slice each quarter diagonally to make 8 little triangles total.

GREEK SALAD
WITH KING OYSTER MUSHROOM RINGS

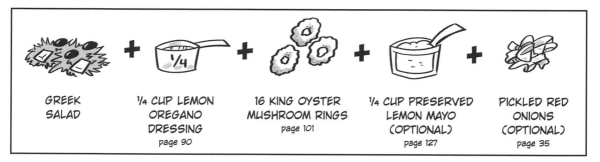

| GREEK SALAD | ¼ CUP LEMON OREGANO DRESSING
page 90 | 16 KING OYSTER MUSHROOM RINGS
page 101 | ¼ CUP PRESERVED LEMON MAYO (OPTIONAL)
page 127 | PICKLED RED ONIONS (OPTIONAL)
page 35 |

SERVES 4

- 1½ cups diced plum tomatoes
- 1½ cups diced hothouse cucumbers
- ¾ cup very thinly sliced fennel
- 1 tablespoon chopped fresh dill
- 2 teaspoons chopped fresh oregano
- 1½ tablespoons chopped flat-leaf parsley
- 16 pitted kalamata olives
- ¼ cup crumbled feta cheese
  Salt
- 1 teaspoon ground sumac
- 1 teaspoon za'atar

The world owes Greece an apology for the crimes it has committed against Greek salad: oily, soggy monstrosities full of canned black olives and rubbery feta. A Greek salad should be bright, loud, and vibrant, like a shouting match inside your mouth. This recipe gets its zip from sumac (a dried berry with a bright, citrus flavor) and za'atar (a vibrant, intensely herbal seasoning), which you can find at pretty much any Middle Eastern or Indian grocery store.

1. In a bowl, mix the tomatoes, cucumbers, fennel, fresh herbs, and olives. Toss gently with the dressing and add the feta. Salt to taste and divide among 4 plates.

2. To serve:

Sprinkle the salad and the plate with sumac and za'atar to add color and a bright herbal flavor.

Preserved Lemon Mayonnaise drizzled from a squeeze bottle or a spoon.

Four fried King Oyster Mushrooms per dish.

Salad goes down first, in a line or a little heap.

Pickled Red Onions (1 tablespoon) for added acidity.

SMOKED SWEET POTATO NICOISE SALAD

WITH FRIED OLIVES AND CHICKPEA DRESSING

NICOISE SALAD + **12 SLICES SMOKED SWEET POTATOES** *opposite* + **½ CUP CHICKPEA DRESSING** *opposite* + **16 FRIED OLIVES (OPTIONAL)** *page 103*

SERVES 4

- ½ **pound haricots verts**
- 4 **cups mesclun mix**
  Salt
- 2 **quartered plum tomatoes**
- ¼ **cup thinly sliced red onion**
- ¼ **cup chopped flat-leaf parsley**
- 1 **hothouse cucumber (optional)**
- 4 **hardboiled eggs (optional), quartered**
- 1 **tablespoon capers**

1. Blanch and shock the haricots verts (page 19).

2. In a bowl, toss the mesclun with ¼ cup of the dressing. Salt to taste, then divide among 4 bowls.

3. To serve:

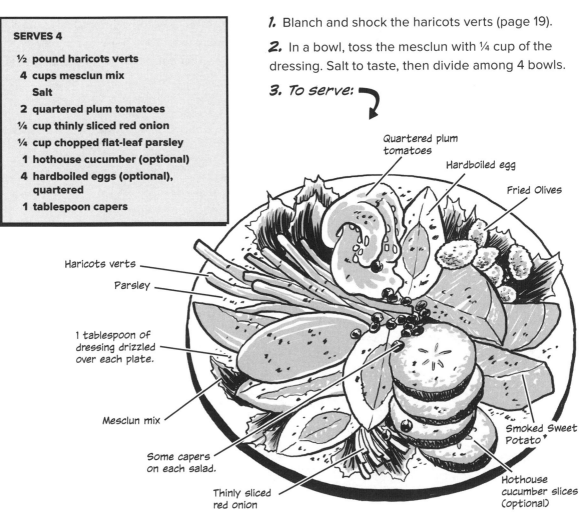

Quartered plum tomatoes

Hardboiled egg

Fried Olives

Haricots verts

Parsley

1 tablespoon of dressing drizzled over each plate.

Mesclun mix

Some capers on each salad.

Thinly sliced red onion

Smoked Sweet Potato

Hothouse cucumber slices (optional)

SMOKED SWEET POTATOES

SERVES 4

2 large sweet potatoes, peeled
½ cup extra-virgin olive oil
Salt

Note: you'll need 1 quart of maple chips, for smoking.

1. Slice the sweet potatoes into ½-inch-thick rounds. You'll want at least 12 slices for the Nicoise salad.

2. Smoke twice (page 78), lifting the lid between smokings to let out the moisture.

3. Prepare a high-heat grill or preheat the oven to 425°F.

4. Coat the potato slices with the oil and sprinkle with salt.

5. Grill the potatoes until they are cooked through and have strong grill marks, about 5 minutes on each side.

CHICKPEA DRESSING

MAKES ABOUT 1 CUP

1 cup cooked chickpeas or rinsed
  and drained canned chickpeas
½ cup extra-virgin olive oil
½ sheet nori (seaweed)
1 teaspoon Dijon mustard
2 tablespoons fresh lemon juice
2 teaspoons minced garlic
2 tablespoons white wine vinegar
1 tablespoon chopped fresh
  rosemary
Salt

In a blender, mix everything except for the rosemary and salt until very smooth. Add water 1 tablespoon at a time if necessary to help keep the mixture moving. Add the rosemary, salt to taste, and pulse no more than twice. Use immediately or cover and refrigerate for up to 1 week.

WILD ARUGULA SALAD
WITH KIMCHI DRESSING

SERVES 4

KIMCHI DRESSING

2 tablespoons grated peeled fresh ginger

Grated zest from 1 lime

2 tablespoons fresh lime juice

2 tablespoons kimchi juice (the liquid the kimchi ferments in; see page 40)

½ teaspoon minced garlic

½ cup extra-virgin olive oil

Salt

SALAD

½ cup thinly sliced peeled watermelon radish

2 tablespoons extra-virgin olive oil

Salt

4 cups wild arugula

½ cup julienned peeled daikon

¼ cup diced avocado

¼ cup diced Asian pear

This goes with Kimchi Doughnuts (page 108). It layers grilled radishes with soft avocado and crunchy daikon while the dressing adds spice.

1. To make the dressing: Put the ginger, lime zest and juice, kimchi juice, and garlic in a blender; pulse until the mixture becomes a chunky paste. With the blender running on low speed, slowly stream in the oil and blend until incorporated. Salt to taste. The dressing will make about ¾ cup; cover and store the remaining dressing in the fridge for up to 1 week.

2. To make the salad: In a small bowl, toss the watermelon radishes with the olive oil and sprinkle with a pinch of salt. Grill them until they turn an intense pink, about 3 minutes. Set aside.

3. In a large bowl, combine the arugula, daikon radish, avocado, and Asian pear. Toss with 2 to 3 tablespoons dressing.

4. Divide the salad among 4 plates. Lay the grilled watermelon radishes on top of the salad and serve.

MAPLE ARUGULA SALAD

SERVES 4

2 tablespoons maple syrup

2 tablespoons fresh lemon juice

1 tablespoon extra-virgin olive oil

Salt

4 cups wild arugula

½ cup julienned green apple

I created this salad to accompany Smoked Cauliflower and Waffles (page 158) but it's a good example of how to jazz up a salad with a sweet, rather than a tart, dressing.

1. Put the maple syrup, lemon juice, oil, and 1 teaspoon salt in a jar or plastic container and cover tightly. Shake the dressing until well mixed.

2. Put the arugula and apple in a large bowl. Add the dressing and toss to coat. Salt to taste. Serve.

RADISH SALAD

SERVES 4

1 cup julienned purple radish

1 cup radish sprouts or alfalfa sprouts

¼ cup toasted pistachios, chopped

2 tablespoons pistachio oil or extra-virgin olive oil

2 tablespoons fresh lemon juice

Salt

This goes best with Radish Ravioli (page 156) but it's another great, crunchy, all-texture summer salad.

In a large bowl, gently toss together all of the ingredients, and salt to taste. Serve.

JICAMA SLAW

SERVES 4

1 cup diced peeled jicama

½ cup thinly sliced Brussels sprouts

½ cup thinly sliced haricots verts

¼ cup thinly sliced Thai basil

2 tablespoons minced Preserved Lemons (page 41)

1 tablespoon extra-virgin olive oil

Salt

Another good summer salad, this pairs with Tomato Spaetzle (page 184).

In a large bowl, gently toss together all of the ingredients, salting to taste. Serve.

CARROT AND CUCUMBER SALAD

SERVES 4

2 cups julienned white carrots

2 cups julienned seeded hothouse cucumbers

¼ cup thinly sliced scallion

2 teaspoons finely julienned peeled fresh ginger

2 tablespoons toasted sesame oil

3 tablespoons fresh lime juice

Salt

This cooling summer salad is all texture and it goes best with the Roasted Carrot Buns (page 112) or any other dish with rich flavors that need a clean, crisp taste to balance them.

In a large bowl, gently toss together all of the ingredients, salting to taste. Serve.

FENNEL SEED DRESSING

MAKES ABOUT 1 CUP

- 1 teaspoon fennel seeds
- 2 tablespoons grated grapefruit zest
- ¼ cup fresh grapefruit juice
- 2 tablespoons fresh lemon juice
- 1 tablespoon finely minced shallot
- ½ teaspoon Dijon mustard
- ¾ cup extra-virgin olive oil
  Salt and freshly ground black pepper

1. In a dry pan over medium heat, toast the fennel seeds until fragrant, 5 minutes. Let cool.

2. Blend all of the ingredients except the oil, salt, and pepper in a blender on high until smooth. Turn the blender to low and slowly stream in the oil. Add salt and pepper to taste. Use immediately or cover and refrigerate for up to 1 week.

LEMON OREGANO DRESSING

MAKES ¾ CUP

- ½ teaspoon minced garlic
- ¾ tablespoon Dijon mustard
- 2 tablespoons red wine vinegar
  Grated zest of 1 lemon
- 1 tablespoon fresh lemon juice
  Salt and freshly ground black pepper
- ¾ cup extra-virgin olive oil
- ¼ cup fresh oregano

1. Put the garlic, mustard, vinegar, lemon zest and juice, and a pinch each of salt and pepper in a blender. Mix on high speed until smooth. Turn the blender to low and slowly stream in the oil.

2. Still on low, add the oregano and blend until it is broken into small pieces. Use immediately or cover and refrigerate for up to 1 week.

CELERY SEED DRESSING

MAKES APPROXIMATELY 1 CUP

- 1 teaspoon celery seeds
  Grated zest of 1 lemon
- 2 teaspoons fresh lemon juice
- 2½ tablespoons white wine vinegar
- ½ garlic clove, minced
- ⅛ teaspoon Dijon mustard
- ½ cup plus 1 teaspoon extra-virgin olive oil
- ½ cup toasted almond oil
  Salt

1. In a dry pan over medium heat, toast the celery seeds until fragrant, about 5 minutes.

2. Blend all of the ingredients except the oils and salt in a blender on high until smooth. Turn the blender to low and slowly stream in the oils until fully incorporated. Do this slowly so that the dressing emulsifies; if the oil is dumped in at once, the dressing will break. Salt to taste. Use immediately or cover and refrigerate for up to 1 week.

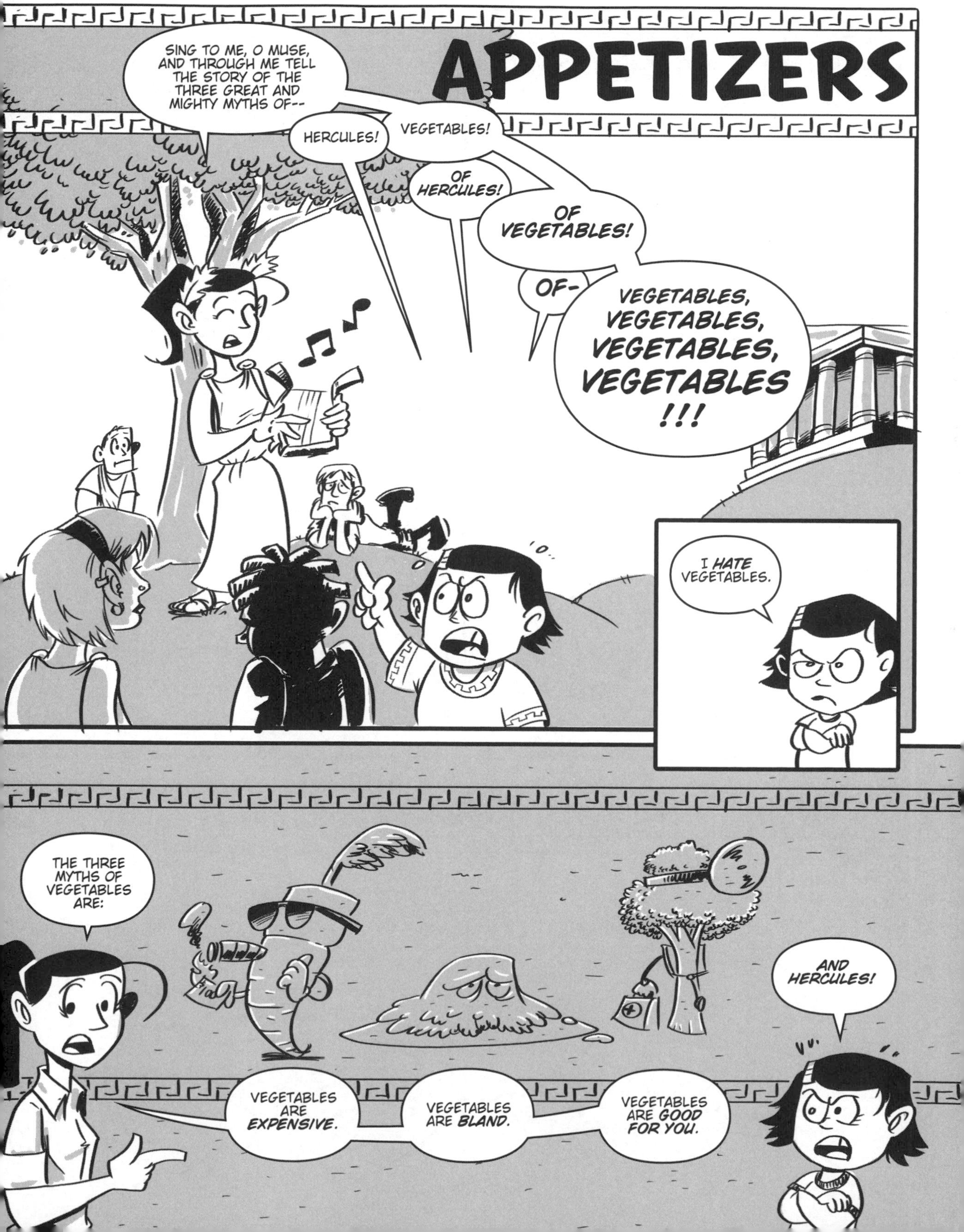
APPETIZERS
SING TO ME, O MUSE, AND THROUGH ME TELL THE STORY OF THE THREE GREAT AND MIGHTY MYTHS OF--
HERCULES!
VEGETABLES!
OF HERCULES!
OF VEGETABLES!
OF-
VEGETABLES, VEGETABLES, VEGETABLES, VEGETABLES !!!
I HATE VEGETABLES.
THE THREE MYTHS OF VEGETABLES ARE:
AND HERCULES!
VEGETABLES ARE EXPENSIVE.
VEGETABLES ARE BLAND.
VEGETABLES ARE GOOD FOR YOU.

A recent study revealed that 75% of American meals don't include vegetables. People just don't like them.

SORRY, PRINCESS, BUT YOU'RE TOO COMPLICATED, TOO EXPENSIVE AND, FRANKLY, YOU'RE BORING.

SEE YOU IN 30 YEARS WHEN I'M WORRIED ABOUT MY HEALTH.

For the most part, people ignore vegetables, and desperate attempts to make us eat them are big turnoffs.

IT'S JUST THAT SAD TOMATO TRYING TO TELL ME HOW GREAT SHE IS.

AGAIN.

I'm as guilty of it as anyone else.

OH, NO. IT'S THAT TOMATO.

AGAIN.

I even stopped being a vegetarian years ago because the same thing happened to me at every single restaurant.

THE CHEF WOULD BE DELIGHTED TO CREATE A VEGETARIAN TASTING MENU FOR YOU. HE RESPECTS THE EARTH'S BOUNTY.

I wanted to keep up with what the big-name chefs were cooking, but time after time I got the exact same thing. They just couldn't bring themselves to care.

Salad.

Another salad.

Grilled vegetable salad.

Yet another salad.

Dessert salad.

Chefs find vegetables *boring.* They'd rather work with the ingredients everyone says are *sexy:* pork belly, foie gras, duck fat, oysters.

Cooking is still very much a boy's club where everyone wants to be *tougher* than everyone else. And vegetables?

VEGETABLES ARE FOR *GIRLS.* I DON'T ALLOW VEGETARIANS IN MY RESTAURANT. SCREW 'EM! THEY *HATE* FOOD.

I'm careful to call Dirt Candy a *vegetable* restaurant to avoid getting tarred with the dismissive "vegetarian" brush, but some people think that's *really* pretentious.

YOU'RE A *VEGETARIAN* RESTAURANT.

WE'RE ACTUALLY A *VEGETABLE* RESTAURANT.

NO, WE'RE A *VEGETABLE* RESTAURANT.

BUT YOU DON'T SERVE *MEAT.*

SO YOU'RE A *VEGETARIAN* RESTAURANT.

RIGHT, WE SERVE *VEGETABLES.*

People have a lot of preconceived notions about vegetarian food and most of them aren't very flattering.

The New Harvest Flavorless, Self-Righteous, Holier Than Thou, Health-Obsessed, Over-cooked Vegetable and Gloopy Brown Sauce Cookbook

This is not entirely unfair.

93

All the way back to the 1800's, a vegetarian diet has *never* been allowed to simply be about the food.

EATING MEAT DESTROYS THE PURITY OF YOUR COLON. 'TIS BETTER TO HAVE DAILY *YOGURT ENEMAS!*

JOHN HARVEY KELLOGG
inventor of corn flakes

MEAT AND MILK CAUSE *LUST.* VEGETARIAN DIETS MAKE FOR CHASTE, HEALTHY CITIZENS.

SYLVESTER GRAHAM
inventor of the graham cracker
(originally created to prevent masturbation)

Starting in the nineteenth century, spas and hot springs appeared every-where, promising to treat a wide variety of health problems.

I CURE *PELVIC CONGESTION!*

French Lick, Indiana

I CURE *SYPHILLIS!*

Hot Springs, Arkansas

I CURE *CLOGGED BOWELS!*

Saratoga Springs, New York

The ideal citizen had clean bowels, ate no meat, and therefore had no inflamed passions.

Men like Kellogg were terrified of disorder and chaos (read: sex). They believed strongly in an *ultra-bland* diet.

GRAHAM FLOUR, OATMEAL, AND RIPE FRUIT ARE THE INDISPENSABLES OF A DIET FOR THOSE WHO ARE SUFFERING FROM *SEXUAL EXCESSES.**

DISCARD ALL STIMULATING FOOD...SPICES, PEPPER, GINGER, MUSTARD, CINNAMON, CLOVES, ESSENCES, ALL CONDIMENTS AND PICKLES TOGETHER WITH FLESH FOOD IN ANY BUT *MODERATE* QUANTITIES.**

* Actual quotes from *Plain Facts for Old & Young.*

Vegetarian and health-food restaurants spread from the hot springs to the cities and became a big turn-of-the-century fad.

OUR SPECIALS ARE NUT GLUTEN WITH PROTOSE SALAD, FIG BROMOSE WITH NUT BUTTER AND NUTTOLENE.

Flavor was *not* on the menu.

People started to think of food as medicine. Vegetables were on the plate to support your health, not to be delicious.

Seventh Day Adventists, Tolstoyans, and even the Salvation Army were early advocates of vegetarianism, but Jews were the ones who made it an ethical issue.

The Yidisher Vegetarian Society of New York, and many left-wing Jewish groups, rejected the "meat diet" because they found it cruel.

WHAT HAPPENED NEXT...

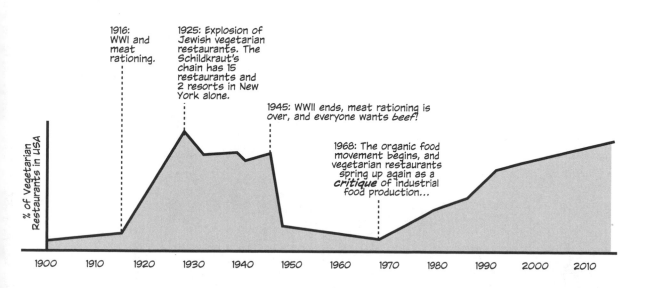

1916: WWI and meat rationing.

1925: Explosion of Jewish vegetarian restaurants. The Schildkraut's chain has 15 restaurants and 2 resorts in New York alone.

1945: WWII ends, meat rationing is over, and everyone wants *beef*!

1968: The organic food movement begins, and vegetarian restaurants spring up again as a *critique* of industrial food production...

% of Vegetarian Restaurants in USA

1900 1910 1920 1930 1940 1950 1960 1970 1980 1990 2000 2010

The problem was, organic vegetables were *expensive* and people came to regard them as a luxury item for the idle rich.

I'M *DYING* FOR SOME ORGANIC EGGS AND KALE, SISTER.

YOU CAN'T *AFFORD* OUR PRICES, "BROTHER."

It didn't help that chefs began to *fetishize* heirloom vegetables.

WHAT KIND OF NAME IS *"EGGPLANT"*? CHANGE YOUR NAME TO *"STICKYBACK FARMS HIGH BUSH ORGANIC EGGPLANT"* AND YOU'LL GET ALL THE HOT CHEF ACTION YOU CAN *HANDLE.*

The three trends-- *organic farming, ethical living,* and *pure healthy bodies*-- merged to influence how most people think of vegetables today.

DON'T YOU WANT TO GROW UP TO BE *BIG* AND *STRONG*?

MEAT IS MURDER!

THINK *GLOBALLY,* ACT *LOCALLY!*

HEALTH

ETHICS

ORGANICS

FINALLY! A *MONSTER!*

But that's just vegetarian food in America. There are *dozens* of vegetarian cuisines around the world that are older, richer, and more fun than our conflicted, crabby history of "health food."

Close to 4,000 years ago, Vedic Indians were *sacrificing* every cow in sight.

I PRAY FOR *GOOD CROPS!*

I PRAY FOR A *SON!*

I PRAY FOR A *HAMBURGER!*

WE'VE GOT A *PROBLEM.* IF THINGS KEEP GOING LIKE THIS, THERE WON'T BE ANY OF US *LEFT.*

IDEAS?

WHAT IF WE STARTED A *RELIGION* THAT SAID COWS WERE *HOLY?*

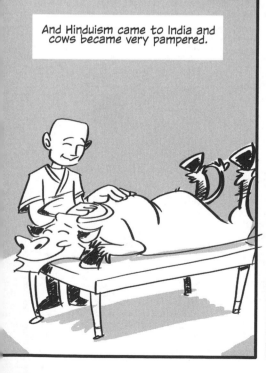

And Hinduism came to India and cows became very pampered.

It's not just the cows who benefited. French cuisine is put on a pedestal in the West, but Southern Indian cuisine is older, more *diverse*, and arguably *more delicious*. And most of it is vegetarian.

THANKS, COWS!

CHINESE TEMPLE COOKING

Then there's Chinese temple cooking. You know what they say about vegetarians who eat fake meat?

I SAY A VEGETARIAN WHO EATS MOCK MEAT DEMONSTRATES AN INFERIORITY COMPLEX WITH SCHIZOID TENDENCIES.

Actually mock meat comes from one of the world's oldest cuisines, invented by Chinese Buddhists.

Thousands of years ago, some Buddhists ate meat, and some didn't. But they *all* lived off charity.

When their rich patrons came to eat, the monks wanted to woo them, but the fat cats only had **one question**:

WHERE'S MY PORK CHOP?

So the vegetarian monks created mock meat out of soy and gluten. However, it wasn't supposed to *duplicate* the *taste* of meat.

The talented chef was supposed to trick the diner into *seeing* one thing and *tasting* another.

LOOKS LIKE *PIG*...

...TASTES LIKE *PUMPKIN!*

And that's just two out of **dozens** of non-Western vegetarian traditions that shatter the chains Western vegetarian food is shackled with.

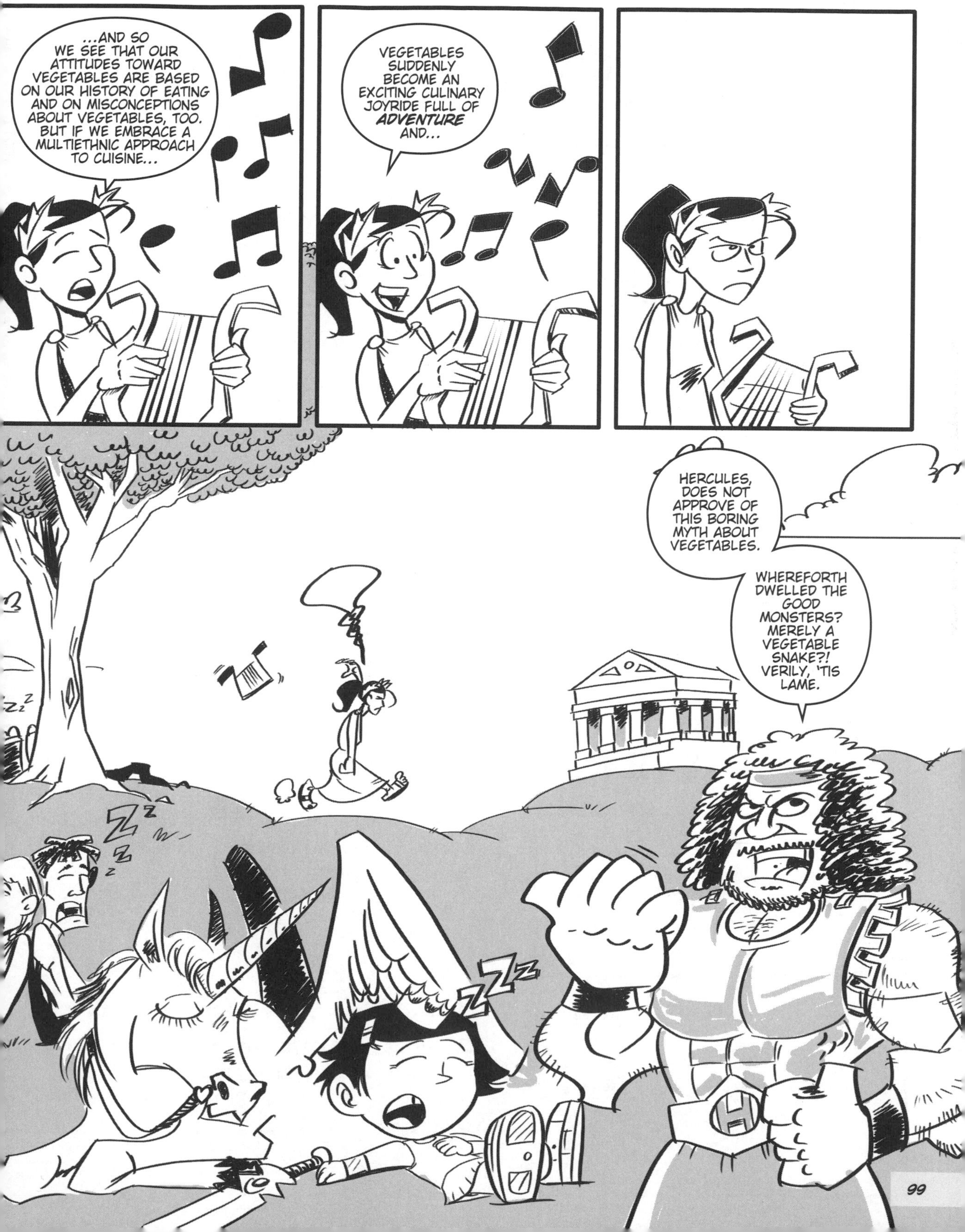
...AND SO WE SEE THAT OUR ATTITUDES TOWARD VEGETABLES ARE BASED ON OUR HISTORY OF EATING AND ON MISCONCEPTIONS ABOUT VEGETABLES, TOO. BUT IF WE EMBRACE A MULTIETHNIC APPROACH TO CUISINE...
VEGETABLES SUDDENLY BECOME AN EXCITING CULINARY JOYRIDE FULL OF ***ADVENTURE*** AND...
HERCULES, DOES NOT APPROVE OF THIS BORING MYTH ABOUT VEGETABLES.
WHEREFORTH DWELLED THE GOOD MONSTERS? MERELY A VEGETABLE SNAKE?! VERILY, 'TIS LAME.

BASIC BATTER WITH PANKO

MAKES 2 CUPS

- 1 cup plus 2 tablespoons unbleached all-purpose flour
- 1 cup seltzer water or beer
- 2 cups panko
- 2 teaspoons salt (or other seasonings as indicated)

This is my go-to deep-frying batter. I use it often in this book, sometimes adjusting the seasonings or quantities depending on what and how much is being fried. To make it a beer batter, just replace the seltzer with delicious beer.

1. In a bowl, mix together the flour and seltzer to form a smooth batter.

2. Pulse the panko a few times in a food processor. Add the salt and pulse once or twice to combine. Transfer to a bowl.

3. Dip the ingredient in the batter and then roll in the panko crumbs. Fry as directed in the recipe.

Food that's deep-fried properly barely touches the oil. Air is trapped between the batter shell and the food, and the food is cooked by steaming as its water content evaporates.

The bubbles you see in the oil are the steam escaping the batter shell.

You want to pull your food out right before the bubbles stop. Once they stop, your food is going to start drying out.

CRISPY VINEGAR POTATOES

SERVES 4 TO 6

- 1 Russet or Idaho potato, peeled
- 2 cups white vinegar
- Canola oil for deep-frying
- Salt

I make these for Roasted Potato Soup (page 55), but Danielle always had to make double because I couldn't stop people from eating them all day long.

1. Using a mandolin, shred the potato into long, thin julienned strips. Soak the strips in the vinegar for 24 hours.

IT MUST BE FOR 24 HOURS! NO MORE, NO LESS. I DON'T KNOW WHY, BUT THIS IS WHAT WORKS.

2. In a large pot, heat the oil to 350°F.

3. Dry the potatoes as much as possible. Working in batches, deep-fry them (page 76) until golden brown, about 45 seconds. Remove from the oil and salt to taste.

KING OYSTER MUSHROOM RINGS

SERVES 4

4 **large King Oyster mushrooms**
Canola oil for deep-frying
Basic Batter with Panko (opposite)
1 **tablespoon ground sumac**
1 **tablespoon za'atar**
2 **teaspoons salt**

Deep-fried mushrooms are superior in every way to onion rings, which are greasy and fall apart when you bite into them. Serve these on top of Greek Salad (page 85) like a vegetable version of calamari, or dip them in Preserved Lemon Mayonnaise (page 127) or hot sauce.

1. In a large pot, heat the oil to 350°F.

2.

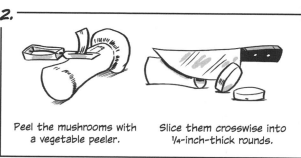

Peel the mushrooms with a vegetable peeler.

Slice them crosswise into ¼-inch-thick rounds.

3.

Using a small, round cookie cutter or ring mold, punch out the center of each musrhroom round, leaving about a ¼-inch outer ring.

(If you feel like MacGyver, use the screw top from a milk carton to punch out the center.)

4. While the oil heats, prepare the batter and pulse the panko crumbs, then add the sumac, za'atar, and salt to the panko and pulse once or twice to combine. Transfer to a bowl.

5. Dip the mushroom rings in batter and then roll them in the panko crumbs. Working in batches, deep-fry (page 76) until they turn golden brown, 2 to 3 minutes.

SPRING PEA FLAN

SERVES 8 TO 10

Nonstick spray for ramekins
1 cup fresh cilantro leaves
½ cup fresh mint leaves
2¼ cups fresh or frozen peas
3 extra-large eggs
¾ cup heavy cream
Salt

Serve with Pea Soup (page 65) or on their own with a salad of pea-shoot leaves.

For the hot water bath, pour in the water until it is about ¾ of the way up the sides of the ramekins.

1. Preheat the oven to 325°F. Lightly coat eight to ten 2-ounce (or slightly larger) ramekins with nonstick spray.

2. Blanch and shock the cilantro, mint, and peas separately (page 19), then roughly chop the cilantro and mint.

3. Put the blanched peas and herbs in a blender. Blend until smooth (don't overprocess, or the color of the peas turns dull). If the mixture is lumpy, push through a chinois (page 23).

4. In a bowl, mix the eggs and cream until well combined, and then gently mix in the pea puree and salt to taste.

5. Divide the mixture among the prepared ramekins. Place the ramekins in a hot-water bath then place the bath in the oven and bake for 8 minutes, rotate, and bake for 8 minutes more. Keep rotating and cooking until fully set, about 20 to 30 minutes. Larger ramekins will take a little longer.

6. Remove the hot-water bath from the oven. Important: do not remove the ramekins from the hot-water bath. Let stand until the water reaches room temperature, and then remove the ramekins.

7. To unmold, turn each ramekin over onto a small plate and ***gently*** ease out the flan. If necessary, run a thin-bladed knife around the edge. Serve, or cover and refrigerate for up to 3 days.

VARIATION
VEGAN SPRING PEA FLAN

SERVES 8 TO 10

1 cup fresh cilantro leaves

½ cup fresh mint leaves

2¼ cups peas

1 cup minus 1 teaspoon silken tofu
(225 milliliters)

2⅛ teaspoons agar agar

Salt

To make this dish vegan, change the eggs for tofu and the cream for agar agar. And don't bake!

1. Follow steps 1, 2, and 3 for Spring Pea Flan.

2. In a small saucepan over medium heat, bring the tofu and agar agar to a simmer. Immediately remove from the heat, transfer to a blender, and blend until smooth.

3. Add the pea mixture and salt to taste and continue blending until smooth.

4. Divide the mixture between the prepared ramekins. Refrigerate, covered, until set, about 30 minutes and up to 1 week.

5. To unmold, turn each ramekin over onto a small plate and ease out the flan. If necessary, run a thin-bladed knife around the edge of the flan. Serve.

FRIED OLIVES

MAKES 20

Canola oil for deep-frying

¼ cup feta cheese

¼ teaspoon minced garlic

20 large pitted black or green olives

Basic Batter with Panko
(page 100)

1. In a large pot, heat the oil to 350°F.

2. In a mini food processor or a bowl, blend the feta and garlic into a paste. Transfer to a pastry bag with an ⅛-inch round tip or a resealable plastic bag with one corner cut off. Stuff each olive with the feta mixture.

3. Dip each olive in the batter and then roll in the panko crumbs. Deep-fry (page 76) until golden, about 30 seconds. Serve warm.

WASABI PEA LEAVES

SERVES 4 TO 6

¼ cup extra-virgin olive oil
2 tablespoons wasabi powder
1 teaspoon salt
¼ pound washed pea leaves with stems

I believe in using as much of a vegetable as possible, including its leaves. These add heat to Spring Pea Flan (page 102) and Pea Soup (page 65) and they are an easier-to-make version of wasabi peas, Japan's supersnack.

1. Blend the oil, wasabi powder, and salt in a blender until incorporated, then toss in a bowl with the pea leaves until they're thoroughly coated.

2. Spread the pea leaves out on a baking sheet with a Silpat liner and turn the oven to dehydrating temperature (page 21). Dehydrate the leaves until crisp, 2 to 4 hours. Let cool, then cover, and store in a cool, dry place for up to 10 days.

PEPITA CLUSTERS

MAKES 4 CUPS

1½ cups chickpea flour
1½ tablespoons rice flour
1½ tablespoons vadouvan or curry powder
½ tablespoon salt
1½ cups pumpkin seeds

Pepitas are roasted pumpkin seeds, a popular Mexican street food. Vadouvan and chickpea flour, both common in French and Indian cuisines, are used to coat the seeds and form the clusters. Use the clusters to add texture to any salad, such as Roasted Squash Salad (page 82).

1. Preheat the oven to 375°F. Line a baking sheet with a Silpat liner.

2. Mix together the flours, vadouvan, and salt; divide between 2 bowls. Add the pepitas and ½ cup water to one of the bowls and mix until well coated.

3. Pour the wet flour mixture into the dry flour mixture and lightly stir together to form clusters. Spread the clusters on the lined baking sheet.

4. Bake for 7 minutes, then stir and bake 15 minutes longer. Increase the oven temperature to 425°F and bake until you hear the pepitas pop, 20 to 30 minutes. Remove from the oven and let cool.

5. Break apart any large clumps into smaller clusters. Store in a cool, dry place for up to 3 weeks.

FRIED CHEESE CURDS

SERVES 4 TO 6

Canola oil for deep-frying
1 tablespoon celery seeds
¼ cup unbleached all-purpose flour
1 extra-large egg
¾ cup bread crumbs
1 teaspoon salt
½ cup cheese curds (broken in half)

Found in the dairy belt (Wisconsin, Ontario, British Columbia), cheese curds should technically be eaten only when they're so fresh, they squeak. But deep-frying is a way to use curds that are more than a day old.

1. In a large pot, heat the oil to 350°F.

2. In a dry pan over medium heat, toast the celery seeds until fragrant, 5 minutes. Set aside.

3.
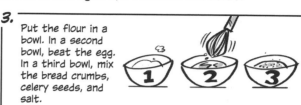
Put the flour in a bowl. In a second bowl, beat the egg. In a third bowl, mix the bread crumbs, celery seeds, and salt.

4.
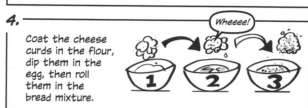
Coat the cheese curds in the flour, dip them in the egg, then roll them in the bread mixture.

5. Deep-fry (page 76) the curds until golden brown, 30 seconds each.

PEAR AND BEET LEATHER

MAKES 8 STRIPS

2 red beets
1 cup diced peeled pear
¼ cup sugar

This is designed to go with Molten Beet Cake (page 210) but it's an awesome additive-free version of fruit roll-ups. Patience is the key to this recipe.

1. Preheat the oven to 375°F.

2. Roast the beets until tender, 45 to 60 minutes. Remove from the oven, peel, and dice. Reserve 1 cup.

3. Turn down the oven to dehydrate (page 21). Line a baking sheet with a Silpat liner.

4. In a pot, simmer the 1 cup beets, the pear, and sugar until the pear is very soft, about 20 minutes. Let cool and puree in a blender until smooth.

5. Spread on the Silpat and dehydrate in the oven, until the leather is slightly tacky to the touch but firm, 2 to 3 hours, flipping the leather over once.

6. Peel off the Silpat and slice into strips. Store, covered, in a cool, dry place for up to a week.

HUSH PUPPIES
WITH MAPLE BUTTER

SERVES 4 TO 6 (MAKES 34 HUSH PUPPIES AND 1¼ CUPS BUTTER)

MAPLE BUTTER
- 1 cup (2 sticks) unsalted butter, softened
- ¼ cup maple syrup
- 1½ teaspoons Dijon mustard
- ¼ teaspoon salt

HUSH PUPPIES
- Canola oil for deep-frying
- 1½ cups cornmeal
- 6 tablespoons unbleached all-purpose flour, plus more as needed
- 1¼ teaspoons plus ⅛ teaspoon baking powder
- 1 teaspoon salt
- ½ cup finely diced red onion
- ½ cup diced jalapeño
- 1¼ cups whole milk
- 1 extra-large egg, beaten

This recipe is like crack: cheap, easy, and people can't get enough of it. Maple butter from Canada and hush puppies from the South make this the recipe where the Deep South meets the Great White North.

1. For the maple butter, put the butter, syrup, and mustard in a stand mixer fitted with the whisk attachment. Beat until fluffy. Salt to taste. Set aside or cover and store in the fridge for up to 1 month. Serve at room temperature.

2. For the hush puppies, in a large pot, heat the oil to 350°F.

3. In a bowl, whisk together the cornmeal, flour, baking powder, and salt.

4. Add the onion and jalapeño to the bowl and mix. Gently fold in the milk, and then very gently fold in the beaten egg.

5. Using 2 spoons or a small ice cream scoop, slowly push a spoonful of batter into the oil. If the batter breaks apart in the fryer, whisk a little flour into the remaining batter to make it stiffer. If the consistency is correct, it'll sink to the bottom and then rise to the top. When it reaches the top, flip it over once and fry (page 76) until golden brown, 2 to 3 minutes. Continue frying until all the batter is used.

6. Serve the hush puppies warm with the maple butter.

VEGAN HUSH PUPPIES WITH VEGAN MAPLE BUTTER

SERVES 4 TO 6 (MAKES 30 HUSH PUPPIES AND 1¼ CUPS BUTTER)

MAPLE BUTTER

- **1 cup Earth Balance**
- **¼ cup maple syrup**
- **1 teaspoon Dijon mustard**
- **Salt**

HUSH PUPPIES

- **Canola oil for deep-frying**
- **1¼ cups cornmeal**
- **¾ cup unbleached all-purpose flour, plus more as needed**
- **1 tablespoon plus 1 teaspoon baking powder**
- **1 teaspoon salt**
- **½ cup finely diced red onion**
- **½ cup diced jalapeño**
- **1½ cups unflavored soy milk**

This recipe is a straight substitution. Just follow the recipe for regular Hush Puppies and Maple Butter (opposite), using the ingredients on this page. Unlike regular maple butter, vegan maple butter should be served cold.

Earth Balance is my preferred vegan butter substitute. It has the least aggressive flavor and is the smoothest of those I've tasted. It's pretty salty, so there's no need to add much extra salt when using it.

1. For the vegan maple butter, put the butter, syrup, and mustard in a stand mixer fitted with the whisk attachment. Beat until fluffy. Add salt, cover, and store in the fridge for up to 1 month. Serve cold.

2. For the hush puppies, in a large pot, heat the oil to 350°F.

3. In a bowl, whisk together the cornmeal, flour, baking powder, and salt.

4. Add the onion and jalapeño to the bowl and mix. Gently fold in the unflavored soy milk.

5. Using 2 spoons or a small ice cream scoop, slowly push a spoonful of batter into the oil. If it breaks apart in the fryer, whisk a little flour into the remaining batter to stiffen it. If the consistency is correct, the batter will sink to the bottom of the pot and then rise to the top of the oil. When it reaches the surface, flip it over once, and fry (page 76) until golden brown, 2 to 3 minutes. Continue frying until all the batter is used.

6. Serve the vegan hush puppies warm with the vegan maple butter.

KIMCHI DOUGHNUTS

WITH WILD ARUGULA SALAD AND CILANTRO SAUCE

KIMCHI
DOUGHNUTS

+

CILANTRO
SAUCE

+

WILD ARUGULA SALAD
WITH KIMCHI DRESSING
page 88

+

1 CUP DRAINED &
CHOPPED KIMCHI
page 40

**SERVES 4 TO 6 (MAKES 25 SMALL
DOUGHNUTS AND ¾ CUP SAUCE)**

- 2 cups fresh cilantro sprigs
- ½ teaspoon minced garlic
- ½ teaspoon minced peeled fresh ginger
- ½ cup coconut cream (page 64)
- Grated zest of 1 lime
- Salt
- Canola oil for deep-frying
- 1 (200-gram) box vadai mix

Arugula Salad (page 88) is bitter and nutty, and the Kimchi Doughnuts are briny and spicy. You can find vadai mix at any Indian grocery store or online.

1. Blanch and shock the cilantro (page 19).

2. Put the cilantro in a blender with the garlic, ginger, coconut cream, and lime zest. Blend until smooth, and salt to taste. Set the sauce aside or store, covered, in the fridge for up to 2 days.

3. In a large pot heat the oil to 350°F.

4. Pour the vadai mix into a bowl and add 220 milliliters of water. Stir, then let sit for 20 minutes.

5. Add the kimchi and gently stir it into the dough. Divide the dough into 25 balls and put them on a baking sheet. This is easier with wet hands.

6.

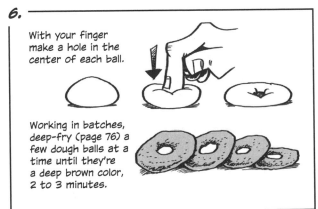

With your finger make a hole in the center of each ball.

Working in batches, deep-fry (page 76) a few dough balls at a time until they're a deep brown color, 2 to 3 minutes.

THIS RECIPE REQUIRES KIMCHI, SO EITHER BUY IT OR SPEND A COUPLE OF WEEKS MAKING THE RECIPE ON PAGE 40.

7. To serve:

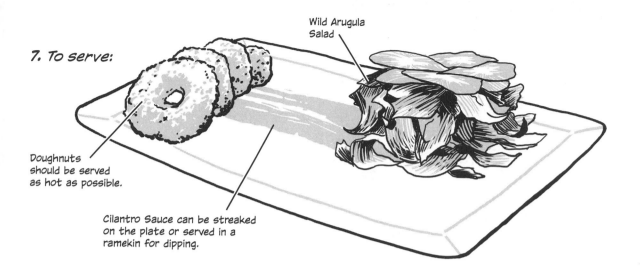

Wild Arugula Salad

Doughnuts should be served as hot as possible.

Cilantro Sauce can be streaked on the plate or served in a ramekin for dipping.

KOREA IS KNOWN FOR ITS BEEF AND PORK, BUT IT ALSO HAS A MAJOR VEGETABLE TRADITION: THE HUNDREDS OF SMALL SIDE DISHES CALLED *BANCHAN*.

BUT THE MOST POPULAR BANCHAN OF THEM ALL IS KIMCHI. 3000 YEARS OLD, WITH 187 VARIETIES DIVIDED BY REGION, SEASONS AND INGREDIENTS, KIMCHI IS OFTEN BURIED AND CAN TAKE FROM 2 WEEKS TO A YEAR TO PROPERLY FERMENT.

THESE KIMCHI DOUGHNUTS BRING TOGETHER THE BEST OF KOREAN AND INDIAN VEGETARIAN FOOD TO BLOW YOUR MIND.

YOU GOT YOUR KIMCHI ON MY VADAI!

YOU GOT YOUR VADAI ON MY KIMCHI!

BROCCOLI CARPACCIO

WITH BROCCOLI STALK SALAD

The latest trend is nose to tail cooking, in which *every single part* of an animal is served...

EAT MY PIG INTESTINES STUFFED WITH PIG'S FEET AND GARNISHED WITH PIG EARS AND PIG TAILS OR YOU'RE A *WIMP*.

...even the gross ones.

By comparison, vegetables don't really have any gross parts, and yet people throw a lot of them away.

This dish makes use of *broccoli stalks*, which are normally tossed in the trash.

LOOK AT MY FIRM, *HARD* STALK... DON'T YOU WANT TO...

...MMM...

...TAKE A *BITE*...?

BROCCOLI CARPACCIO

+

BROCCOLI STALK SALAD
opposite

SERVES 4 TO 6

- 3 tablespoons minced Thai basil
- 1 teaspoon minced peeled fresh ginger
- 1 teaspoon minced garlic
- ¼ teaspoon chopped red bird's-eye chile
- 1 teaspoon kosher salt
- 3 large broccoli stalks
- 3 tablespoons fresh lime juice
- 2 avocadoes
- 2 tablespoons extra-virgin olive oil

1. In a small bowl, mix the basil, ginger, garlic, chile, and ½ teaspoon of the salt into a rough paste.

2.

Trim the tough outsides of the broccoli stalks, shaping them into long rectangles.

Then slice them thinly with a mandolin.

3. Put the broccoli slices in a bowl and add the lime juice and remaining ½ teaspoon salt. Toss to coat.

4.

Peel the avocado, then use a vegetable peeler to slice it into rectangles.

5. On a plate, overlap the strips of broccoli and avocado and trim edges so the sizes match.

6. To serve:

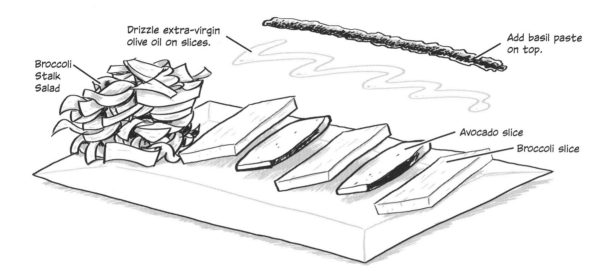

Drizzle extra-virgin olive oil on slices.

Add basil paste on top.

Broccoli Stalk Salad

Avocado slice

Broccoli slice

BROCCOLI STALK SALAD

SERVES 4 TO 6

Canola oil for deep-frying
3 broccoli stalks
1 cup cornstarch
2 cups mesclun mix
¼ cup thinly sliced red onion
1 tablespoon extra-virgin olive oil
1 tablespoon fresh lime juice
1 teaspoon salt
Pinch of ground black pepper

1. In a large pot heat the oil to 250°F.

2. Using a vegetable peeler, peel the broccoli stalks, then shave them into thin strips.

3. Coat half of the broccoli stalks in cornstarch and deep-fry (page 76) until they hold their shape, about 30 seconds.

4. Julienne the remaining half of the broccoli stalks and put in a large bowl. Add the remaining ingredients. Toss to coat. Right before serving, garnish the salad with the fried broccoli strips so they don't get soggy.

ROASTED CARROT BUNS

WITH CARROT AND CUCUMBER GINGER SALAD

 + **+** **+**

| CARROT BUNS | CARROT AND CUCUMBER SALAD
page 89 | CARROT HALVAH (OPTIONAL)
page 116 | CARROT HOISIN SAUCE (OPTIONAL)
page 116 |

MAKES 25 BUNS PLUS 2 EXTRA BATCHES OF FILLING

BUN FILLING

- 4 cups diced carrots
- 2 cups carrot juice, plus more as needed
- ¼ cup vegetarian oyster sauce
- 1 teaspoon fresh lime juice
- 2 tablespoons dark brown sugar
- 2 tablespoons rice wine vinegar
- 1 tablespoon plus 1 teaspoon extra-virgin olive oil
- 1 tablespoon plus 1 teaspoon toasted sesame oil
- 2 teaspoons shoyu or soy sauce
- 1 teaspoon hot sauce
- Salt
- ¼ cup sesame seeds
- 1 teaspoon chopped garlic
- 1 teaspoon chopped peeled fresh ginger
- 1 cup diced seeded hothouse cucumbers
- ½ cup sliced scallions
- ¼ cup chopped water chestnuts

1. To prepare the filling: Preheat the oven to 425°F.

2. In an 8-inch square or other small baking dish (as small as possible), combine the carrots, carrot juice, oyster sauce, lime juice, brown sugar, vinegar, 1 tablespoon olive oil, 1 tablespoon sesame oil, shoyu, hot sauce, and 1 teaspoon salt.

3. Bake until the carrots have softened and browned on the outside, about 1 hour, stirring every 15 minutes. If after an hour there's a lot of liquid in the pan, drain off and reserve the liquid, and then crisp the carrots in the oven for 5 more minutes. Older carrots are drier and will soak up the liquid, but fresher carrots will release additional juices of their own. Remove from the oven and set aside.

Take them out of the oven when they get like this.

crisp & chewy

soft & moist

4. In a dry pan over medium heat, toast the sesame seeds until light brown, 5 minutes. Set aside to cool.

These roasted carrot buns are based on dim sum, specifically char siu bao, or roast pork buns.

Char siu bao became famous in the West for their part in the Hong Kong true crime movie *Human Meat Roast Pork Buns: The Untold Story*, about a chef who takes over a restaurant by killing the owner's family and turning them into char siu bao.

This recipe uses carrots instead of humans. Easier to source.

These buns aren't supposed to taste like pork (or human), but the rich, juicy filling is supposed to resemble the *texture* of char siu bao.

5. In a large pan over medium heat, soften the garlic and ginger in 1 teaspoon olive oil and 1 teaspoon sesame oil. Add the carrot mixture and cook until the oil starts to bubble, about 3 minutes. Add the cucumbers, scallions, water chestnuts, and any reserved cooking liquid. If your carrots didn't have a lot of liquid and the pan looks dry, you can add some carrot juice to the pan at this point to get the mix juicy looking.

6. Bring the mixture to a simmer and immediately remove the pan from the heat. It should be a rich orange-brown color. Salt to taste. Set aside to cool to room temperature. The filling can be covered and refrigerated for up to 5 days or frozen for up to 2 months. Return the filling to room temperature before you fill the buns.

7. To prepare the dough: In a food processor fitted with the dough-blade attachment, combine the cake flour, baking powder, yeast, and sugar. Pulse a few times.

8. Turn the food processor to normal speed, and slowly pour in the carrot juice. Gluten strands will form and the dough will come together in a ball. Slowly pour in the olive oil. Continue to process for 3 to 5 minutes as the dough comes together into a ball and then breaks open.

BUN DOUGH	
300	grams cake flour (see Note)
3	grams baking powder
3	grams instant yeast
30	grams white sugar
160	milliliters carrot juice
15	grams extra-virgin olive oil, plus more for bowl

THE BUN DOUGH RECIPE IS MEASURED IN METRIC FOR ACCURACY.

RECIPE CONTINUES ➔

9. Touch the dough; it should feel hot and sticky. If it does not, then let it mix longer. This has activated the yeast. Normally yeast is pre-activated in a bowl of warm water, but this recipe activates the yeast *in the dough itself!!!*

10.

Oil a bowl and form the dough into a ball as you move it from the food processor to the bowl. Cover with plastic wrap and draw a circle on the plastic that's the same size as the dough. Cover it with a towel and stick it in a warm, dry place for 1 hour.

Check the circle. Has the dough doubled in size? If so, it's activated. If it didn't activate, you can't save it. Throw it out and start over.

11.

Punch the dough to get rid of air.

Divide it into about 25 .7-ounce balls.

Roll each ball into a small disc about 2 inches in diameter.

Put slightly less than 1 tablespoon of filling into the center of each.

Pinch four small pleats into the dough.

While holding in the filling with your finger, fold each corner to the center and then pinch them together with a half-twist.

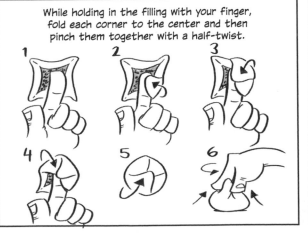

1 2 3

4 5 6

Fold over to seal. Cut small squares of parchment paper and place one under each bun. Cover with a towel. Let rise for 30 minutes.

12. Prepare a steamer. Working in batches, steam the buns for 15 minutes.

13. Remove the buns from the steamer and serve immediately, or let cool completely. When ready to serve, steam again for 6 to 10 minutes.

14. To serve:

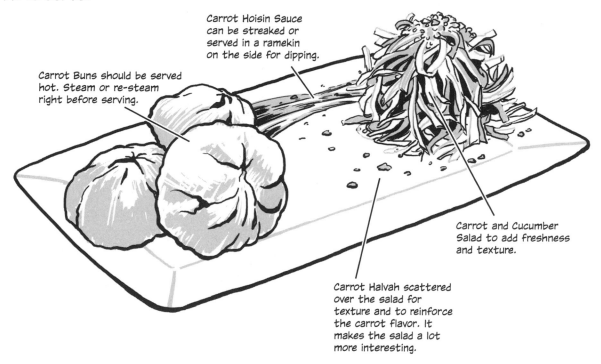

Carrot Hoisin Sauce can be streaked or served in a ramekin on the side for dipping.

Carrot Buns should be served hot. Steam or re-steam right before serving.

Carrot and Cucumber Salad to add freshness and texture.

Carrot Halvah scattered over the salad for texture and to reinforce the carrot flavor. It makes the salad a lot more interesting.

CARROT HOISIN SAUCE

MAKES ½ CUP

- 1 cup carrot juice
- 1 teaspoon extra-virgin olive oil
- 1 teaspoon toasted sesame oil
- 1 teaspoon chopped peeled fresh ginger
- 1 teaspoon chopped garlic
- ¼ teaspoon crushed red pepper flakes
- ¼ cup hoisin sauce
- 2 teaspoons cornstarch
- Salt

1. In a small pan over medium heat, reduce the carrot juice to ½ cup, about 15 minutes.

2. In a clean, small pan over low heat, add the olive and sesame oils, ginger, and garlic, and cook for 2 minutes. Add the red pepper flakes and cook for 3 more minutes. Add the hoisin sauce and reduced carrot juice and whisk to combine.

3. Bring to a simmer and whisk in the cornstarch. When bubbles start to form, remove the pan from the heat, pour the sauce into a blender, and mix until smooth. Salt to taste and let cool. Use immediately or cover and store in the fridge for up to 1 week.

CARROT HALVAH

MAKES 3 CUPS

- ¾ cup sesame seeds
- 6 tablespoons carrot juice
- ¾ cup tahini
- ½ cup plus 2 tablespoons sugar

1. In a dry pan over medium heat, toast the sesame seeds until light brown, about 5 minutes. Let cool.

2. In a pan over low heat, cook the carrot juice until it reduces to 3 tablespoons, about 15 minutes. Remove from the heat and let cool.

3. Put the tahini in a heatproof bowl. In a small pot over very low heat, heat the sugar and reduced carrot juice until the mixture reaches 275°F on a candy thermometer. The mixture should be golden orange, not brown. If it turns brown, it's ruined and you must begin again. Immediately transfer the syrup to the tahini bowl. Quickly mix with a spatula and then immediately pour in the sesame seeds. Keep stirring until fully incorporated and clumps form.

4. Set aside and let cool. Keep covered in a cool, dry place for up to 1 month.

FALAFEL BALLS

**SERVES 4 TO 8
(MAKES 16 FALAFEL BALLS)**

SPICE MIX

- 1 tablespoon cumin seeds
- 1 tablespoon coriander seeds
- 1 tablespoon dried parsley
- 2 teaspoons granulated garlic or garlic powder
- 1 teaspoon granulated onion or onion powder
- Pinch of ground allspice
- 2 teaspoons chili powder
- Pinch of crushed red pepper flakes
- Pinch of freshly ground black pepper
- ½ teaspoon ground sumac
- ½ teaspoon za'atar

FALAFEL BALLS

- Canola oil for deep-frying
- ½ cup dried chickpeas, soaked overnight and drained
- ¾ cup chopped fresh cilantro, carefully dried
- ¾ cup chopped flat-leaf parsley, carefully dried
- ½ cup diced red onion
- 5 garlic cloves, chopped
- ⅛ teaspoon baking soda
- Salt

1. *To make the spice mix:* In a dry pan over medium heat, toast the cumin and coriander until fragrant, 5 minutes. Let cool and then grind or blend into a fine powder.

2. Put the powder in a bowl and add all of the remaining spice mix ingredients. Mix together until well combined. The spice mix will keep for up to 1 month.

3. *To make the falafel:* In a deep pot, heat the oil to 350°F.

4. Put 1½ tablespoons of the spice mix and all of the remaining falafel ingredients in a food processor. Pulse until the chickpeas are the size of fish-tank gravel (about 60 pulses).

5. Gently roll the mixture into about 16 small balls. You need a gentle touch with them or they will fall apart. Deep-fry (page 76) until the outside is dark brown, about 1 minute.

One of Middle Eastern cuisine's most popular vegetarian dishes is falafel. These falafel balls go with Mint and Tarragon Fettuccine (page 176), or use them to make a falafel sandwich. Toss the spice mix with rice or beans to make a zesty side dish.

PORTOBELLO MOUSSE
WITH PEAR AND FENNEL COMPOTE

| PORTOBELLO MOUSSE | GRILLED PORTOBELLOS page 120 | TRUFFLE TOAST page 120 | BALSAMIC VINEGAR REDUCTION page 20 | PEAR AND FENNEL COMPOTE (OPTIONAL) page 41 |

SERVES 14

PORTOBELLO MOUSSE
- **8 portobello mushrooms**
- **1 cup (2 sticks) unsalted butter**
- **¼ cup finely chopped yellow onion**
- **½ cup heavy cream**
- **1¾ teaspoons agar agar**
- **½ teaspoon salt**
- **½ teaspoon truffle oil**

GRILLED PORTOBELLOS
- **10 large portobellos**
- **¼ cup extra-virgin olive oil**
- **1 teaspoon salt**

TRUFFLE TOAST
- **½ cup extra-virgin olive oil**
- **1 teaspoon truffle oil**
- **1 baguette, sliced thinly on the diagonal**
- **Salt**

Contrary to popular belief, there are no truffles in truffle oil. Instead, it contains a chemical additive, 2,4-dithiapentane, that doesn't taste like truffles at all. Its rich, oily mushroom flavor makes it a perfect flavor enhancer for dishes like this, though.

1. To prepare the mousse, remove and discard the stems from the mushrooms, then scrape the gills from the underside of the caps. Chop the mushroom caps to yield 6 cups chopped portobello.

2. In a small saucepan over medium heat, melt 2 tablespoons of the butter. Add the onion and cook until very soft, about 15 minutes. Add the cream, reduce the heat to low, and cook for 10 minutes. Add the rest of the butter and cook for 10 minutes.

3. Add the agar agar, stir gently, and let come to a simmer. Immediately remove from the heat and pour the mixture into a blender. Start blending on low and as the mixture smoothes out, gradually increase to high speed.

4. Add the mushrooms to the blender and blend until extremely smooth. Add the salt and truffle oil and blend until incorporated, about 10 seconds.

5. Pour the mousse into any mold you have. I generally use a cube. Rap the mold on the counter once or twice to get out any air bubbles. Refrigerate for at least 1 hour.

6. When ready to serve, tip the mousse out of the mold.

RECIPE CONTINUES ➜

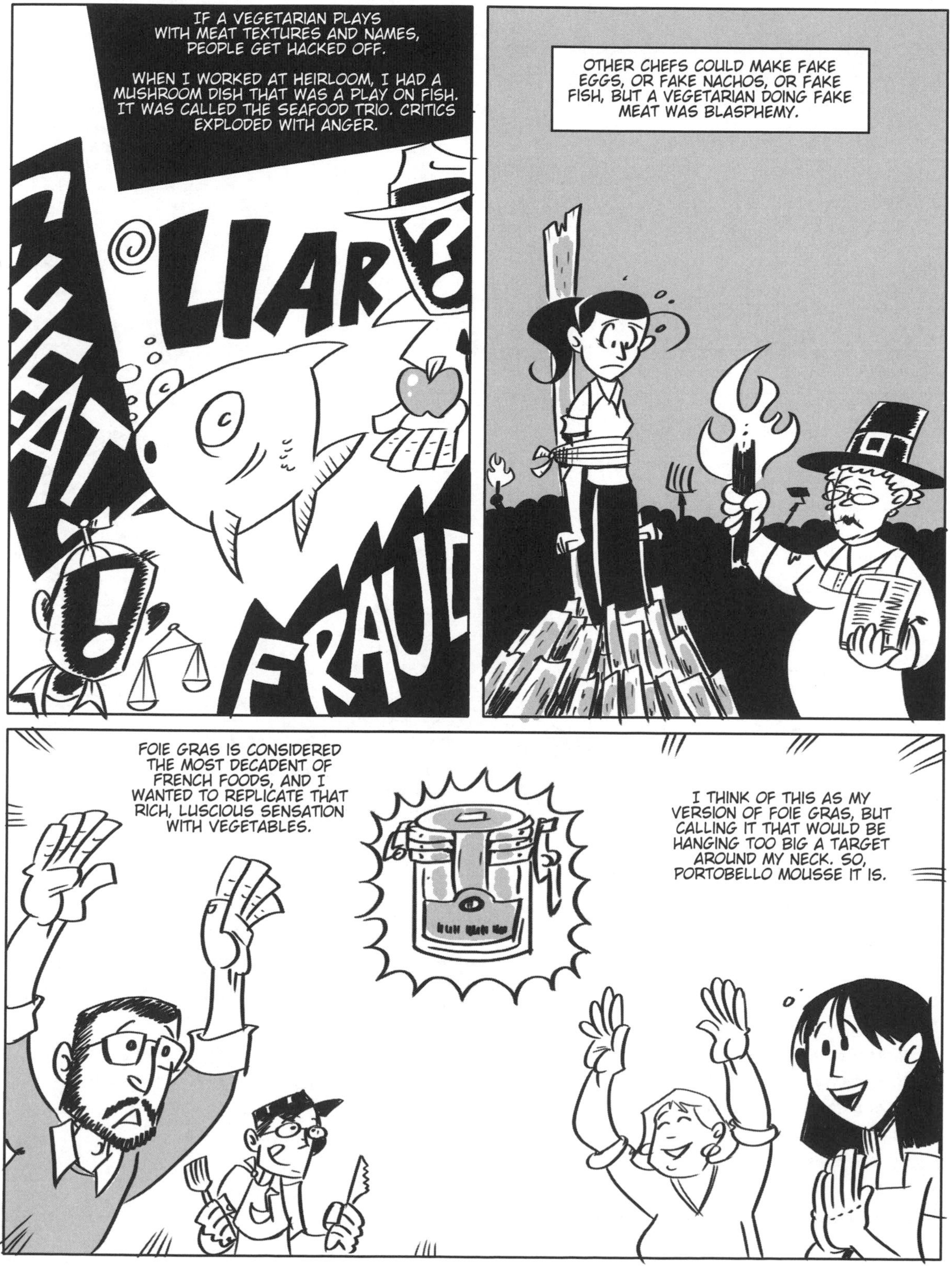
IF A VEGETARIAN PLAYS WITH MEAT TEXTURES AND NAMES, PEOPLE GET HACKED OFF.
WHEN I WORKED AT HEIRLOOM, I HAD A MUSHROOM DISH THAT WAS A PLAY ON FISH. IT WAS CALLED THE SEAFOOD TRIO. CRITICS EXPLODED WITH ANGER.
LIAR
OTHER CHEFS COULD MAKE FAKE EGGS, OR FAKE NACHOS, OR FAKE FISH, BUT A VEGETARIAN DOING FAKE MEAT WAS BLASPHEMY.
FOIE GRAS IS CONSIDERED THE MOST DECADENT OF FRENCH FOODS, AND I WANTED TO REPLICATE THAT RICH, LUSCIOUS SENSATION WITH VEGETABLES.
I THINK OF THIS AS MY VERSION OF FOIE GRAS, BUT CALLING IT THAT WOULD BE HANGING TOO BIG A TARGET AROUND MY NECK. SO, PORTOBELLO MOUSSE IT IS.

7. For the grilled portobellos: Heat a grill. Remove and discard the stems from the mushrooms, and then scrape off the gills from the underside of the caps. With a vegetable peeler, slice the caps into long, thin strips. Toss the strips with the olive oil and salt.

8. Grill until the mushrooms have softened. Alternatively, heat a pan over high heat. Add the strips and sauté until they soften, about 2 minutes.

9. For the truffle toast: Combine the olive and truffle oils and brush evenly on one side of each baguette slice, and then sprinkle with salt. Grill until grill marks form on both sides. Alternatively, toast in oven until lightly browned.

10. To serve:

Drizzle the Balsamic Vinegar Reduction on the plate first.

Grilled Portobellos served hot.

Truffle Toast served warm or at room temperature.

A dollop (1½ tablespoons) of Pear and Fennel Compote served cold or at room temperature.

RESTAURANT TRICK #241: DRIZZLING ADDS CLASS

Squeeze bottles are your drizzling BFFs, but a spoon can substitute. Use a small spoon, fill it ¾ of the way with the sauce, then tilt and drizzle.

ALWAYS have a plan before you start drizzling—circle, streak, squiggle, dots— and execute it **fast**.

VARIATION
VEGAN PORTOBELLO MOUSSE

SERVES 9

- **4 portobello mushrooms**
- **½ cup Earth Balance**
- **¼ cup finely diced white onions**
- **½ cup unflavored soy milk**
- **1 teaspoon agar agar**
- **¼ teaspoon salt**
- **⅛ teaspoon truffle oil**

The steps in this recipe are exactly the same as they are in the nonvegan mousse, just with these ingredients substituted.

Several times I've run out of regular portobello mousse and substituted vegan. No one ever noticed the difference, even regulars who'd had it before.

No country has had a bigger impact on American food than France. They've convinced us that their cuisine is the gold standard of food.

French haute cuisine* and nouvelle cuisine** hit the American foodscape like extinction level events, destroying everything...

* traditional grand cuisine
** post-1960s new-style cuisine

...except themselves!

MY CUISINE REIGNS SUPREME!!!! TREMBLE BEFORE MY SOUFFLÉS! HONOR MY HORS D'OEUVRES! SHIVER BEFORE MY

SAUCES!

The Essential French Formula:

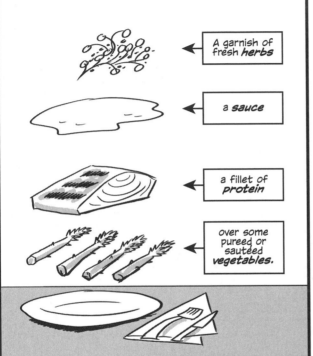

→ A garnish of fresh **herbs**

→ a **sauce**

→ a fillet of **protein**

→ over some pureed or sautéed **vegetables.**

It's a formula strong enough to survive every passing trend.

1980s Minimalist

1990s Bull-Market Food

2000s Haute Comfort Food

America may be a melting pot of food traditions, but one thing that hasn't melted is the dominance of the French-style main course, which favors large protiens.

This had made it almost impossible for vegetables to become the main course. How can you make celery the center of a dish the way you can roast chicken?

One way vegetarian food deals with the dominance of the French formula is by forcing some poor vegetable protein to assume the role of meat.

Quorn: fake meat made of extruded plant fungus. Seriously.

Vegetarian food is being forced to compete in a game that plays to its **weaknesses**, not its **strengths**. It's become about imitating what a meat-centric cuisine values, rather than looking for models outside the French tradition.

Vegetarian food has become about saying "No" to meat rather than about saying "Yes" to vegetables. It focuses on what it's **not** rather than what it is. At Dirt Candy I obsess about what I **can** serve, not about what I **can't**.

NO

YES!

BASIL BROTH

MAKES 2 CUPS

    5 cups basil leaves and stems
    4 garlic cloves, smashed
   ¼ cup diced yellow onion
       Salt

I serve this with Olive Fettuccine (page 173), but it can be used on any pasta. To make Basil Broth, first you have to make basil stock, which needs to get refrigerator cold, so give yourself enough time.

1. In a large pot over medium heat, simmer 1 cup of the basil, the garlic, onion, and 2½ cups water until the onions are soft, about 25 minutes. Strain, let cool, and refrigerate until cold. This is the basil stock.

2. Blanch and shock the remaining 4 cups basil (page 19).

3. Blend the stock and blanched basil in a blender until the basil is broken down, 2 to 3 minutes.

4. Push through a chinois (page 23) to remove any chunks. Salt to taste. The sauce will keep covered in the fridge for up to a week.

YELLOW TOMATO SAFFRON BROTH

MAKES 6 CUPS

    2 tablespoons extra-virgin olive oil
    1 cup diced yellow onion
   ¼ cup minced garlic
 1¼ teaspoons saffron
    6 cups roughly chopped yellow or
        red tomato
    1 tablespoon salt
    1 piece of kombu (seaweed)
 3½ cups Asparagus Stock (page 54)
        or other stock

Add vegetables and this doubles as a perfectly good summer soup. I use asparagus stock here because this sauce is going to accompany my Asparagus Paella (page 150), but feel free to replace it with Basic Stock (page 54).

1. Start a pot over medium heat with the olive oil, onion, and garlic (page 17). When the garlic is very soft, add the saffron and cook, stirring, for 2 minutes.

2. Increase the heat to medium, and add the tomato and salt. Cook, stirring occasionally, until the tomatoes start to break down, about 10 minutes. Add the kombu and stock. Bring to a simmer, turn the heat to low, and cook for 30 minutes. Remove from the heat and let cool slightly.

3. Working in batches, puree the mixture in a blender until smooth. Push through a chinois (page 23) to make it silky. The sauce will keep covered in the fridge for up to a week.

YELLOW TOMATO COCONUT CURRY SAUCE

MAKES 4 CUPS

¾ cup unsweetened coconut flakes

8 large yellow or red tomatoes, roughly chopped

2 tablespoons extra-virgin olive oil

1 cup diced yellow onion

2 tablespoons chopped garlic

2 tablespoons chopped peeled fresh ginger

2 tablespoons berber seasoning or curry powder

1 stalk lemongrass, cut into 1-inch pieces (page 54)

2 cups coconut milk

Grated zest of 2 lemons

¼ teaspoon crushed red pepper flakes

Salt

I pair this with Tomato Spaetzle (page 184), but it's a good sauce for any vegetable curry, or served with basmati rice.

1. Preheat the oven to 350°F.

2. Spread the coconut flakes on a baking sheet and toast in the oven until golden brown, about 10 minutes. Set aside.

3. Pulse the tomatoes in a blender until they form a chunky sauce.

4. Start a large pot over low heat with the olive oil, onion, garlic, and ginger (page 17). Cook until the onions are translucent, about 5 minutes, then add the toasted coconut flakes and mix well. Cook for 5 minutes. Add the berber seasoning and lemongrass and cook for 5 more minutes.

5. Add the tomatoes, coconut milk, lemon zest, and red pepper flakes, and bring to a simmer over medium heat. Simmer for 30 minutes, stirring occasionally. Remove from the heat and push through a chinois to break down any chunks. Salt to taste and serve. The sauce will keep covered in the fridge for up to a week.

CORN CREAM

MAKES 2 CUPS

2 cups fresh or frozen corn kernels

Salt

Though this sauce is just water and corn, the starch released by the corn kernels thickens into a sweet, all-vegetable version of a hollandaise sauce.

1. Put the corn kernels in a blender and cover them with water. Blend until smooth, about 3 minutes.

2. Push through a chinois (page 23) to remove chunks. Salt to taste. The sauce will keep covered in the fridge for up to a week.

YOGURT SAFFRON SAUCE

MAKES 2 CUPS

16 ounces labneh
¼ teaspoon saffron
   Salt

One of my favorite ingredients is labneh, a strained yogurt that's creamier and tangier than the regular stuff. It doesn't curdle when you heat it, and you can find it in any Middle Eastern grocery store. This sauce accompanies the Mint and Tarragon Fettuccine (page 176) but it also makes a good dip for pita or crudités.

1. In a blender, mix the labneh and saffron until smooth. If it's too thick to blend properly, add a little water to get it moving. You should wind up with a light yellow sauce. The sauce will keep covered in the fridge for up to a week.

2. When ready to serve, heat in a pan until warm and salt to taste.

 *VARIATION*

VEGAN YOGURT SAFFRON SAUCE

MAKES 3 CUPS

1 cup macadamia nuts
¼ teaspoon saffron
1 teaspoon fresh lemon juice
   Salt

1. Cover the macadamia nuts with water and let them soak overnight. Drain and rinse the nuts, and puree in a blender with 3 cups water. Push through a chinois (page 23) and blend again.

2. Line the chinois with cheesecloth and push the mixture through again, then put it back in the blender with the saffron. Blend until smooth. If it's too thick to blend well, add a little water to get it moving.

3. The sauce will keep covered in the fridge for up to a week. When ready to serve, warm in a pan and add the lemon juice. Salt to taste.

LEMON CORN SAUCE

MAKES 2 CUPS

- ½ cup (1 stick) unsalted butter
- 5 cups fresh or frozen corn kernels
- 2 cups Radish Stock (page 54) or other stock
- 2 tablespoons minced garlic
- 2 teaspoons grated lemon zest (page 43)
- Salt

This is a decadent cream sauce, only without any cream. I use radish stock in the recipe because I originally created this to go with Radish Ravioli (page 156), but pick whatever stock best matches the dish you're serving (carrot stock with a carrot dish, corn stock with a corn dish), or use Basic Stock (page 54).

1. In a saucepan over medium heat, melt the butter, and then add the remaining ingredients, salting to taste. Cook until the corn is soft, about 5 minutes.

2. Remove from the heat and let cool slightly. Pour into a blender and blend.

3. Push through a chinois to remove chunks (page 23). Salt to taste and serve. The sauce will keep covered in the fridge for up to a week.

 **TO MAKE IT VEGAN**

Replace the butter with Coconut Cream (page 64) or 2 tablespoons extra-virgin olive oil.

CAUTION:
IF YOU BLEND WHILE THE MIXTURE IS HOT, THE BLENDER WILL EXPLODE.

PRESERVED LEMON MAYONNAISE

MAKES 1 CUP

- ¼ cup chopped, seeded Preserved Lemons (page 41)
- 1 cup Vegenaise

This Middle Eastern–flavored mayo is part of my Greek Salad (page 85) but you can use it anywhere, from sandwiches to deviled eggs to a dipping sauce for King Oyster Mushroom Rings (page 101).

Vegenaise is even **better** than mayonnaise. It has a more savory taste and a creamier texture.

In a blender, blend the lemons and Vegenaise until smooth. The mayo will keep covered in the fridge for up to a week.

YOGURT CUMIN SAUCE

MAKES 2 CUPS

>   2 teaspoons cumin seeds
>   2 teaspoons coriander seeds
> 2½ tablespoons extra-virgin olive oil
>   ½ cup diced yellow onion
>   2 tablespoons chopped garlic
>   2 tablespoons chopped peeled
>   fresh ginger
>   1 cup plain yogurt
> 1½ cups Basic Stock (page 54)
> 1½ tablespoons unbleached
>   all-purpose flour
>   2 ounces goat cheese
>   Salt

One of the most popular (and ancient) spices in the world, cumin—with its bitter, oily taste—gets balanced by cooling yogurt and goat cheese. Serve this with Beet Pappardelle (page 178) or on any beet dish.

1. In a dry pan over medium heat, toast the cumin and coriander seeds until fragrant, about 5 minutes. Pulse them together in a blender or spice grinder into a fine powder.

2. Start a pot over medium heat with the olive oil and onion (page 17). Add the garlic, ginger, and the cumin-coriander powder and cook for 4 minutes.

3. Pour in the yogurt and turn the heat to low *so it doesn't boil.* Let simmer for 2 minutes and then whisk in the stock. Turn the heat back up to medium and simmer for 10 minutes. Remove from the heat and push through a chinois.

4. Put ½ cup of the yogurt sauce in a small bowl and stir in the flour to make a slurry. Add the slurry to the rest of the yogurt sauce and cook over medium heat for 10 minutes.

5. Add the goat cheese and whisk until incorporated. Remove from the heat and salt to taste. The sauce will keep covered in the fridge for up to a week.

VARIATION

VEGAN YOGURT CUMIN SAUCE

MAKES 3 CUPS

- 2 teaspoons cumin seeds
- 2 teaspoons coriander seeds
- 3 tablespoons extra-virgin olive oil
- ½ cup diced yellow onion
- 2 tablespoons minced garlic
- 2 tablespoons chopped peeled fresh ginger
- 1 quart unflavored soy milk
- 2 teaspoons nutritional yeast
- 2 tablespoons unbleached all-purpose flour
  Salt

This recipe is almost identical to Yogurt Cumin Sauce (opposite), except that it uses soy milk and nutritional yeast instead of yogurt. Both recipes are thickened with a slurry (a bit of the sauce mixed with flour) instead of a roux (which is thickened with both butter and flour). Not only is a slurry easy to make, but it also can be added at the end, while a roux has to be the base of the sauce from the very beginning. Slurries are an easy way to vary the thickness of a sauce: Use less flour for a looser sauce, more for a thicker one. It's a nice, simple trick to thicken almost any sauce.

1. In a dry pan over medium heat, toast the cumin and coriander seeds until fragrant, about 5 minutes. Pulse them both together in a blender or spice grinder until they are a fine powder.

2. Start a pot over medium heat with the olive oil and onion (page 17), and cook until the onion is very soft. Add the garlic, ginger, and the cumin-coriander powder and cook for 4 minutes.

3. Add the soy milk and let simmer over medium heat for 10 minutes.

4. Whisk in the nutritional yeast and simmer for 5 more minutes. Strain the mixture and pour it back into the pot on medium heat.

5. Put ½ cup of the sauce in a small bowl and stir in the flour to make a slurry. Add the slurry back into the rest of the sauce and whisk to fully incorporate the slurry with the sauce.

6. When the mixture comes back to a simmer, about 5 minutes, remove the pan from the heat and salt to taste. The sauce will keep covered in the fridge for up to a week.

BEURRE BLANC SAUCE

MAKES 2 CUPS

- **1 cup white wine**
- **¼ cup finely diced shallot**
- **1 stalk lemongrass, chopped (page 54)**
- **1 garlic clove, minced**
- **Salt**
- **Flavorings for flavored beurre blanc (see step 2)**
- **2 cups (4 sticks) unsalted butter, refrigerator-cold**

Beurre blanc is a basic French butter sauce. I make three versions of it, and they all start and end the same way.

 **TO MAKE IT VEGAN**

Replace the butter with 1 (13.5-ounce) can of coconut milk, adding it all at once. Let it simmer for 10 minutes, but don't let it come to a boil.

1. Put the wine, shallot, lemongrass, garlic, and ¼ teaspoon salt in a large pot and reduce over medium-low heat until you have approximately 1 tablespoon of liquid left, about 30 minutes.

2. Add the ingredients below depending on which beurre blanc sauce you're making.

ORANGE BEURRE BLANC

- **Grated zest of 2 oranges (page 43)**
- **1 cup fresh orange juice**
- **1 tablespoon sliced peeled fresh ginger**

GRAPEFRUIT BEURRE BLANC

- **Grated zest of 1 grapefruit (page 43)**
- **1 cup fresh grapefruit juice**
- **1 tablespoon sliced peeled fresh galangal**

KAFFIR LIME BEURRE BLANC

- **Grated zest of 2 limes (page 43)**
- **1 cup fresh lime juice**
- **6 kaffir lime leaves**

3. Over medium-low heat, reduce the ingredients to ¼ cup liquid, 30 to 35 minutes. Strain and discard the solids. This is the base for your beurre blanc sauce. **Do not taste.** It's pretty gross at this point.

4. Pour the sauce base back into the pot over very low heat, then stir in the butter 1 tablespoon at a time, letting it melt completely before adding the next tablespoon.

5. Remove from the heat and salt to taste. Serve immediately; beurre blanc sauce will not keep.

HORSERADISH CREAM SAUCE

MAKES 2 CUPS

½ cup chopped peeled fresh
 horseradish or ½ cup jarred
 horseradish (NOT the pink kind!)
2 cups heavy cream
 Salt to taste

Horseradish adds heat to a dish, but because it's related to wasabi and other mustards, the kick is more savory and rounded than the sharp heat of chile peppers. This sauce was specifically designed for Smoked Cauliflower and Waffles (page 158), but it balances all sweeter vegetables, like broccoli, Brussels sprouts, or carrots.

 **TO MAKE IT VEGAN**

Use 6 tablespoons horseradish and substitute unflavored soy milk for the cream.

1. Put the fresh horseradish chunks in a blender and add a little water (unless it's already very juicy). Blend until it forms a thick paste. Do not put your face over the blender when you open it. The fumes will **knock you out!**

2. Put the horseradish paste (or the jarred horseradish) and the heavy cream in a saucepan and bring to a simmer over medium heat. Reduce the heat to low and cook for 30 minutes. Remove from the heat and let cool.

3. Push through a chinois (page 23), really **jamming** the bits of horseradish through the holes. This will break them up and release their juices, which is where the horseradish flavor comes from.

4. Throw out the pulped horseradish, and salt the cream to taste. The sauce will keep covered in the fridge for up to a week.

You can buy horseradish in a jar if you want to skip step 1 of this recipe, but fresh horseradish has a zing that jarred horseradish lacks.

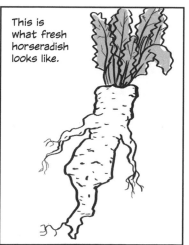

This is what fresh horseradish looks like.

Peel the horseradish and cut it into big chunks to use in the recipe.

Entrées

Cooking for other people is the hardest thing you'll ever learn. Everyone's tastes are different.

THIS PAELLA TASTES LIKE SUMMER IN A BOWL.

THIS PAELLA TASTES A LITTLE BIT BLAND.

THIS PAELLA TASTES LIKE DIRTY SOCK WATER WITH DAY-OLD FRIED RICE FLOATING IN IT.

Sometimes customers just don't get the food.

HERE'S YOUR PORTOBELLO MOUSSE AND YOUR SPINACH SOUP.

WHICH ONE IS THE SOUP?

THIS ONE IS THE *MOUSSE* ...

...AND THIS ONE IS THE *SOUP*.

SO *THIS* IS MY SOUP?

NO, THE ONE ON THE *PLATE* IS THE MOUSSE. THE ONE IN THE *BOWL* IS THE SOUP.

SO YOU'RE SAYING *THIS* IS MY *SOUP*?

Other times we have **NO CLUE** what a customer thinks.

MARTHA STEWART WOULD LIKE TO COME FOR DINNER TONIGHT.

I DON'T HAVE ANY TABLES TONIGHT--BUT IT'S MARTHA STEWART. I NEVER GIVE CELEBRITIES PRIORITY--BUT IT'S *MARTHA STEWART.* I CAN'T DO THIS--BUT IT'S *MARTHA STEWART.*

OK!

Fortunately, I had a regular customer booked that night and I knew she would understand.

SARA, CAN I BUMP YOU? I NEED TO GIVE YOUR TABLE TO MARTHA STEWART.

OMG *MARTHA STEWART!*

I HAVE A TABLE FOR *TWO* FOR MARTHA AT *8*.

GREAT. SHE'LL BE A PARTY OF *FOUR* AT 8:30.

I had other customers that night, but they weren't quite so understanding.

CAN I OFFER YOU A FREE MEAL?

SIX FREE MEALS.

TWO?

SIX.

DONE.

Martha's party arrived. They ordered. We sent out food. And after that... we were in the dark.

DID YOU LIKE THE KIMCHI DOUGHNUTS?

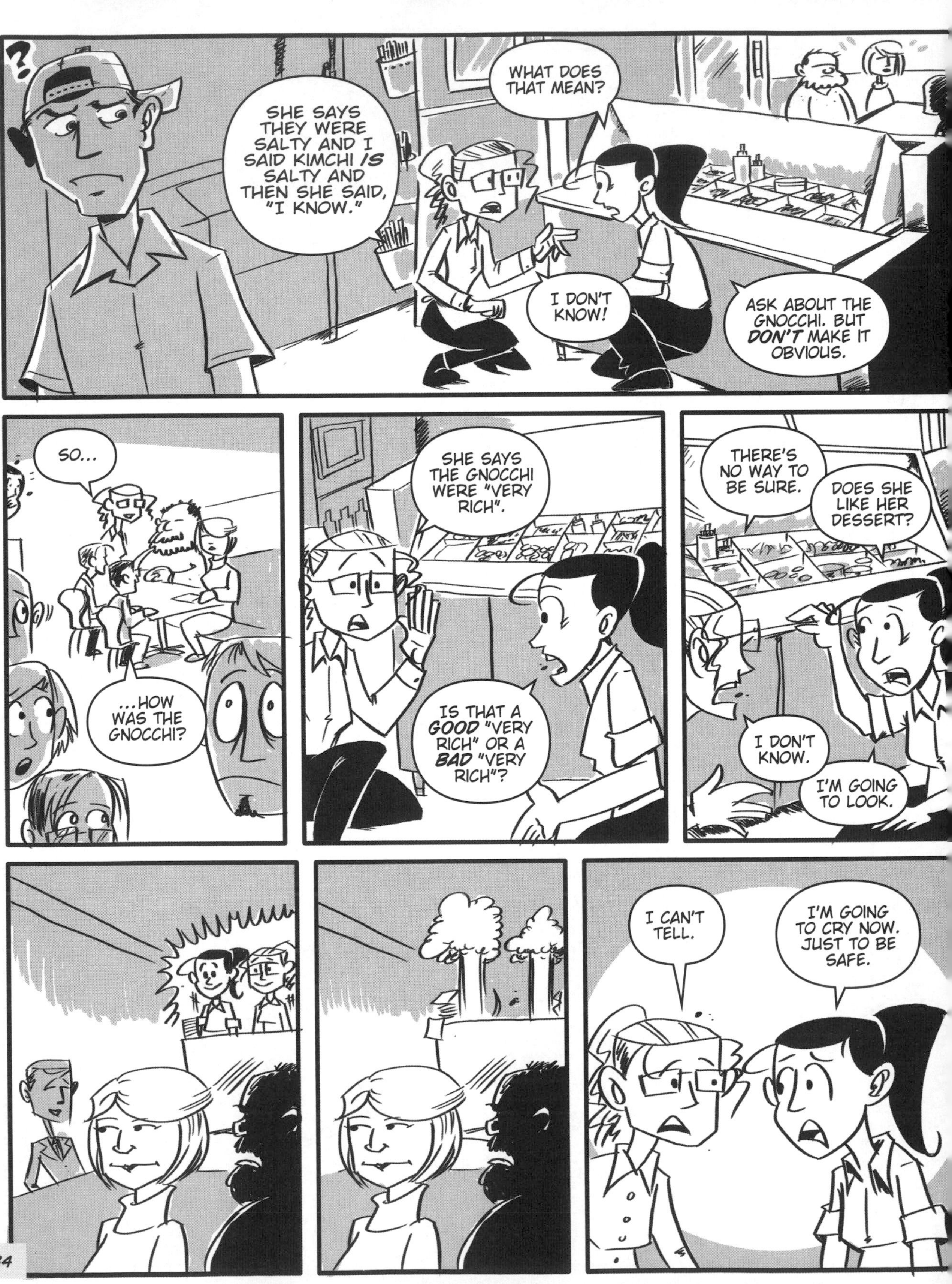
?
SHE SAYS THEY WERE SALTY AND I SAID KIMCHI *IS* SALTY AND THEN SHE SAID, "I KNOW."
WHAT DOES THAT MEAN?
I DON'T KNOW!
ASK ABOUT THE GNOCCHI. BUT *DON'T* MAKE IT OBVIOUS.
SO...
...HOW WAS THE GNOCCHI?
SHE SAYS THE GNOCCHI WERE "VERY RICH".
IS THAT A *GOOD* "VERY RICH" OR A *BAD* "VERY RICH"?
THERE'S NO WAY TO BE SURE.
DOES SHE LIKE HER DESSERT?
I DON'T KNOW.
I'M GOING TO LOOK.
I CAN'T TELL.
I'M GOING TO CRY NOW. JUST TO BE SAFE.

But sometimes the problem isn't the **customer**. Sometimes the problem is me.

I was a good girl, until I met my **match** in that plate of *Roasted Cauliflower Pappardelle*. They all tried to warn me...but I wasn't listening! I was **blind** that winter because...

I FELL IN LOVE WITH THE WRONG DISH!

SHAMELESS!

SHE'S GOT TOMATO SAUCE ALL OVER HER *FACE*!

UGH!

I DON'T CARE WHAT THEY SAY...I KNOW YOU'RE *PERFECT*!

I had met plates of pappardelle before but they were all so coarse...so *rural*!

YEW WANNA KNOW HOW AH TAYSTE SEW GOOD? CUZ AH'M FULLA WILD BOAR! THAS RIGHT! WILD BOAR!

MORE LIKE A WILD *BORE*.

And then I saw *you*...across the kitchen that night...and right away I knew you were *different*! You were subtle, delicate, *SENSITIVE*!

So **light** and **flavorful!** The **sweetness** of your raisins, the **subtlety** of your roasted cauliflower, and your pine nuts!

They were dehydrated, rolled into sheets, then crumbled. So **deconstructed!** So **sophisticated!**

You made me feel smarter, more grown-up, like a **real** chef.

I... I LOVE YOU!

There were problems from the start. No one understood you the way I did.

IT'S UNDULY COMPLICATED.

≈SOB≈... ≈CHOKE≈

Night after night I listened to them tear you apart and finally I couldn't take it anymore!

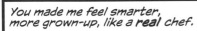

BLAND FUSSY Cloying Flavorless VAPID Pointless BIZARRE

I'LL **NEVER** LOVE A DISH AS MUCH AS I LOVED YOU!

And so I left you on the **Island of Retired Dishes,** but every night I'm still serving you...in my heart!

It's the **hardest thing** about being a chef. You can go to school. You can read books. You can watch your mother.

But **no one** ever teaches you how to cook for other people. You learn those lessons at the School of Hard Knocks.

My school changed names the way most people change socks. It was called Mooza, then Cafe Lika, then One 91. Later it was called Core 191 and the Sixth Ward.

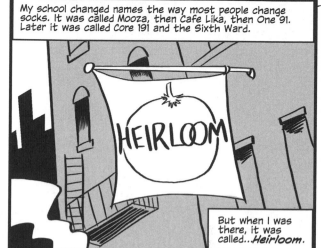

HEIRLOOM

But when I was there, it was called...*Heirloom*.

Matthew Kenney hired me to open Heirloom in six weeks. It was **cursed** from the beginning. I tore ligaments in my shoulder when I fell down the stairs.

My sous chef grabbed what she thought was an empty pot off the stove. Turned out to be full of **boiling oil**. She was in the hospital for two weeks.

At the second friends and family dinner we were down a chef, I had one arm, and we had 70 people on the books. But no one had managed the guest list...

WE'VE GOT 150 PEOPLE OUT THERE!

COOK! COOK FOR YOUR **LIVES**!

Food couldn't go out. Plates weren't being cleared. The owners kept sending free booze to tables, and the dining room devolved into *chaos*.

We ran out of food. By the end of the night we were serving people who'd waited *three hours* boxed pasta and canned tomato sauce.

But over the next few weeks, things were going to get *worse*.

No matter how hard I tried, a lot of my dishes kept coming *back*.

THEY SAY IT'S BLAND.

BLAND.

THEY LOVED IT!

JUST KIDDING. BLAND.

THEY DON'T UNDERSTAND ME! THEY CAN'T TASTE THE *SUBTLETY* OF MY FOOD.

THEY'RE FOOLS! BLIND FOOLS! I'M A GENIUS! MY FOOD IS *PERFECT*!

The press were waiting to jump all over Matthew, and I got mugged by proxy. A few weeks in, the *New York Observer* called my food bland one time too many, and that night...

HELLO! IT IS I, *JULIA CHILD!* I COME TO CHEFS WHEN THEY ARE AT THEIR LOWEST TO REMIND THEM OF SOMETHING.

THE CUSTOMER IS *NOT* YOUR ENEMY. THEY'VE COME TO YOU TO BE EXCITED! THEY GO OUT TO EAT BECAUSE IT IS A TREAT!

WE GROW UP BEING FED BY OUR MOTHERS, AND SO WHEN WE TRUST SOMEONE ELSE TO COOK FOR US IT IS THE *ULTIMATE INTIMACY.*

COOKING IS LIKE LOVE: IT SHOULD BE ENTERED INTO WITH *ABANDON* OR NOT AT ALL.

TASTE IT. FIND THE FLAVOR. NOW *ADD MORE.* DOUBLE IT! TRIPLE IT! *MORE* SALT! *MORE* BUTTER! BE *FEARLESS,* DUCKLING! NO REGRETS!

I woke up the next morning and it was all just a dream...

...or *was* it?

From that moment on, my cooking changed forever.

You have to use *more* salt. *More* butter. *More* fat. *More* spice. *More* vinegar. *More* wine. *More* sugar. *More* flavor. More! MORE! *MORE!*

PLATE'S EMPTY, CHEF.

THEY LOVED IT.

THEY SAID IT WAS THE BEST THEY'D EVER HAD.

Two months later I left when Matthew decided to turn Heirloom into a spa-food restaurant. No frying. No flavors. No *fun.*

One month after that, Heirloom closed for good. But I finally knew how to cook for other people.

RAW	GOOD PLACE	"THE BAD PLACE"	ROAST

Vegetables need to cook way **more** than you think, or way **less**.

Most people get timid and cook things too long and not hot enough.
Result: blah, colorless vegetables.

Fast-cooking on high heat keeps them bright and seals in flavor.

If you're roasting, leave it in **longer** than you think you should so that the vegetables release their sugars and caramelize **completely**.

Add **citrus** at the **end** of a recipe to brighten the flavors.

Add a tablespoon of butter or fat, like an oil or a cream, to finish a dish--most restaurants do this to make it rich and creamy.

For vegetables you need to **go big** or **go home**.

Fat isn't going to deliver all of your flavor, so you have to blow it up big **yourself**.

BIG FLAVA

141

CARROT RISOTTO

WITH CARROT DUMPLINGS AND CARROT RIBBONS

CARROT
RISOTTO

+

CARROT
DUMPLINGS
page 144

+

CARROT RIBBONS
(OPTIONAL)
opposite

SERVES 4

- 6 cups Carrot Stock (page 54)
- ¼ cup extra-virgin olive oil
- 1 cup diced yellow onion
- 1 tablespoon minced garlic
- 2 cups arborio rice
- ⅓ cup white wine
- 1 tablespoon fresh lemon juice
- 1 cup carrot juice
- ¼ cup diced carrot
- 3 tablespoons unsalted butter
- 5 tablespoons grated Parmesan, optional
- 1 tablespoon fresh thyme leaves
- Salt

A lot of what folks consider the taste of a vegetable is really its texture. Remove the texture, and your tongue gets confused. This risotto is all about changing the texture of a vegetable to see how that changes its taste.

TO MAKE IT VEGAN

Omit the butter and Parmesan.

1. In a small pot over medium-low heat, simmer the stock.

2. In another pan, start the oil, onion, and garlic over medium heat (page 17). Add the rice and cook, stirring, until it's translucent, about 7 minutes. Add the wine and stir until it has evaporated, about 2 minutes. Add the lemon juice and stir until it, too, has evaporated, about 1 minute.

3. Add 1 cup of the simmering Carrot Stock to the hot rice (both need to be the same temperature). Stir until it's absorbed, about 5 minutes. Continue adding stock 1 cup at a time and stirring until it's absorbed. When you have 2 cups stock left, pour the carrot juice into the simmering stock, and let it come back up to a simmer. Add 1 cup of the stock-juice mixture to the rice and cook until it's absorbed. Add the diced carrot to the rice and then add the last 2 cups stock, 1 cup at a time.

4. When the rice looks wet and juicy, but there's no liquid sloshing around, add the butter, 3 tablespoons of the Parmesan (if using), thyme, and salt to taste; stir until the butter is melted. Divide among 4 plates.

5. To serve:

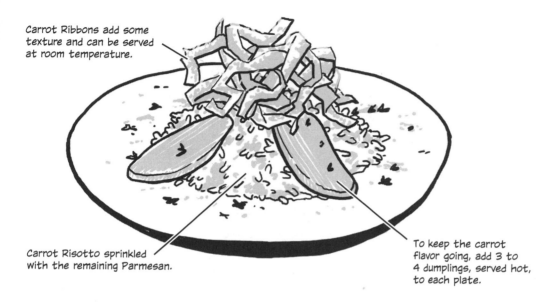

Carrot Ribbons add some texture and can be served at room temperature.

Carrot Risotto sprinkled with the remaining Parmesan.

To keep the carrot flavor going, add 3 to 4 dumplings, served hot, to each plate.

CARROT RIBBONS

Use a vegetable peeler to peel 2 carrots. Toss them in cornstarch, and deep-fry (page 76) them quickly, just until they hold their shape.

½ cup cornstarch

Canola oil for deep-frying

CARROT DUMPLINGS

**SERVES 4 TO 6
(MAKES ABOUT 18 DUMPLINGS)**

- ¼ cup Carrot Stock (page 54)
- 4 cups sliced carrots
- 1 teaspoon salt
- ½ cup potato starch
- ⅛ teaspoon baking soda
- 2 tablespoons agave nectar

This recipe isn't 100% necessary, but it adds another texture of carrot to the dish and it impresses the heck out of people if you can pull it off. These dumplings are not Chinese-style filled dumplings, but more like British dumplings, which are simply cooked dough.

TO MAKE THE CARROTS FUNKY, CUT THEM DIAGONALLY WITH A SERRATED KNIFE.

1. In a pot over medium heat, bring the stock to a boil and then reduce the heat so that it simmers. Add the carrots, cover, and simmer until tender, about 20 minutes. Drain the carrots and let cool.

2. Break down the carrots in a food processor until smooth, about 3 minutes. Add the salt, potato starch, baking soda, and agave and process again until very smooth.

3.

Divide the dough into 2 equal logs and wrap each with plastic. Make sure *no air* is trapped inside the plastic.

Then wrap with tinfoil.

4. Bring a large pot of water to a boil and poach the wrapped dumpling logs for 30 minutes. Remove and refrigerate the logs until cool. They will keep for up to 1 week in the fridge or in the freezer for up to 1 month.

5.

When ready to serve, bring a large pot of water to a boil. Unwrap the logs and cut each into 10 to 12 slices.

6. Reboil slices for 3 minutes, until cooked through.

CRISPY TOFU

WITH GREEN RAGOUT AND BEURRE BLANC SAUCE

Tofu gets a bad rap as bland and tasteless.

I'VE BEEN FRAMED!

Most people drown it in cloying sauces, but when you make tofu, you want to **taste** tofu.

GLUB

Tofu is subtle: nutty, creamy, slightly sweet. This dish uses citrus to make the flavor pop.

DON'T CRY. I CAN HELP YOU.

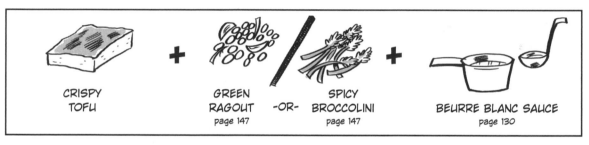

CRISPY TOFU + GREEN RAGOUT page 147 -OR- SPICY BROCCOLINI page 147 + BEURRE BLANC SAUCE page 130

SERVES 4

- 1 (14-ounce) block extra-firm tofu
- 6 cups Basic Stock (page 54)
- About 20 sheets tofu skin (aka *yuba*)
- ¼ cup potato starch
- 2 tablespoons extra-virgin olive oil

If you cook tofu long enough to make it crispy, you're going to overcook it. My cheat is to meld sheets of yuba (tofu skin) to one side of the tofu with a flour-and-water slurry. It crisps quickly without ruining the tofu. To save time, you can poach the tofu and make the Basic Stock in the same pan, at the same time.

1. Wash the disgusting package juice from the tofu. Wrap the tofu in a dishtowel and press between 2 stacks of plates for 1 hour to drain water.

2.

Slice the tofu into four even pieces.

In a pan, poach the tofu in the stock for 1 hour over low heat. Remove from poaching liquid and let the tofu cool in the fridge to room temperature.

3.

Slice the yuba into four stacks of about five sheets each. Cut each stack so that it's ¼ inch smaller on all sides than the pieces of tofu. (The yuba expands when wet.)

RECIPE CONTINUES ➜

4.

Fill a shallow bowl with water. In a separate bowl, whisk the potato starch with 6 tablespoons water to make a slurry. Spread the slurry on top of each piece of tofu.

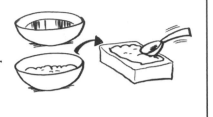

5.

Dip each stack of yuba in the water and lay it on the slurry-coated side of the tofu. Let dry for 15 minutes to lock the yuba to the tofu.

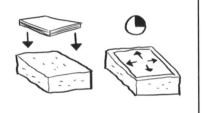

6.

Heat the olive oil in a nonstick pan over medium heat. Gently place the tofu pieces in the pan yuba-side down. Cook until the skin is golden brown and crispy, about 2 minutes on each side.

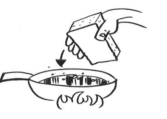

7. To serve:

The Green Ragout or Spicy Broccolini goes on the plate first, right out of the pan. Lift it out with tongs so no extra liquid gets on the plate.

Crispy Tofu goes down next, right out of the pan so it's hot.

TO MAKE IT VEGAN

Use Vegan Beurre Blanc Sauce (page 130).

Simmer ½ cup of Beurre Blanc Sauce per serving, and pour it over the tofu so it saturates the vegetables.

GREEN RAGOUT OR SPICY BROCCOLINI

SERVES 4

GREEN RAGOUT

- **2 tablespoons extra-virgin olive oil**
- **2 tablespoons minced garlic**
- **2 tablespoons minced peeled fresh ginger**
- **½ cup julienned peeled kohlrabi**
- **½ cup julienned snow peas**
- **½ cup sliced sugar snap peas**
- **2 cups sliced baby bok choy**
- **½ cup steamed edamame**
- **½ cup peeled and quartered Brussels sprouts**
- **½ cup Basic Stock (page 54)**
- **Salt**

SPICY BROCCOLINI

- **2 tablespoons extra-virgin olive oil**
- **2 tablespoons minced garlic**
- **2 tablespoons minced peeled fresh ginger**
- **4 whole dried chili peppers**
- **3 cups chopped broccoli (stems and florets)**
- **3 cups chopped broccolini**
- **½ cup minced fresh cilantro**
- **½ cup Basic Stock (page 54)**
- **Salt**

These two recipes are both prepared the same way, just with different ingredients. Green Ragout goes with Kaffir Lime Beurre Blanc Sauce (page 130) or Grapefruit Beurre Blanc Sauce (page 130). Spicy Broccolini is better with Orange Beurre Blanc Sauce (page 130).

1. For the ragout or broccolini, start a large pan on medium heat with the oil, garlic, and ginger (page 17). If you're making the Spicy Broccolini, also add the dried chili peppers.

2. Add all the vegetables and toss a few times, then add the stock. This will steam the vegetables quickly while keeping their color, about 2 minutes.

3. Lift the vegetables out of the pan with tongs, so no excess stock gets on the plate.

COCONUT-POACHED TOFU

WITH CUCUMBER THREE WAYS

| COCONUT-POACHED TOFU | CUCUMBER MIX | SHISO GALANGAL SAUCE _opposite_ | AVOCADO RELISH (OPTIONAL) _opposite_ | FRIED PICKLES (OPTIONAL) _page 38_ |

TOFU

- 1 (14-ounce) package extra-firm tofu
- 1 (13.5-ounce) can coconut milk
- 2 cups Basic Stock (page 54)
  About 20 sheets tofu skin (aka _yuba_)
- ¼ cup potato starch
- 2 tablespoons extra-virgin olive oil

CUCUMBERS

- 2 tablespoons extra-virgin olive oil
- 1 tablespoon minced garlic
- 1 tablespoon minced peeled fresh ginger
- 1 tablespoon minced fresh galangal
- 3 cups seeded diced cucumber
- ¼ cup diced peeled (remove outer layer) fresh hearts of palm
- ¼ cup thin rounds peeled salsify
- ¼ cup chopped fresh Chinese chives
- 2 tablespoons white wine
- ½ cup fresh cilantro
- ¼ cup seeded diced hothouse cucumber
  Salt

TO MAKE IT VEGAN

Substitute coconut cream (page 64) for the butter in the sauce.

1. To cook the tofu: Prepare exactly as in the Crispy Tofu recipe (page 145), except in Step 2, instead of poaching the slices of tofu in stock, poach them in the coconut milk and 2 cups of the stock for 1 hour, then continue with the recipe just as written.

2. To cook the cucumbers: Start a pan on medium heat with the olive oil, garlic, ginger, and galangal (page 17). Add 3 cups of the cucumbers along with the hearts of palm, salsify, and Chinese chives. Stir twice and add the wine. Continue cooking for 3 minutes. Add the cilantro and hothouse cucumber. Salt to taste and remove from the heat.

3. To make the sauce: Put the galangal, ginger, garlic, shallot, and lemongrass into a saucepan with 2 cups water and bring to a boil. Reduce to ½ cup, about 45 minutes, and let cool.

_4._ Blanch and shock the shiso, parsley, and cilantro all together (page 19). Squeeze dry the herbs, rough chop them, and put them in a blender. Add the galangal stock and blend until smooth.

SHISO GALANGAL SAUCE

- 2 tablespoons chopped galangal
- 1 tablespoon chopped peeled fresh ginger
- 1 tablespoon chopped garlic
- 2 teaspoons chopped shallot
- ¼ stalk of lemongrass, bruised (page 54)
- 1 cup packed fresh shiso leaves
- ¾ cup flat-leaf parsley leaves
- 2 tablespoons fresh cilantro leaves
- ¾ cup Basic Stock (page 54)
- 1 tablespoon unsalted butter
- Salt

5. Pour the sauce into a saucepan and heat on medium with the stock and butter or coconut cream until bubbling, about 2 minutes. Salt to taste and remove from the heat.

6. *To serve:* Divide among 4 plates. Heat the Shiso Galangal Sauce to a simmer and pour slightly less than ¼ cup per plate. Layer as shown below.

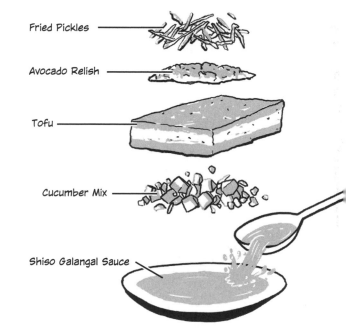

Fried Pickles

Avocado Relish

Tofu

Cucumber Mix

Shiso Galangal Sauce

THE AVOCADO RELISH BRINGS SPICINESS, AND THE FRIED PICKLES GIVE IT SOME CRUNCH SINCE THE VEGETABLES ARE SOFT AFTER COOKING.

AVOCADO RELISH

SERVES 4 TO 6

- 2 teaspoons minced fresh galangal
- 1 teaspoon minced peeled fresh ginger
- 1 teaspoon minced garlic
- ½ teaspoon minced bird's-eye chiles
- ¼ cup seeded small diced hothouse cucumbers
- ¼ cup small diced avocado
- 2 tablespoons fresh lime juice
- 1½ tablespoons extra-virgin olive oil
- Salt

Mince the galangal, ginger, garlic, and chiles together until they form a paste. Mix with the remaining ingredients in a bowl. Use immediately.

ASPARAGUS PAELLA

WITH GRILLED VEGETABLES AND YELLOW TOMATO SAFFRON BROTH

 **+** **+** **+**

| GRILLED VEGETABLES | PAELLA RICE | 4 CUPS YELLOW TOMATO SAFFRON BROTH *page 124* | PAELLA CRISP (OPTIONAL) *page 152* |

SERVES 4

GRILLED VEGETABLES

- ¼ cup extra-virgin olive oil
- 2 tablespoons grated lemon zest
- 1 tablespoon salt
- 2 tablespoons chopped garlic
- 1 pound asparagus, cleaned and bottom of stems broken off
- 1 pound frozen baby artichoke hearts
- ½ pound chanterelle mushrooms, cleaned and quartered

PAELLA

- 1 cup canned tomatoes, with juice
- 2 cups Basic Stock (page 54)
- ¼ cup extra-virgin olive oil
- ½ cup diced yellow onion
- ½ cup chopped garlic
- 2 tablespoons chopped green olives
  Salt
- 2 cups bomba rice
- 1 teaspoon sweet red paprika
- 1 teaspoon smoked paprika
- ¼ cup white wine
- ½ cup chopped flat-leaf parsley

1. To grill the vegetables: Preheat the grill.

2. In a blender, blend the olive oil, lemon zest, salt, and garlic until smooth. Then toss all the vegetables in a large bowl with the oil mixture until every piece is coated.

3. Lay the vegetables on the grill, one type of vegetable at a time, and cook until they have a slight char but are still firm, about 5 minutes.

4. To make the paella: Puree the canned tomatoes in a blender until smooth. In a pot over medium heat, simmer the tomato saffron broth and stock.

5. Start a large pot on low heat with the oil, onion, and garlic (page 17). Add the green olives and a pinch of salt; cook until heated through, about 2 minutes. Add the pureed tomatoes and cook until they break down into a loose paste, about 5 minutes.

6. Stir in the rice and cook for 10 minutes. Add the paprikas and cook for 1 minute. Add the wine and cook until it's evaporated, about 2 minutes. Stir in the parsley. **Don't stir the dish again.**

7. Cover the pot, turn the heat down to low, and cook for 10 minutes. Then remove the pan from the heat and let stand, covered, for 10 minutes.

8. *To serve:*

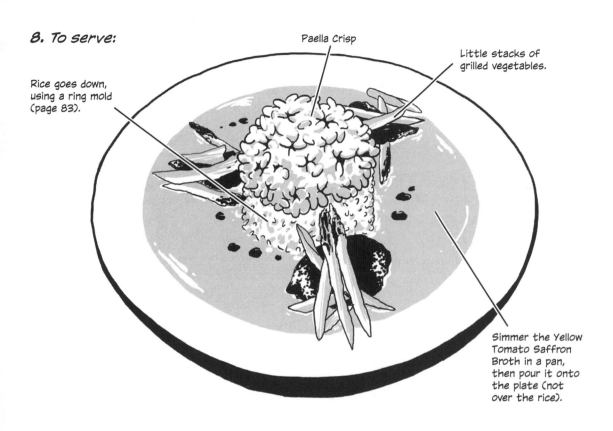

Paella Crisp

Little stacks of grilled vegetables.

Rice goes down, using a ring mold (page 83).

Simmer the Yellow Tomato Saffron Broth in a pan, then pour it onto the plate (not over the rice).

EVERY COUNTRY HAS A NATIONAL DISH:

PASTA

POUTINE

SCHNITZEL

CURRY RICE

HAMBURGER

AND FROM SPAIN? *PAELLA*.

YOU *CANNOT* MAKE ME IN YOUR RESTAURANT. YOU *CANNOT* MAKE ME IN YOUR HOME.

MAKING *TRUE* PAELLA REQUIRES A SPECIAL PAN AND A SPECIAL HEAT SOURCE.

IT IS A *RIGOROUS* UNDERTAKING.

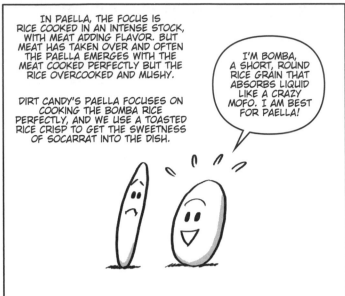

PAELLA CRISP

SERVES 4 TO 6

- ¼ cup extra-virgin olive oil
- ¼ cup corn syrup
- ¼ cup sugar
- ½ teaspoon salt
- 1 teaspoon smoked paprika
- 3 cups Rice Krispies or another puffed rice cereal

Socarrat is the toasted rice from the bottom of a paella pan, and it adds sweetness to the dish. It's impossible to get good *socarrat* in the restaurant, so this is our version.

1. Line a baking sheet with a Silpat.

2. Put the oil and syrup in a large pan. Pour in the sugar so it's evenly distributed on the bottom. Heat over medium heat without stirring until the sugar has melted, about 3 minutes. Remove the pan from the heat and add the salt, paprika, and Rice Krispies.

3. Toss the Rice Krispies in the pan until they're thoroughly coated. Pour the mixture onto the Silpat-lined baking sheet.

4. Spread the Rice Krispies across the liner with a spatula, pressing down to form a thin layer. Allow to cool slightly. While still warm, cut into any shape on earth. Bunnies are cute! Circles are easy! Squares are modern!

STONE-GROUND GRITS

WITH PICKLED SHIITAKES AND TEMPURA POACHED EGG

Most people cook grits by pouring them into boiling water. The grits absorb the flavorless water and taste like glue.

I cook grits the way I cook risotto, adding flavor from the start and using corn cream to make them light n' fluffy.

Grits are a vegetable in disguise: corn. So the trick is to enhance the corn flavor.

 + **+** **+**

| STONE-GROUND GRITS | TEMPURA POACHED EGG page 154 | PICKLED SHIITAKES page 36 | HUITLACOCHE CREAM (OPTIONAL) page 155 |

SERVES 4 TO 6

- 3 tablespoons extra-virgin olive oil
- ¼ cup diced yellow onions
- 1 tablespoon minced garlic
- 2 cups stone-ground grits
- 2 tablespoons white wine
- 5 cups Corn Stock (page 54), at room temperature
- Salt
- 2 cups Corn Cream (page 125)
- 2 cups chopped watercress
- 1 cup fresh or frozen corn kernels
- 2 tablespoons unsalted butter, optional
- ¼ cup crumbled ricotta salata cheese
- 2 tablespoons chopped fresh cilantro

1. Start a pan over medium heat with the olive oil, the onion, and garlic (page 17). Add the *dry* grits to the pan and stir until they coat the garlic and onion, about 2 minutes. This toasts the grits. Add the wine and cook until the liquid is gone, about 2 minutes.

2. Turn the heat to low and add ½ cup Corn Stock. Stir until the grits start to expand and the liquid is absorbed. Continue to stir and add the stock ½ cup at a time until all the stock is used.

3. Stir in 1½ cups of the Corn Cream, making sure to break down any lumps in the grits.

RECIPE CONTINUES ➡

4. Add the watercress to the pan as well as the Pickled Shiitakes and stir into the grits. Add the corn kernels and 6 tablespoons Corn Cream. Mix in the butter if you want it and salt to taste.

5. *To serve:*

**TO MAKE IT VEGAN**

Leave out the Tempura Poached Egg and use Tempura Watercress (opposite) instead.

Huitlacoche Cream

Corn Cream

Tempura Poached Egg

Stone-Ground Grits

Crumble ricotta salata cheese over the grits to add saltiness, and chopped cilantro to add fresh green notes.

TEMPURA POACHED EGG

SERVES 4

2 tablespoons white vinegar
4 extra-large eggs
Basic Batter with Panko (page 100)
Canola oil for deep-frying

1. Fill a large pot with 6 cups water, add the vinegar, and bring to a boil. Put a bowl of ice water next to the stove.

2. One by one, crack eggs in a bowl and slide them into the boiling water. Don't stir the water. Stirring the water will keep the poached eggs tighter, but tempura frying requires lots of ridges and flakes and pieces for the batter to stick to.

3. When the whites start to solidify, after 1 to 2 minutes, lift the eggs out with a slotted spoon and put them directly into the ice bath. The eggs MUST be cold for tempura frying.

4. In a large pot, heat the oil to 350°F.

5. Pour the batter into one bowl, and the panko crumbs into another. Drain the eggs, dip them in the basic batter, and then roll them in the panko crumbs.

6. Deep-fry (page 76) the eggs one at a time until golden, about 2 minutes. Serve hot.

TEMPURA WATERCRESS

SERVES 4

Canola oil for deep-frying
2 cups watercress, stemmed
Basic Batter (page 100, *without* panko)

1. In a large pot, heat the oil to 350°F.

2. Mix ½ cup of the watercress into the batter. Pull it out with tongs and drop it immediately into the oil. Use the tongs to keep pushing the watercress pieces together so that they bind to one another while frying. Fry until golden, about 1 minute. Remove with the tongs.

3. Repeat until all the watercress has been fried.

HUITLACOCHE CREAM

MAKES APPROXIMATELY 1 CUP

1 (7-ounce) jar or can of huitlacoche

Pour the huitlacoche in a blender. If it's dry, add a little water to help it move. Blend until super-smooth and creamy. It will keep covered for up to 1 week in the fridge.

Huitlacoche is Mexican corn fungus— like a corn truffle. It's used to add one more layer of corn to this dish, but you can use it as a condiment on scrambled eggs, burritos, or enchiladas.

RADISH RAVIOLI

WITH RADISH SALAD AND LEMON CORN SAUCE

DAIKON RADISH
RAVIOLI SKIN
+
RAVIOLI
FILLING
+
LEMON CORN
SAUCE
page 127
+
RADISH SALAD
(OPTIONAL)
page 89

SERVES 4

- ½ cup Sicilian or plain pistachios
- 1 cup radish tops
- ½ cup chopped red radish
- 3 tablespoons extra-virgin olive oil
- 1 teaspoon minced garlic
- 3 tablespoons ricotta cheese
- 1 teaspoon grated lemon zest
- 1 teaspoon salt
- ½ teaspoon freshly ground black pepper
- 20 thin slices daikon radish
- 1 extra-large egg
  Basic Batter with Panko (page 100)

I use a few raw cuisine tricks at Dirt Candy. One of them is making ravioli out of thinly sliced daikon radishes.

 **TO MAKE IT VEGAN**

Substitute crumbled soft tofu for the ricotta, and seal the raviolis with a slurry of 1 tablespoon cornstarch and ¼ cup water.

Peel a daikon.

Slice into thin rounds on the mandolin.

You should be able to see the shadow of your fingers through it.

1. Preheat the oven to 350°F and toast the pistachios until lightly browned, about 15 minutes. Set aside.

2. Blanch and shock (page 19) the radish tops, then chop them.

3. Pulse the pistachios in the food processor until they're crumbled and the size of fish-tank gravel. Add the blanched radish tops, red radish, olive oil, garlic, ricotta, lemon zest, salt, and pepper, and pulse until the mixture is a chunky paste.

4. To assemble:

Lay pieces of daikon on the counter or a baking sheet.

Place 1 tablespoon filling in the middle of each.

Paint the rim with egg wash (1 beaten extra-large egg plus 1 tablespoon water).

Place a second piece of daikon over it and press the edges to seal. You've got a ravioli!

Dip the ravioli in Basic Batter.

Dredge it in panko crumbs.

Deep-fry (page 76) or pan fry until the outside is golden and crisp, about 2 minutes if deep-frying and 3 minutes on each side if pan frying.

5. To serve:

Bring Lemon Corn Sauce to a simmer in a pan and then pour it onto the plate until it's covered, but not too deep (unless you like your ravioli super saucy).

Place the ravioli down next. They can be warm, not hot out of the pan.

Top with Radish Salad. Using a raw and a cooked version of the same vegetable in a dish reinforces its flavor.

SMOKED CAULIFLOWER AND WAFFLES

WITH HORSERADISH CREAM SAUCE

SMOKED CAULIFLOWER + WAFFLES + HORSERADISH CREAM SAUCE page 131 + MAPLE ARUGULA SALAD (OPTIONAL) page 88 + CAULIFLOWER BITS (OPTIONAL) page 160 + PICKLED CAULIFLOWER (OPTIONAL) page 38

SERVES 4

SMOKED CAULIFLOWER

- 1 head cauliflower
  Canola oil for deep-frying
- 1½ cups buttermilk
- 2 tablespoons unbleached all-purpose flour
- 1 extra-large egg
- ½ cup cornstarch
- 4 cups cornflakes
- ¼ cup smoked paprika
- 1 tablespoon salt
- 1 tablespoon garlic powder
- 1 tablespoon onion powder

Stealing a page from soul food, this recipe is a vegetarian riff on chicken and waffles. You can use any kind of waffles you want. You need only two waffles for the recipe, but the rest freeze well.

TO MAKE IT VEGAN

Substitute 1 cup unflavored soy milk for the buttermilk and leave out the egg. Use vegan waffles (page 160).

1. To smoke the cauliflower, cut it into wedges and remove as much of the stem as possible, then smoke twice with maple chips (page 78), lifting the lid between smokings to let out the moisture. The smoked cauliflower can be stored in the fridge overnight.

2. Make the waffle batter: In a medium bowl, whisk together the flour, cornstarch, baking powder, baking soda, salt, and sugar. In another bowl, whisk together the milk, buttermilk, oil, and egg. Whisk the milk mixture into the flour mixture to blend, so no lumps remain. Set aside to rest for 30 minutes.

3. Preheat a waffle iron to its medium-high setting. Preheat the oven to warm at its lowest setting (150–200°F).

4. Following the manufacturer's instructions, cook each waffle until golden. Plan on the first waffle being a "test." Put the waffles on a baking sheet and keep them warm in the oven.

YOU'LL NEED 1 QUART MAPLE CHIPS FOR SMOKING.

5. To fry the cauliflower, heat the oil in a large pot to 350°F.

6. To make the batter for the cauliflower, mix the buttermilk, flour, and egg in a bowl until smooth.

7. Put the cornstarch in a second bowl.

8. Put the cornflakes, paprika, salt, garlic powder, and onion powder in a food processor and pulse until the cornflakes are the size of half a pea (about 10 pulses). Transfer to a third bowl.

WAFFLES
- ¾ **cup unbleached all-purpose flour**
- ¼ **cup cornstarch**
- ½ **teaspoon baking powder**
- ¼ **teaspoon baking soda**
- ½ **teaspoon salt**
- 1½ **teaspoons sugar**
- ½ **cup whole milk**
- ½ **cup buttermilk**
- ⅓ **cup canola oil**
- 1 **extra-large egg, beaten**

9.

Dip each piece of smoked cauliflower in cornstarch...

...then in the buttermilk mixture.

Shake off the excess liquid and...

...roll in the cornflake mixture. Coat all the cauliflower before moving on to the next step.

10. Deep-fry (page 76) the battered cauliflower until golden brown, 2 to 3 minutes.

11. To serve:

Toss 4 cups dressed Maple Arugula Salad with ¼ cup Cauliflower Bits, then add about 1 cup of it to each dish.

Pour Horseradish Cream Sauce on the plate, enough to cover it, but not too deep.

Smoked Cauliflower, served as hot as possible.

Waffles, which can be at room temperature, go down next.

A few Pickled Cauliflower pieces to cut the richness of the sauce.

VARIATION
VEGAN WAFFLES

1½ cups unbleached all-purpose flour
2 teaspoons baking powder
½ teaspoon salt
2 tablespoons sugar
1½ cups unflavored soy milk
4 tablespoons canola oil

Follow the procedure for the waffles (page 158), swapping in these ingredients and leaving out the egg in step 2.

CAULIFLOWER BITS

You can leave these out, but they add a lot of cauliflower flavor into this (or any) dish.

Take 1 head cauliflower and cut the florets the size of a corn kernel, with as little stem as possible.

Mix the florets with ¼ cup extra-virgin olive oil and 1 teaspoon salt, then spread them on a baking sheet and roast at 425°F until golden brown, about 30 minutes.

Then turn the oven to dehydrating temperature (page 21) and leave the florets in for 2 hours.

Keep an eye on them because you want them to turn dark brown and crunchy, not black.

They can be stored, covered, in a cool, dry space for up to 2 weeks.

PASTA

Interview in progress...

YOU PROBABLY HAVE SO MUCH *FUN* GOING TO THE FARMER'S MARKET AND GETTING *INSPIRED* BY ALL THAT LOVELY PRODUCE.

YES... GOING TO THE FARMER'S MARKET.

Farmer's markets are nice to visit, but they can't give you 40 pounds of arugula *every single day*. Restaurants mostly order their food from purveyors.

IT'S ROTTEN *AGAIN*. SEND IT BACK.

ARUGULA

Ordering your ingredients isn't some *inspirational journey*, it's a part of your business. Do you only want your doctor to treat you with whatever medicine he was inspired to buy that day?

RX

WELL, MY MAGAZINE WOULD *LOVE* TO COME TAKE PHOTOS OF WHAT'S IN YOUR FRIDGE AT HOME. IT'S SO *GREAT* TO SEE THE SECRETS OF A CHEF'S LARDER!

YEAH, THAT'D BE GREAT.

Now I have to go buy groceries on my way home. The last time I cooked at home was 2005. I live on takeout and leftovers.

At *least* one year old.

WHAT KIND OF *TREATS* DO YOU LIKE TO COOK UP FOR YOUR HUBBY ON YOUR NIGHT OFF?

LISTEN!!!

YOU HAVE SOME WEIRD ROMANTIC IDEA OF WHAT A CHEF IS. *ALL* OF THE PRESS DOES.

I *GET* IT! SELLING THAT IMAGE IS HOW YOU SELL MAGAZINES. BUT LET ME TELL YOU SOMETHING.

YOU DON'T *ACTUALLY* WANT TO HANG AROUND WITH REAL CHEFS.

WE MAKE *RAIN MAN* LOOK *OUTGOING*. THERE'S A REASON WE PICKED THIS JOB. WE'RE OBSESSIVE, NEUROTIC, AND THIN-SKINNED. BECAUSE INSIDE *EVERY* CHEF THERE LIVES A--

URK!

... A MONKEY AND A PANDA!

The monkey is *ALWAYS* stressed out, *ALWAYS* freaking out, *always* scrambling to keep up. The problem with the monkey...

...is that when things don't work out, the monkey goes *bananas*.

THE PORTOBELLO MOUSSE DIDN'T SET.

THE PORTOBELLO MOUSSE *DIDN'T* SET.

THE PORTOBELLO MOUSSE DIDN'T SET.

THE PORTOBELLO MOUSSE DIDN'T SET!

THE PORTOBELLO MOUSSE DIDN'T SET!!!

THE PORTOBELLO MOUSSE DIDN'T SET!!!!!!

My monkey freaks out the most when we've run out of a dish. *Normal* people would just take it off the menu, but my monkey doesn't go for that.

WHAT DO YOU MEAN THERE'S NO MORE PEANUT ICE CREAM??? WE GOTTA HAVE PEANUT ICE CREAM! WE GOTTA HAVE IT!!!!! WHERE'S MY PEANUT ICE CREAM!!!!!!!!

If people are moving slowly, the monkey takes over.

I'm always amazed he's never lost a finger. I have no idea how he does it.

The problem with the monkey is that he's lost me friends. Debbie Lee worked with me for years, and she came to Dirt Candy as the pastry chef. But I wanted more from her than she was willing to give.

I WANT BETTER DESSERTS! MORE DESSERTS! MORE ORIGINAL DESSERTS! NOW! NOW! NOW!

I haven't heard from her since.

I'D RATHER WORK FOR *MY MOM* THAN PUT UP WITH THIS.

EXIT

BUT AT LEAST THE FAMILY MEALS MUST BE FUN? A REAL BONDING MOMENT FOR YOUR STAFF TO BREAK BREAD TOGETHER?

YOU KNOW WHAT'S THE BEST THING ABOUT *FAMILY MEALS?*

TAP TAP

You can sit down for a few minutes and no one *talks* to you.

In a kitchen, you stand up for your entire 11-hour shift. All day. Every day. But that's what the monkey's for. He's *strong*.

Working in a kitchen is about hard, repetitive labor. To get two days' worth of King Oyster mushrooms we have to break down a case of mushrooms. It takes an intern *three* hours. It takes the monkey *one*.

It takes three hours to reduce a case of cauliflower to a quart of dehydrated florets for Smoked Cauliflower and Waffles (page 158). That's *hours* of work, just for a little bit of extra crunch in a salad.

The monkey can break down all the cauliflower I need for a night in *20 minutes*. The monkey *never* gets tired. The monkey *never* feels pain.

AND THERE'S *ALWAYS* PAIN.

Working in a kitchen takes a *toll* on your body.

Working in a raw-food restaurant temporarily made my eyebrows red.

Shoulder torn from fall (page 137)

Wrists shot from lifting fry baskets

Burns from pulling trays from oven

Scar from spilling one gallon of boiling soup down pants

Scars from two chopping disasters

No scars here, because this is my knife hand

High blood pressure from stress

High cholesterol from tasting rich food all day

As you get promoted off the line you don't get hurt as much, but there's a *trade-off.* I haven't slept through the night since I became responsible for locking up a restaurant.

WHAT ABOUT THE PANDA?

THE *BEST* WAY TO KNOW THE PANDA IS TO TALK ABOUT *PASTA.*

If an old Italian grandmother wants to make pasta, she first has to draw the water.

Then she has to get flour from the mill.

Then she kneads the dough to the perfect consistency. If it isn't perfect, out it goes.

Not the panda. The panda knows his *limitations.* The panda knows how to *compromise.*

The panda's not a master pasta maker. He knows he can never make that perfect, lighter-than-air pasta. So he makes pasta that's *easier* to work with.

The more you work your dough, the more you *stretch* the gluten. The more you stretch your gluten, the *tougher* the dough is. That makes it easier to work with, but less delicate.

Kneading by hand is hard. The panda mixes his dough in a *mixer*. The second it comes together in a ball he moves it to the pasta machine.

The panda puts the dough through the pasta machine over and over until it's smooth. The machine stretches the gluten for the panda.

The dough will break at first. The panda just keeps folding it and putting it back through the machine. *Don't panic.* Eventually it'll come back together again.

Don't sweat the long recipes. The panda knows you can eat these pastas dressed simply with oil and salt, or just make the sauces and use *dried* pasta. Depends on how complicated you're feeling.

Pasta machines aren't as complicated as you might think. Your dough should be narrow when you put it in. It'll get **wider** as it flattens and you don't want it to touch the sides.

Set the size here. All machines have different settings, but start on your **thickest** one and put it through again and again, slowly approaching your **thinnest** setting.

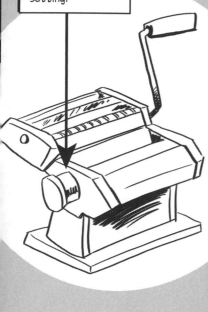

Make sure you have enough room to work. Your pasta is going to get really, **really** long.

If your dough is sticking to the rollers, sprinkle some flour on the dough--**NOT** on the rollers. It should slide right through.

Don't be afraid to **cut** your dough sheet in half or quarters if it's too long to work with. You're going to be cutting it at the end anyway.

No matter what happens, don't give up. Keep **folding** and **rolling**, **folding** and **rolling**. You're done when the dough is smooth, soft, and silky.

To store, divide into servings, lay them on a tray, and sprinkle with semolina flour so they don't stick to themselves. Wrap the tray in plastic and it'll keep in your fridge for up to a week.

Cook fresh pasta really fast in boiling water. Always remove with a basket or a slotted spoon, then finish cooking it in a pan with your sauce.

COOKING TIMES

20-30 SECONDS spaetzle	**30-40 SECONDS** fettuccine	**40-50 SECONDS** gnocchi & pappardelle

The panda understands that people want pasta to be **comforting**, not **complex**.

Although these recipes look complicated, they have fewer components than the salads. Salad should be a fun explosion. Pasta should be **straightforward**.

People want a creamy sauce. They don't want sauce-less pasta, and they don't want a sauce that's overwrought. They want a smooth, rich feel in their mouths.

People say they want this and that, but when it comes to pasta, the panda has seen what's truly in their **hearts**: comfort and simplicity.

When you're a chef, your entire life is a balancing act between the monkey and the panda. Some days the monkey wins, and some days, the panda.

BROCCOLINI FETTUCCINE
WITH PORCINI MUSHROOMS AND TEMPURA POACHED EGG

BROCCOLINI
FETTUCCINE

+

TEMPURA
POACHED EGGS
page 154

SERVES 4

BROCCOLINI FETTUCCINE

- 2 **bunches broccolini**
- 2 **cups unbleached all-purpose flour**
- 1 **extra-large egg**
- 1 **egg white**
- ½ **teaspoon salt, plus more for pasta water**
- **Semolina flour for storing**
- ¼ **cup (½ stick) unsalted butter**
- 2 **teaspoons minced garlic**
- 2 **cups sliced porcini or other mushroom**
- 2 **cups broccoli rabe, thinly sliced**
- 1 **tablespoon porcini oil**
- ¼ **cup grated Parmesan**
- ¼ **cup chopped fresh basil**

This is a dish I made for *Iron Chef,* and I lost. Which means that if you like it, television thinks you're wrong. But it's easy to make, so use it to practice your pasta skills.

1. Blanch and shock the broccolini (page 19). Chop it as finely as possible, and then pulse in a blender until pureed. If it clumps, add water to loosen. This should yield 1¼ cups puree.

2. Put ¼ cup of the puree in a mixer with the flour, egg, egg white, and salt and mix until it forms a ball. Wrap the dough in plastic and let rest for 30 minutes.

3. Feed the dough through the pasta machine until it reaches a relatively thin setting (I use setting #6 on a machine with nine settings) and it feels smooth and silky. Using the fettuccine attachment, cut the dough. (In other dishes, I like noodles heartier, so I cut them by hand.) Divide the noodles into 4 portions and sprinkle with semolina flour to keep from sticking.

4. Bring a pot of salted water to a boil.

5. Start a separate pan with butter and garlic (page 17), sauté the mushrooms on medium heat for about 2 minutes, then add the broccoli rabe and 1 cup reserved broccolini puree. Cook for 1 minute.

6. Cook the pasta in the boiling water until al dente, 30 to 40 seconds. Remove from the water, put in the pan with the mushroom mixture, and add the porcini oil. Mix once to combine and immediately add the Parmesan and basil.

OLIVE FETTUCCINE

WITH PICKLED EGGPLANT AND EGGPLANT JAM

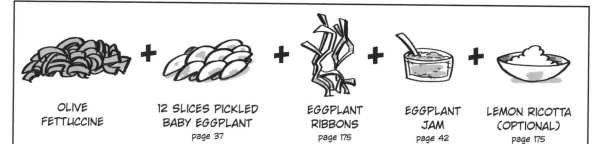

OLIVE FETTUCCINE	12 SLICES PICKLED BABY EGGPLANT	EGGPLANT RIBBONS	EGGPLANT JAM	LEMON RICOTTA (OPTIONAL)
	page 37	page 175	page 42	page 175

SERVES 4

OLIVE FETTUCCINE

- 2 cups pitted kalamata olives
- 2 cups unbleached all-purpose flour
- 1 extra-large egg
  Semolina flour for storing
- 2 cups Basil Broth (page 124)

PICKLED EGGPLANT

- 12 slices Pickled Baby Eggplant (page 37)
- ¾ cup unbleached all-purpose flour
  Basic Batter (page 100, *without* panko)
- 2 cups bread crumbs
- 1½ teaspoons dried oregano
- 1½ teaspoons dried basil
- 1 teaspoon salt, plus more for pasta water
- ½ cup extra-virgin olive oil

People have plenty of preconceived notions about pasta, and you poke them at your peril. This dish came with a complex broth instead of a rich, thick sauce, and that bummed some people out. Lesson learned? Pasta requires a hearty sauce.

1. Rinse the olives in hot water to remove excess oil. Break down the olives in a food processor for 3 minutes, then in a blender with 2 tablespoons water for 2 minutes. Push through a chinois. It should yield 1 cup very smooth olive puree.

2. Mound the 2 cups flour in the bowl of a stand mixer fitted with the paddle attachment, and make a well in the center. Add the olive puree and the egg and mix until incorporated, then switch to the dough hook attachment. Keep going until the dough forms a ball. Wrap the ball of dough in plastic and let sit for 30 minutes.

3. Roll out the dough to a relatively thin setting on a pasta machine. (I use #6 on a machine with nine settings.) Cut into ⅛-inch-wide strips by hand. (Olive fettuccine is too delicate to cut by machine, but cutting by hand is very easy.) Divide the fettuccine into 4 portions, sprinkle with semolina flour, and set aside.

4. Bring a large pot of salted water to a boil. In a smaller pot, heat the Basil Broth on low until it reaches a simmer.

RECIPE CONTINUES ➡

5. To fry the pickled eggplant: Put the ¾ cup flour in a bowl. Prepare the Basic Batter in another bowl. In a third bowl, mix together the bread crumbs, oregano, basil, and salt.

6. Drain or blot the excess oil from the pickled eggplant. Roll each piece in the flour, dip in the batter, and then roll in the bread crumb mixture. Continue until all of the slices are breaded.

7. Heat the olive oil in a pan over medium heat. Lower the eggplant slices into the pan and fry until golden brown, 2 to 3 minutes on each side.

8. Cook the fettuccine for 30 to 40 seconds in boiling water, drain, and toss in the pan with the warm Basil Broth, coating the fettuccine completely.

9. To serve:

TO MAKE IT VEGAN

Leave out the egg and use 2¼ cups semolina flour instead of all-purpose flour. Also skip the lemon ricotta.

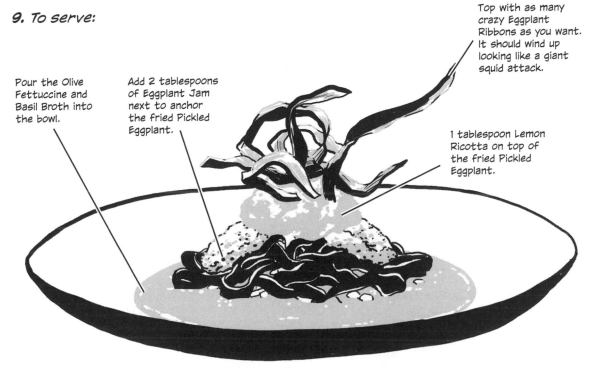

Top with as many crazy Eggplant Ribbons as you want. It should wind up looking like a giant squid attack.

Pour the Olive Fettuccine and Basil Broth into the bowl.

Add 2 tablespoons of Eggplant Jam next to anchor the fried Pickled Eggplant.

1 tablespoon Lemon Ricotta on top of the fried Pickled Eggplant.

LEMON RICOTTA

MAKES 1 CUP

- 1 cup fresh ricotta cheese
- 1 tablespoon grated lemon zest
- Salt

Whip the ricotta in a stand mixer fitted with the whisk attachment until fluffy, about 1 minute. Add the lemon zest and salt to taste, then whip until they're incorporated. Set aside or chill until ready to use.

EGGPLANT RIBBONS

SERVES 4

- Canola oil for deep-frying
- 2 cups eggplant peels
- ½ cup cornstarch

1. In a large pot, heat the oil to 325°F.

2. In a bowl, toss the peels with the cornstarch, then deep-fry (page 76) in batches until crispy enough to hold their own shape. This will take 1 minute or less, but be careful: the eggplant will get bitter if fried too long.

USE THE PEELS LEFT OVER FROM MAKING THE EGGPLANT JAM (PAGE 42).

MINT AND TARRAGON FETTUCCINE

WITH YOGURT SAFFRON SAUCE AND ZUCCHINI RELISH

| MINT & TARRAGON FETTUCCINE | YOGURT SAFFRON SAUCE page 126 | GRILLED ZUCCHINI RELISH opposite | FALAFEL BALLS (OPTIONAL) page 117 | PICKLED RED ONIONS (OPTIONAL) page 35 |

SERVES 4

MINT AND TARRAGON FETTUCCINE

- ¾ cup packed fresh tarragon leaves
- 2 cups packed fresh mint leaves
- 1 cup unbleached all-purpose flour
- 1 extra-large egg, beaten
- ½ teaspoon plus 2 tablespoons extra-virgin olive oil
- Salt
- Semolina flour for storing

- 2 large zucchini
- 2 teaspoons chopped garlic

I use yogurt sauces in pasta because it makes them creamy but keeps them light. This dish, with yogurt sauce, saffron, and falafel balls, is the closest to an Italian/Middle Eastern marriage you'll ever see in a bowl. The zucchini fettuccine is augmented with raw ribbons of zucchini, another trick learned during my days in the raw-food world.

1. Blanch and shock (page 19) the tarragon and mint. Chop them, then puree the herbs separately in a blender, adding a little water if necessary to keep it moving.

2. Put the flour in a mixer and make a well in the center. Pour in 2 tablespoons tarragon puree, 6 tablespoons mint puree, the egg, ½ teaspoon olive oil, and 1 teaspoon salt. Mix with the paddle attachment until the dough incorporates, then switch to the dough hook, and mix until the dough forms a ball. Wrap the ball in plastic and let rest for 30 minutes.

3. Roll the pasta out to a thicker setting on a pasta machine. (I use #3 on a machine with nine settings.) Use a knife or the cutting attachment to cut each sheet of dough into ⅛-inch-wide strands. Divide into 4 portions, sprinkle with semolina flour, and store (page 169).

4. Bring a large pot of salted water to a boil.

5. Using a spiraling machine or a mandolin, slice long, thin strips of raw zucchini. The ribbons should be as long and noddle-y as possible.

6. Start a pan over medium heat with 2 tablespoons olive oil and the garlic (page 17). Add the

Yogurt Saffron Sauce to the pan. If it's too thick, thin with water or stock. Add the zucchini ribbons to the pan.

7. Cook the pasta for 30 to 40 seconds in the boiling water. Remove from the water and add the pasta to the pan with the saffron sauce. Cook for 30 seconds. Salt to taste, and divide among 4 plates.

8. To serve:

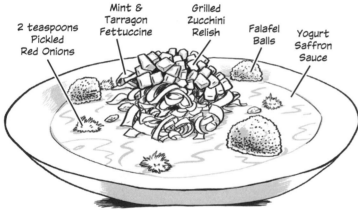

2 teaspoons Pickled Red Onions

Mint & Tarragon Fettuccine

Grilled Zucchini Relish

Falafel Balls

Yogurt Saffron Sauce

TO MAKE IT VEGAN

VEGAN MINT AND TARRAGON FETTUCCINE:

Follow the procedure for the fettuccine (opposite), but make the following substitutions:

- **Use ½ teaspoon of salt instead of 1 teaspoon in step 2.**
- **Use 2 tablespoons of extra-virgin olive oil instead of ½ teaspoon in step 2.**
- **Add 2 tablespoons semolina flour to the dough in step 2.**
- **Leave out the egg from the fettuccine recipe and serve with Vegan Yogurt Saffron Sauce (page 126).**

GRILLED ZUCCHINI RELISH

MAKES 1 CUP

This relish is made from two recipes: Pickled Squash Blossoms (page 36) and Preserved Zucchini (page 39).

1. First, remove 6 squash blossoms from their liquid and let drain. A little wetness is okay, but they shouldn't drip.

2. Heat a grill to medium-high (page 77) and grill 12 slices of Preserved Zucchini until grill lines have formed.

3. Dice the grilled zucchini and roughly chop the squash blossoms.

4. Toss the blossoms and zucchini together and salt to taste.

BEET PAPPARDELLE
WITH YOGURT CUMIN SAUCE AND ROASTED BEETS

This dish had a fatal flaw: pesto placement.

How you eat a dish has to be *instinctive*.

No one ever ate the **beet greens pesto** because it was served on the side.

Don't make the same mistake.

Put it right in the center of your pasta.

 **+**  **+**

| BEET PAPPARDELLE | ROASTED BEETS | 2 CUPS YOGURT CUMIN SAUCE
page 128 | BEET GREENS PESTO (OPTIONAL)
page 180 |

SERVES 4

ROASTED BEETS
- 1 **pound red beets with tops**
- 1 **pound golden beets with tops**
- 1 **pound candy cane beets with tops**
- 4 **tablespoons extra-virgin olive oil**
- 1 **tablespoon chopped fresh tarragon**
- **Salt**
- ½ **tablespoon chopped garlic**

1. To roast the beets: Preheat the oven to 375°F.

2. Remove the beet greens and save. Either go the monkey way and make pesto with them (see below) or sauté them at the end, like a panda.

3. Scrub each beet but leave the skins on. Toss in the olive oil, put them on a sheet tray, and roast until fork tender, about 1 hour. Remove from the oven and let cool.

4. Remove the beet skins and dice the beets. Do not mix the colors! To keep the colors pretty, dice them from lightest to darkest on the cutting board, beginning with the candy cane beets, then the golden beets, and finally the red beets. Store each type of beet in a separate container.

5. To make the pappardelle: In a pot, bring the beet juice to a boil over high heat immediately after juicing. Instantly take it off the heat when it boils. Boiling keeps the juice from oxidizing and turning black. Let cool.

6. Pour the flour and salt into the bowl of a stand mixer fitted with the paddle attachment and form a well in the center. Into the well pour the beet juice, 1 tablespoon of the oil, the egg, and ½ tablespoon salt; mix until incorporated. Then, using the dough hook attachment, keep mixing until the dough forms a ball. Wrap the ball of dough in plastic and let rest for 30 minutes.

7. Put the dough through the pasta machine until it reaches a medium-thin setting. (I use #5 on a machine with nine settings.) Cut the dough into 1-inch-wide strips with a knife. It should look "rustic," so uneven is fine.

8. When ready to serve, preheat the oven to 375°F. Bring a large pot of salted water to a boil.

9. On a sheet tray, toss the diced beets with 2 tablespoons of the olive oil, the tarragon, and 1 teaspoon salt. Heat through in the oven for 15 to 20 minutes.

10. Start a pan on medium heat with the remaining 2 tablespoons oil and the garlic (page 17). Add the Yogurt Cumin Sauce to the pan (with the beet tops if using here instead of in the pesto) and cook for 1 minute.

11. Meanwhile, cook the pasta in boiling water for 45 seconds. Remove from the water.

12. When the yogurt sauce is bubbling, add the pasta to the pan. Salt to taste, and divide among 4 plates.

RECIPE CONTINUES ➡

BEET PAPPARDELLE
- ¾ cup yellow beet juice (page 22)
- 2¼ cups unbleached all-purpose flour
- Salt
- 5 tablespoons extra-virgin olive oil
- 1 extra-large egg

 **TO MAKE IT VEGAN**

VEGAN BEET PAPPARDELLE:
Follow the procedure for the pappardelle, swapping in these ingredients, leaving out the egg, and using Vegan Yogurt Cumin Sauce (page 129):

- 1 cup yellow beet juice
- 2 cups semolina flour
- ½ tablespoon salt
- 1½ tablespoons extra-virgin olive oil

I LIKE THE WAY THE DIFFERENT BEETS LOOK TOGETHER BUT THIS IS CLEARLY INSANE. FEEL FREE TO JUST USE 3 POUNDS OF ONE KIND OF BEET.

13. To serve:

Beet
Pappardelle
(sauced)

Top with 1 cup Roasted
Beets per serving, right
out of the oven.

Place 1 tablespoon of the
Beet Greens Pesto right in
the center. You can mix it
in yourself as you eat.

RESTAURANT TRICK #893:
Make a quenelle of the Beet
Greens Pesto to impress the
high rollers in your life.

Take two
spoons and
scoop some
of the pesto
up in one
of them.

You're making
a football by
scraping it from
one spoon to
the other. Each
pass should
smooth
out more
of its
rough edges.

Then just
slide it
onto the
pasta.

BEET GREENS PESTO

MAKES 1 CUP

½ cup Sicilian or regular pistachios
1 cup beet greens from the roasted
beets (page 178)
2 tablespoons extra-virgin olive oil
1 garlic clove
Salt

1. Preheat the oven to 350°F.

2. Toast the pistachios on a baking sheet in the oven until light brown, 8 to 12 minutes, stirring once. Let cool.

3. Blanch and shock (page 19) the beet greens, then squeeze completely dry and roughly chop.

4. Pulse the pistachios, olive oil, and garlic in a food processor until the mixture forms a loose paste (about 50 pulses). There should still be chunks of pistachios. Add the beet greens and pulse 20 to 25 times, until they're incorporated. Salt to taste.

PARSNIP GNOCCHI

WITH SOUR RED CABBAGE AND CARROT CRUMBS

 **+** **+** **+**

PARSNIP
GNOCCHI

¾ CUP SOUR
RED CABBAGE
page 39

¼ CUP CHEDDAR
POWDER (OPTIONAL)
page 183

½ CUP CARROT
CRUMBS (OPTIONAL)
page 183

SERVES 4

- 3 pounds whole parsnips, peeled, plus 1 cup julienned peeled parsnips
- 1 cup roughly chopped turnips, plus 1 cup julienned peeled turnips
- 1 cup roughly chopped peeled rutabaga, plus 1 cup julienned peeled rutabaga
- 1 cup roughly chopped peeled celeriac, plus 1 cup julienned peeled celeriac
- ½ cup roughly chopped yellow onion
- 12 garlic cloves, smashed, plus ½ teaspoon chopped garlic
- 1 cup unbleached all-purpose flour
  Salt
- 3 tablespoons extra-virgin olive oil, plus more to store gnocchi
- 2 cups heavy cream
- ½ cup (1 stick) unsalted butter

Making gnocchi is really hard. And parsnip gnocchi is even harder. This recipe has to be exactly right to work, so expect it to drive you crazy.

1. Preheat the oven to 375°F.

2. In a roasting pan, combine the whole parsnips; the roughly chopped turnips, rutabaga, celeriac, and onion; and the 12 garlic cloves. Cover with water. Roast until the parsnips are soft and brown, about 2 hours.

3. Remove the parsnip stock from the oven. Reserve the parsnips and 1 cup of the parsnip stock separately. Discard the rest of the vegetables and store any remaining stock in the fridge or freezer.

4. Puree the parsnips in a food processor, then press them through a potato ricer.

5. Bring a pot of salted water to a boil on medium high.

6. Place the parsnip puree on a floured board. Slowly incorporate the flour ¼ cup at a time. While forming the dough, add 1 tablespoon salt. **This must be done by hand** as a mixer will overwork gnocchi dough.

RECIPE CONTINUES ➡

AS YOU INCORPORATE THE FLOUR, OCCASIONALLY TEAR OFF A GNOCCHI-SIZED PIECE OF DOUGH, DROP IT IN BOILING WATER, AND TASTE IT AFTER IT FLOATS TO THE SURFACE. IF THE CHEW IS TOUGH, YOU'VE ADDED TOO MUCH FLOUR AND THE BATCH IS RUINED.

7. ───────────────────────────

Once a test gnocchi has succeeded, form the dough into a ball and divide it into 6 portions.

Roll each portion into a rope about ¾-inch thick.

Cut each rope crosswise into 1-inch-long pieces, then press the back of a fork into each piece to leave little ridges.

8. Working in batches, drop the gnocchi into the boiling water until they are cooked through, 40 to 50 seconds. They'll rise to the top when they're ready. Remove with a slotted spoon. Use immediately, or toss with olive oil, cover, and refrigerate for up to 4 days.

9. In a large pan, heat 3 tablespoons olive oil on high and add the gnocchi, constantly shaking the pan so they don't stick. When the gnocchi have started to brown, about 3 minutes on each side, turn down the heat to medium.

10. Add the chopped garlic and the julienned parsnip, turnip, rutabaga, and celeriac. Add the 1 cup reserved parsnip stock and cook for 2 minutes. Add the cream and let it reduce until the sauce is thick. Add the butter and salt to taste. When the butter has completely melted, remove it from the heat.

11. To serve:

TO MAKE IT VEGAN

Substitute unflavored soy milk for the heavy cream and 2 tablespoons Earth Balance for the butter. And, of course, leave out the cheese powder.

The gnocchi, sauce, and root vegetables are divided evenly among four bowls.

Next, sprinkle about 2 tablespoons of Carrot Crumbs on top.

Top with 1 tablespoon of Cheddar Powder.

Dot three 1-tablespoon portions of Sour Red Cabbage around the plate.

CHEDDAR POWDER

MAKES ⅓ CUP

¼ pound grated cheddar cheese

1. Turn the oven to dehydrating temperature (page 21) and line a baking sheet with a Silpat liner.

2. Spread the grated cheese on the lined baking sheet and dehydrate in the oven for 4 hours. The cheese will have released a lot of grease, so let it drain on paper towels while they cool to room temperature.

3. Put the dry, cooled cheese in a blender and pulse until it crumbles into powder. Store in a sealed container for up to 2 weeks.

CARROT CRUMBS

MAKES 2½ CUPS

½ cup plus 1 tablespoon unbleached all-purpose flour

½ teaspoon baking powder

½ teaspoon baking soda

¼ teaspoon salt

1 tablespoon cinnamon

¼ cup sugar

6 tablespoons canola oil

½ teaspoon vanilla extract

1 cup grated carrots

1. Preheat the oven to 400°F and grease a 9 × 9-inch baking pan.

2. In a bowl, mix the flour, baking powder, baking soda, salt, cinnamon, and sugar. Add the canola oil and vanilla extract to the flour mixture, and then add the carrots, mixing thoroughly after each addition.

3. Spread the batter in the baking pan and bake until cooked through, 20 to 30 minutes.

4. Turn the oven down to 375°F. Crumble the cake onto a sheet pan and let it dry out in the oven for 10 minutes. Remove the crumbs from the oven and let cool. Store covered in a cool, dry place for up to 2 weeks.

TOMATO SPAETZLE
WITH COCONUT CURRY SAUCE AND FRIED GREEN TOMATOES

| TOMATO SPAETZLE | FRIED GREEN TOMATOES | YELLOW TOMATO COCONUT CURRY SAUCE page 125 | JICAMA SLAW page 89 | COCONUT CREAM (OPTIONAL) page 64 |

SERVES 4

TOMATO SPAETZLE

- ¾ cup tomato paste
- 2 teaspoons salt
- 1¾ cups unbleached all-purpose flour
- 1 tablespoon extra-virgin olive oil

FRIED GREEN TOMATOES

- Canola oil for deep-frying
- 1 cup unsweetened coconut flakes
- 2 cups Basic Batter with Panko (page 100)
- 1 teaspoon salt, plus more for pasta water
- 2 green tomatoes, cut into ¼-inch-thick rounds
- ¾ cup cornstarch

1. To make the spaetzle: In a bowl, mix the tomato paste, salt, and 1¼ cups water by hand until smooth. Sift the flour into the bowl and whisk together until just incorporated. Let the dough rest for 10 minutes.

2. Bring a large pot of salted water to a gentle boil. Set a large bowl of ice water on the counter.

3.

Press the dough through a colander or sieve directly into the water to form spaetzle.

The colander should be 6 inches above the water or steam will cook the spaetzle as it falls.

4. Once the spaetzle has risen to the top and the water has returned to a gentle boil, about 3 minutes, drain the spaetzle and immediately put it into the ice bath. If it's clumping that means there's still starch stuck to it. Don't panic, monkey. Just rinse and drain a few times. Drain, toss with the olive oil, and refrigerate until ready to use.

Spaetzle is just gnocchi for lazy people.

TOSS!

5. *To make the fried green tomatoes:* Preheat the oven to 350°F. In a large pot, heat the oil to 350°F.

6. Spread the coconut flakes on a baking sheet and toast in the oven until golden brown, about 10 minutes. Let cool, then pulse in the food processor until reduced to crumbs.

7. Put the Basic Batter in a shallow bowl and the cornstarch in another bowl. Mix the salt, panko, and coconut together in a separate bowl.

8. Dredge the tomatoes in the cornstarch, then the batter, and finally in the coconut mixture.

9. Working in batches, deep-fry (page 76) the tomatoes until lightly browned, 30 to 40 seconds.

10. When ready to serve, put the coconut curry sauce in a pan and bring it to a simmer over low heat. Add the spaetzle. It will have clumped, so gently break it up in the pan. Cook until the spaetzle is heated through, about 5 minutes.

11. *To serve:*

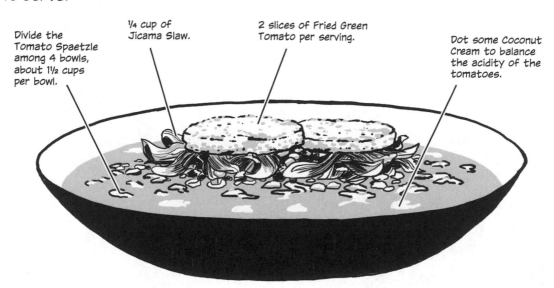

Divide the Tomato Spaetzle among 4 bowls, about 1½ cups per bowl.

¼ cup of Jicama Slaw.

2 slices of Fried Green Tomato per serving.

Dot some Coconut Cream to balance the acidity of the tomatoes.

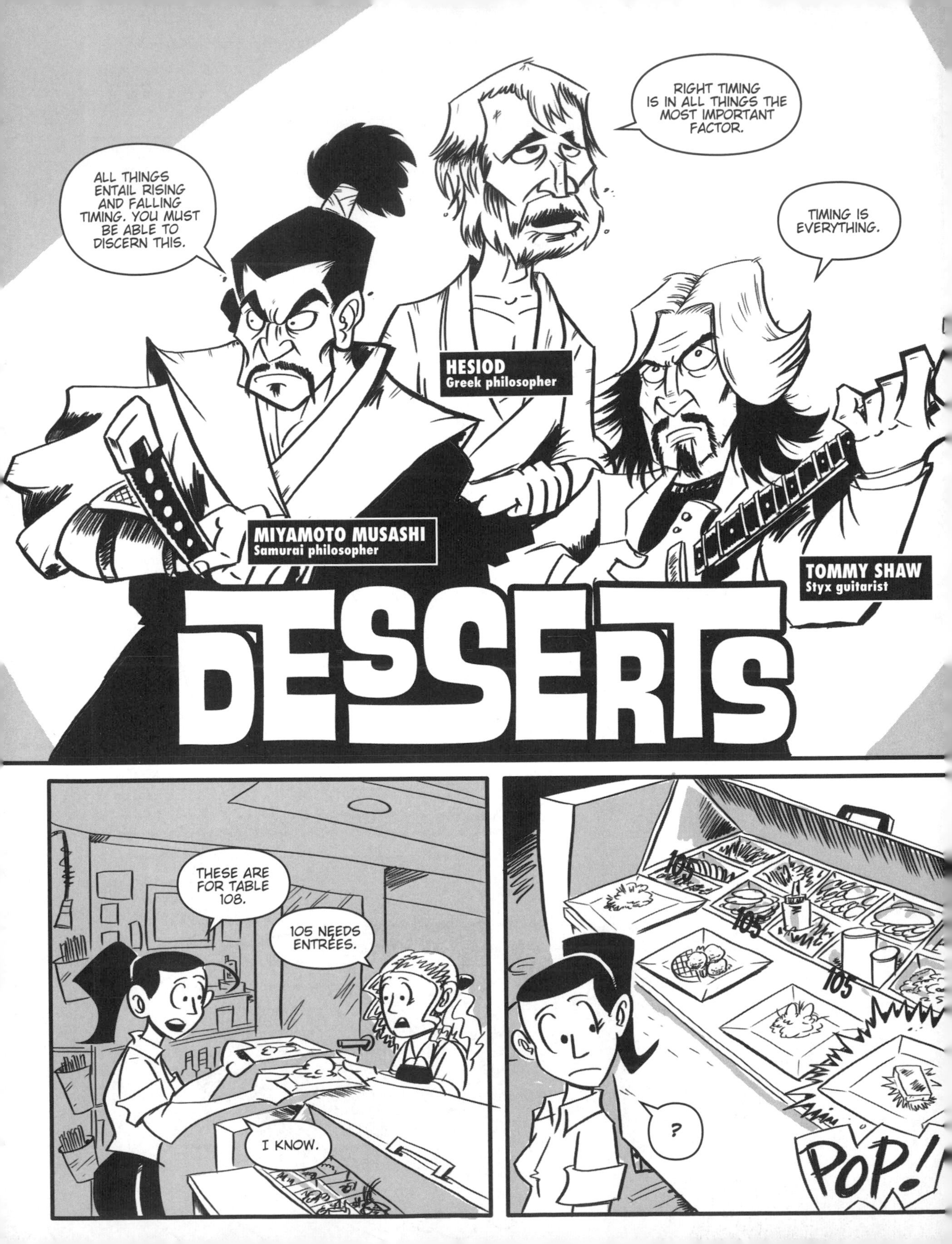
ALL THINGS ENTAIL RISING AND FALLING TIMING. YOU MUST BE ABLE TO DISCERN THIS.
MIYAMOTO MUSASHI Samurai philosopher
RIGHT TIMING IS IN ALL THINGS THE MOST IMPORTANT FACTOR.
HESIOD Greek philosopher
TIMING IS EVERYTHING.
TOMMY SHAW Styx guitarist
DESSERTS
THESE ARE FOR TABLE 108.
105 NEEDS ENTRÉES.
I KNOW.
105
105
105
?
POP!

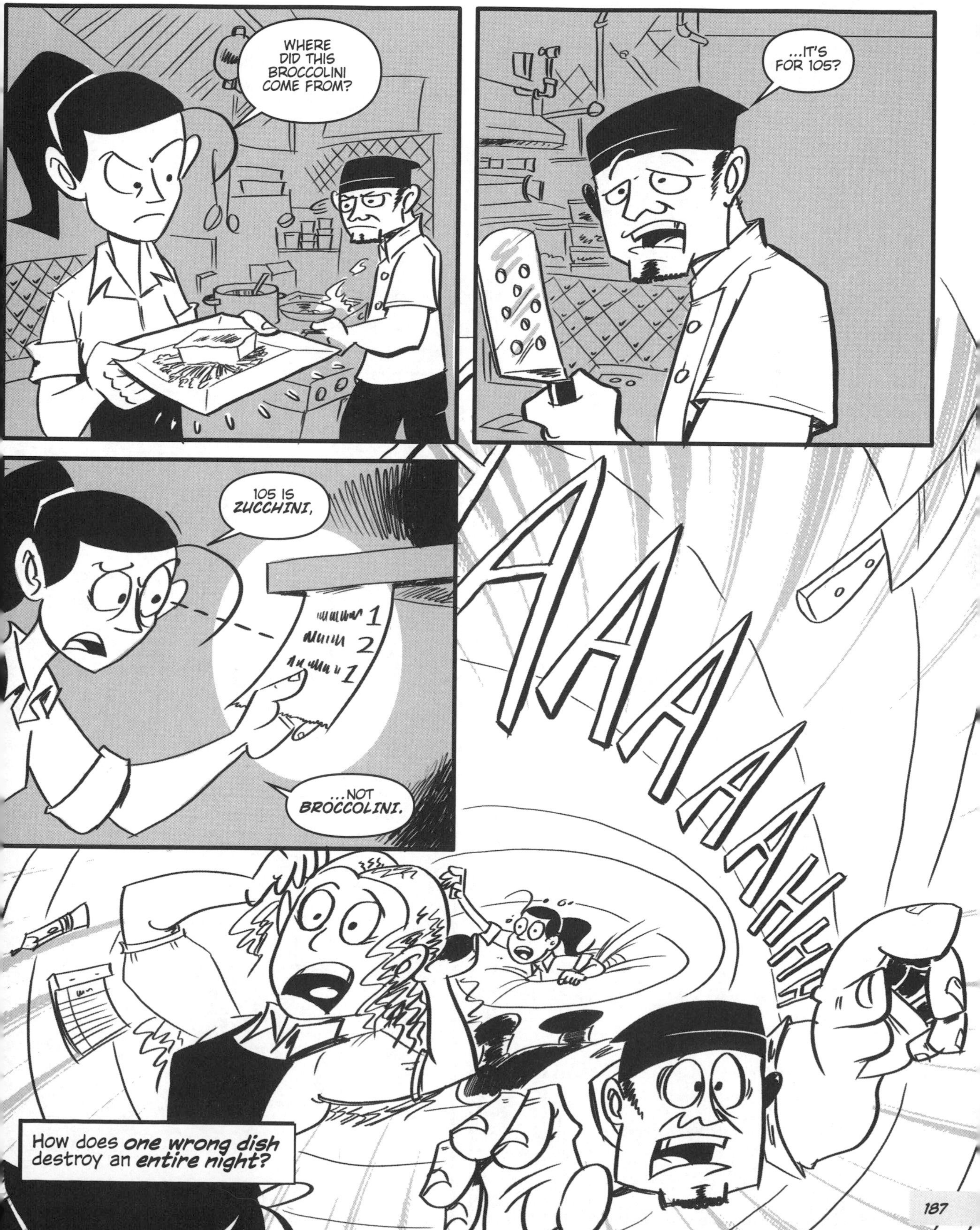
WHERE DID THIS BROCCOLINI COME FROM?
...IT'S FOR 105?
105 IS ZUCCHINI,
...NOT BROCCOLINI.
AAAAAAHHHHH
How does one wrong dish destroy an entire night?

By the time we've replaced the broccolini with zucchini, the other three dishes have to be fired again because they're *cold*.

HEY, DUDES! SORRY TO MAKE YOU WAIT.

Which pushes table 105 back by *20 minutes.*

HEY, DUDES! WHERE'S OUR FOOD?

Which pushes back the orders that were going to be fired right after 105.

Which means 105 isn't finished until 9:20 p.m. and the people who had a 9 p.m. reservation are *not* happy.

And while we struggle to fire tables that are late, the tables we already fired go *neglected.*

I DON'T EVEN WANT DESSERT ANYMORE.

I HOPE THIS PLACE EXPLODES.

One timing mistake starts a chain of dominoes falling that will eventually destroy the entire night.

Dirt Candy has nine tables and they each need to turn *three times* in one night if I'm going to make any money. So reservations are like a game of *Tetris*.

8:30
8:00
7:30
7:00
6:30
6:00
5:30
5:00

Each table gets two hours to eat. Their order is taken at 15 minutes. They should get their entrées at one hour.

Dessert menus go down at 90 minutes. One mistake at the beginning will screw up the entire night.

Working in a kitchen is all about the timing. The formula is simple.

[INGREDIENTS + TECHNIQUE] x TIMING = SUCCESS!

LIMP

Salad dressed too early.

GLUEY

Grits go down too early.

FALL APART

Over-steamed carrot buns.

BURNT

Green sauce overcooked.

MELTED

Ice cream goes down too early.

SOGGY

Waffles sauced too early.

On a good night, it's like a *ballet*.

On a bad night, it turns into a *brawl*.

There's only one way to learn the kitchen ballet...

...experience.

After 9/11 the restaurant business crashed. I landed a job at an upscale diner in Harlem. On my first day of work I showed up at 8 a.m. for a 10 a.m. breakfast shift. I was all alone.

HELLO? *HELLO?*

As the minutes ticked by and 10 a.m. crept closer I realized no one else was coming. Except *customers*.

I was going to have to make dishes I'd never seen before. I asked the bartender to describe them to me.

WHAT'S A "SPANISH HARLEM OMELET"? WHAT THE HELL DOES IT LOOK LIKE?!?!

Eventually Cliff, the line cook, showed up. He was the angriest Rastafarian on the planet. He would be my Yoda.

SHOULDN'T HAVE TO PUT UP WITH THIS SHIT NO ONE SHOULD HAVE TO PUT UP WITH THIS GARBAGE I HATE THIS PLACE GET YOUR STATION READY ALWAYS TALKING DOWN TO ME BACK HOME NO ONE TREATS ME LIKE THIS AND.

Later, Cliff and I did almost 180 covers every night. But when the tickets started coming in that first day, I was overwhelmed.

I realized that lots of these tickets needed **fries**, and so I started throwing them in the basket.

FRIES

FRIES

FRIES

I had no timing. I had too many orders going at once and all my fries were either too early--and got cold--or too late, and the mains got cold.

STOP. **THINK.** LOOK AT THE TICKET **IN FRONT** OF YOU. NOT ALL THE OTHER TICKETS.

LEARN *YOUR* **TIMING.**

My brain evolved. Orders of fries went in **one at a time,** but timed so they were ready when Cliff had finished the rest of the order.

I was learning the Kitchen Ballet.

- Plate bread, onions, tomatoes, lettuce
- Drop one order chicken wings
- Cliff 60 seconds from having proteins ready
- Drop two orders fries
- Get chili bowl, give to Cliff
- Proteins plated
- Plate two orders fries
- Cliff cutting chicken, get rice and beans on plate
- Burger order out
- Chicken order out
- Chicken wings plated
- Plate bread, onions, tomatoes, lettuce
- Cliff 60 seconds from having protein ready
- Drop one order fries

It's *Chef ESP* --the second someone needs something you already have it for them. You're attuned to their every movement.

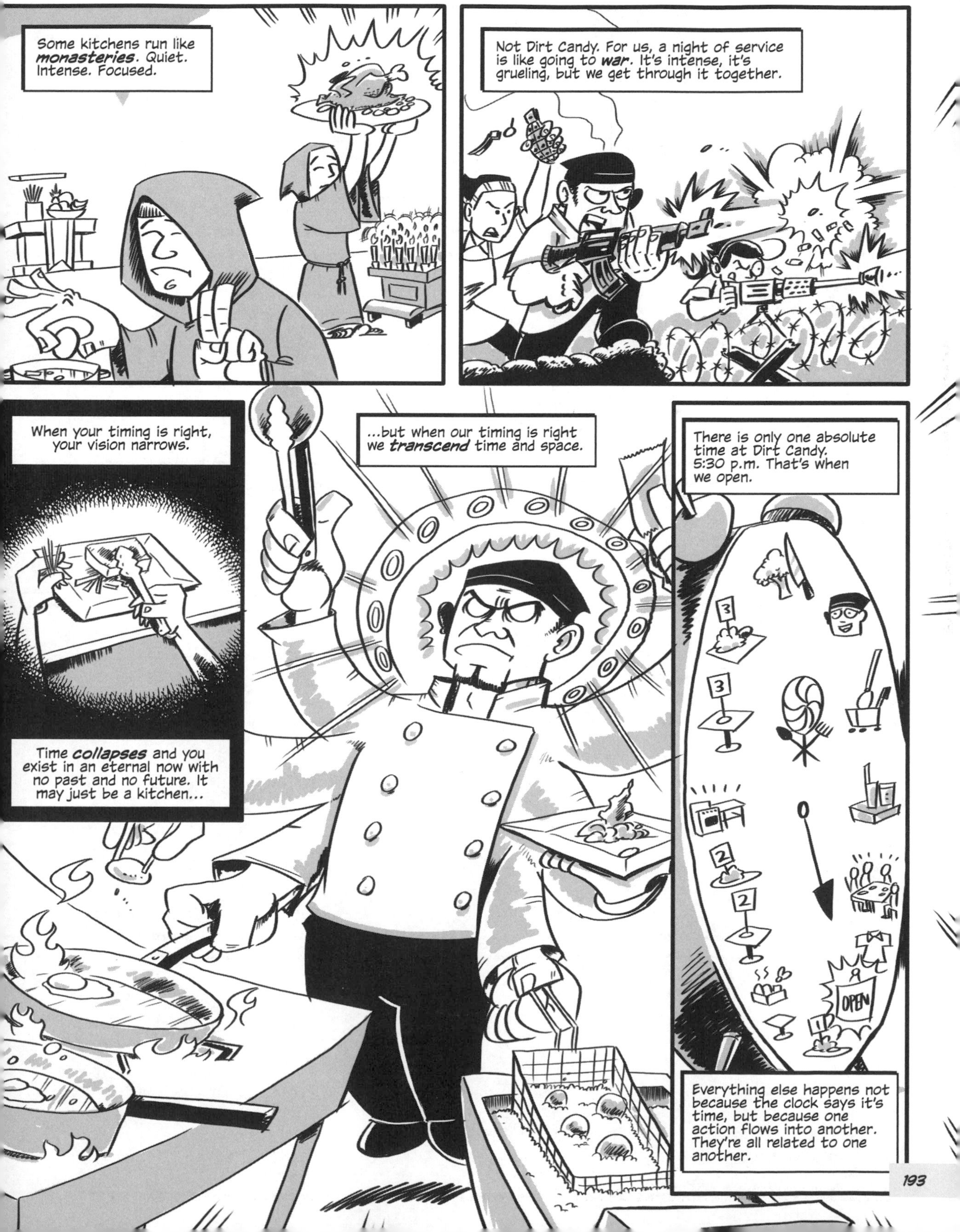
Some kitchens run like ***monasteries***. Quiet. Intense. Focused.
Not Dirt Candy. For us, a night of service is like going to ***war***. It's intense, it's grueling, but we get through it together.
When your timing is right, your vision narrows.
Time ***collapses*** and you exist in an eternal now with no past and no future. It may just be a kitchen...
...but when our timing is right we ***transcend*** time and space.
There is only one absolute time at Dirt Candy. 5:30 p.m. That's when we open.
3
3
2
2
OPEN
Everything else happens not because the clock says it's time, but because one action flows into another. They're all related to one another.

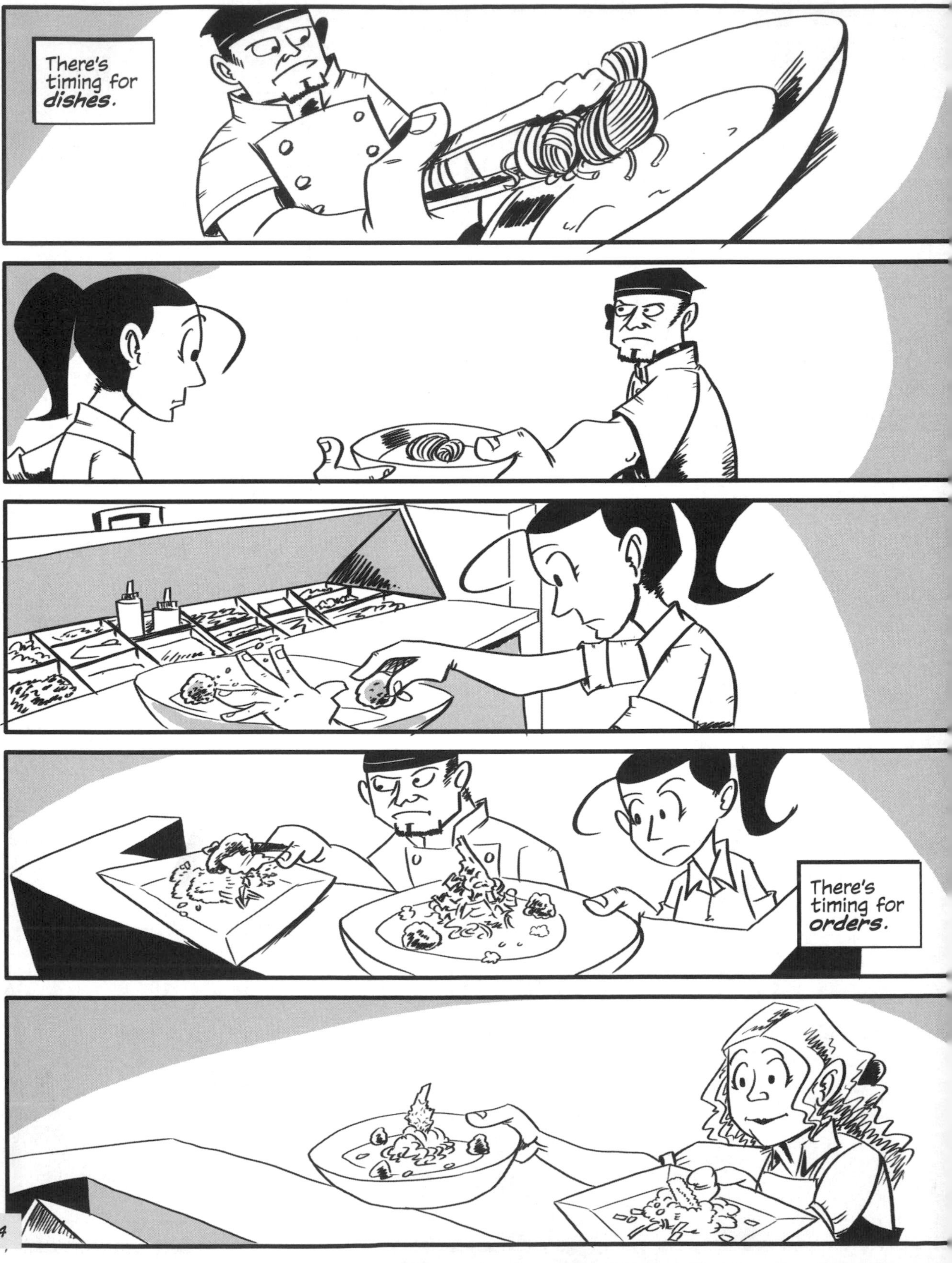
There's timing for *dishes*.
There's timing for *orders*.

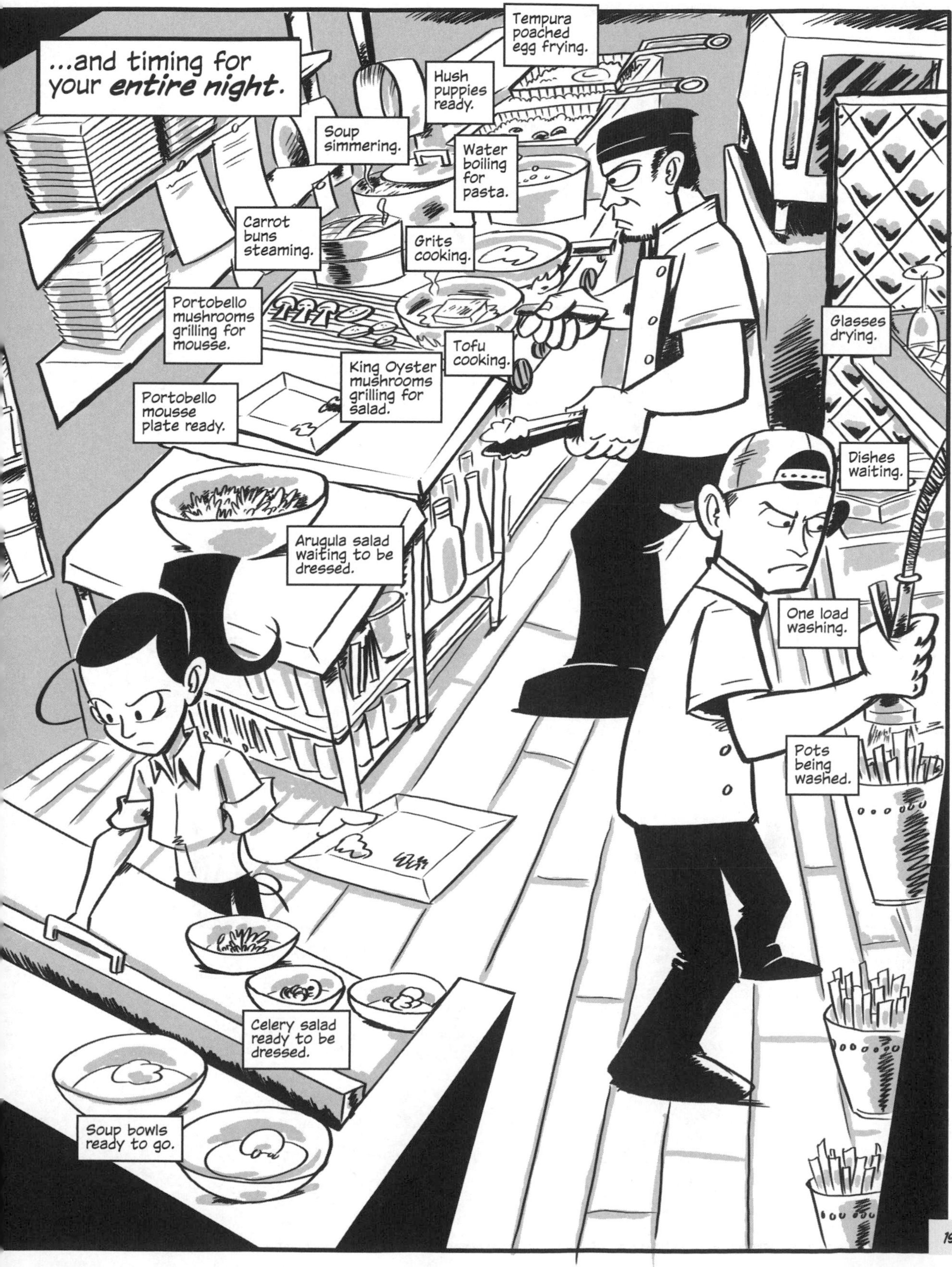

...and timing for your ***entire night***.
Tempura poached egg frying.
Hush puppies ready.
Soup simmering.
Water boiling for pasta.
Carrot buns steaming.
Grits cooking.
Portobello mushrooms grilling for mousse.
Tofu cooking.
King Oyster mushrooms grilling for salad.
Glasses drying.
Portobello mousse plate ready.
Dishes waiting.
Arugula salad waiting to be dressed.
One load washing.
Pots being washed.
Celery salad ready to be dressed.
Soup bowls ready to go.

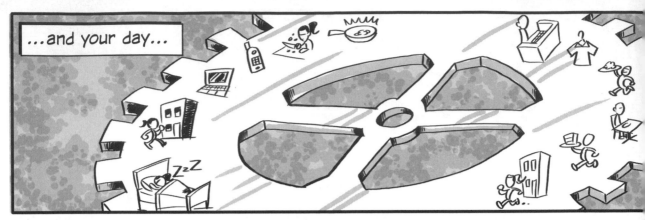

...and your day...

...and your week...

...and your month...

...and your year.

And for your entire life.

And then the lives...

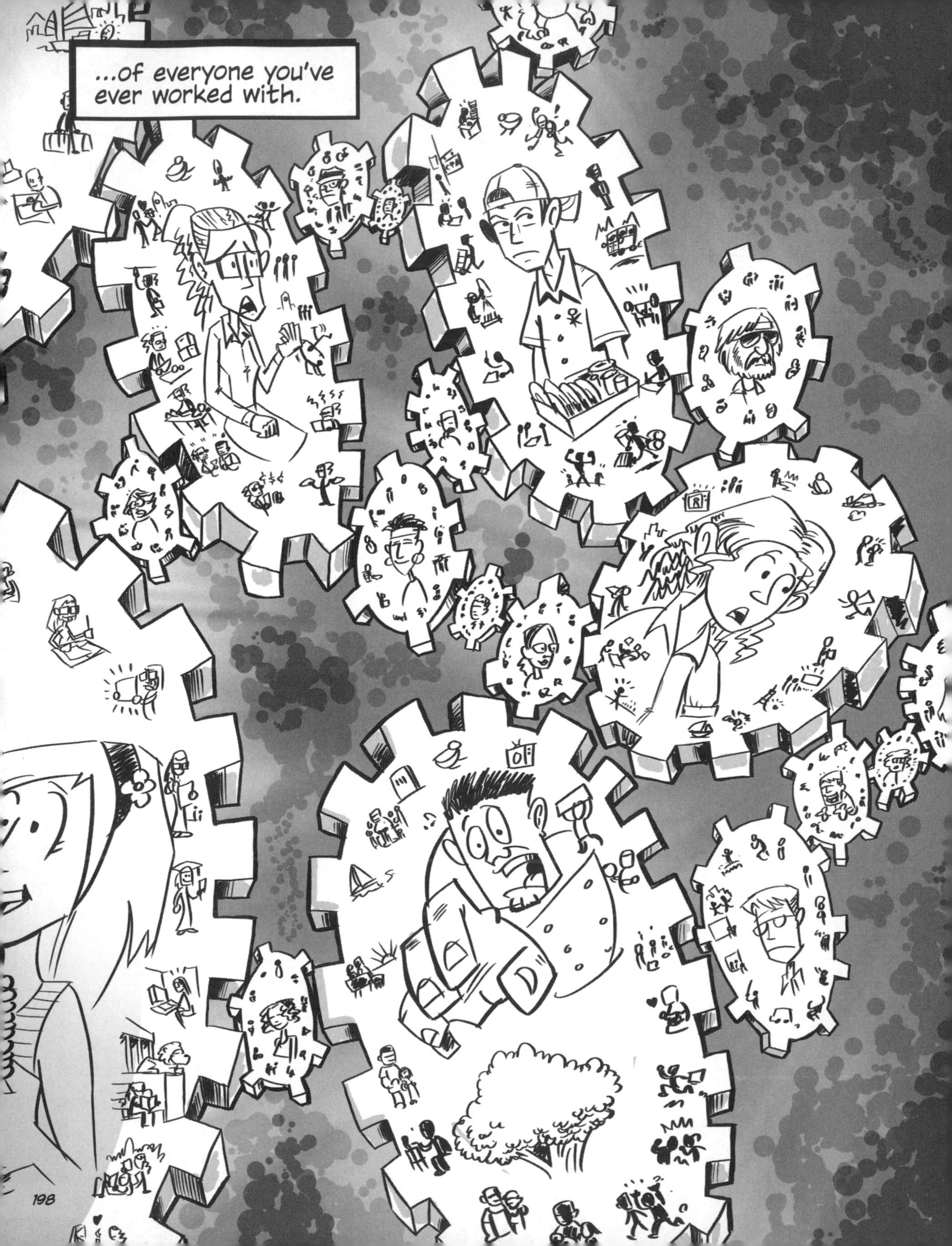
...of everyone you've ever worked with.

From cradle to grave, from sunup to sundown, from moment to moment, it's all about *timing*.

CANDIED GRAPEFRUIT POPS

MAKES 10 POPS

1 large grapefruit
3 cups sugar

Candied orange segments are a traditional Chinese street food, with the sweetness of the sugar balancing the tartness of the citrus. This riff on that idea was originally designed to accompany Fennel Salad (page 79) but people inhaled them on their own, so here they are as a stand-alone recipe.

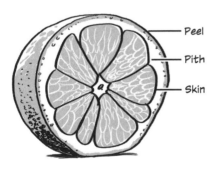

Peel
Pith
Skin

1. Peel the grapefruit and separate into individual segments.

2. Push the skewers through the bottom of the grapefruit segments until they're about halfway in.

3. Put the sugar and ½ cup water into a heavy-bottomed pot over medium heat. Cover and cook until the syrup is 275° to 300°F (covered because you want steam). It takes about 20 minutes to dissolve and form a syrup. **Do not stir** during this process.

4. Dip the skewered grapefruit pieces into the hot syrup one at a time, coating each piece thoroughly. Make sure the grapefruit isn't too wet or the sugar won't stick. This is a great way to get third-degree burns, so be **really careful** with the molten sugar.

5. Stick the skewers into a piece of foam and let the grapefruit stand and dry until a hard shell forms. Use immediately. These do not keep for more than a couple of hours.

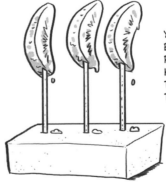

YOU'LL NEED TEN 8-INCH BAMBOO SKEWERS AND A PIECE OF FLORAL FOAM OR HEAVY STYROFOAM TO HOLD THE SKEWERS UPRIGHT WHILE THE GRAPEFRUIT DRIES.

POPCORN PUDDING

WITH CARAMEL POPCORN

SERVES 4 TO 6

- 1 tablespoon canola oil
- ¼ cup popcorn kernels
- 4 cups whole milk
- 1 cup fresh or frozen corn kernels
- 2 extra-large eggs
- ¾ cup plus 2 tablespoons sugar
- ¼ cup plus 3 tablespoons cornstarch
- ¼ fresh vanilla bean, split and scraped
- ½ cup (1 stick) unsalted butter
- 2 cups Caramel Popcorn (page 202)

My friend Debbie Lee was the pastry chef when Dirt Candy opened. The dessert menu has morphed a million times since then, but her Popcorn Pudding has survived every incarnation for three years. It's just that popular. For the best results, pour Caramel Popcorn onto the pudding and eat it that way.

 TO MAKE IT VEGAN

Replace the milk with soy milk and the butter with Earth Balance. Skip step 2 and the first sentence of step 3, and instead just whisk the sugar and cornstarch together and then whisk into the popcorn milk. Also, in step 5, the mixture needs to cook for only 5 minutes.

1. In a large pot over medium heat, pop the popcorn in the oil. Add the milk and corn to the pot, and simmer over low heat for 30 minutes.

2. Beat the eggs, then remove a quarter of the mixture (approximately 1 tablespoon) and discard it. In a separate bowl, whisk the sugar with the cornstarch. Add the eggs and whisk until incorporated.

3. *Very, very slowly* pour the popcorn milk into the sugar-and-egg mixture, stirring constantly. Pour the mixture back into the saucepan, stirring constantly, over medium heat until the mixture reaches 165°F, about 8 minutes.

4. Add the vanilla bean seeds and butter to the milk, stirring continually until the back of the spoon is thickly coated or the temperature reaches 185°F, about 10 minutes.

5. Remove from the heat and push through a chinois (page 23). Cool to room temperature and then cover and put in the fridge until cold.

6. *To serve:*

1 cup of Popcorn Pudding per person.

It's hard to measure Caramel Popcorn because of the shape, but you're trying to give ¼ cup to each person.

CARAMEL POPCORN

MAKES 5 CUPS

Nonstick cooking spray, optional
1 tablespoon canola oil
¼ cup popcorn kernels
¼ cup unsalted butter
¾ cup packed light brown sugar
¼ cup corn syrup
¼ teaspoon vanilla extract
¼ teaspoon baking soda
¼ teaspoon fine salt
⅛ teaspoon fleur de sel or any coarse salt

 **TO MAKE IT VEGAN**

Replace the butter with Earth Balance and leave out the salt.

1. Spray a baking sheet with nonstick spray or line with a Silpat liner.

2. In a large pot over medium heat, pop the popcorn in the oil. Discard any unpopped kernels.

3. In a small pot over low heat, bring the butter, sugar, and corn syrup to a boil. Do not stir. Cook until the mixture reaches 300°F, about 15 minutes. Remove from the heat immediately and stir in the vanilla extract, baking soda, and fine salt. Pour the syrup over the popcorn. Stir until well mixed.

4. Spread the mixture onto the baking sheet or Silpat with a spatula. It will cool very, very fast, so spread it to the edges of the baking tray as quickly as possible. It doesn't have to be even. While still warm, sprinkle the fleur de sel over the popcorn.

5. Let cool completely and break into pieces. Store in a covered container for up to 1 week.

PEANUT BRITTLE

MAKES 1½ CUPS

Nonstick cooking spray, optional
½ cup (1 stick) unsalted butter
½ cup plus 1 teaspoon sugar
⅓ cup plus 1 tablespoon chopped roasted unsalted peanuts
Pinch of fleur de sel or other coarse salt

1. Spray a baking tray with nonstick spray or line with a Silpat liner.

2. In a small pot over medium heat, whisk the butter and sugar very quickly until the mixture turns golden brown and reaches 300°F, about 10 minutes.

3. Stir in the peanuts to coat, then quickly pour the mixture onto the tray. Using a spatula, spread the mixture in a ¼-inch-thick layer. Sprinkle with fleur de sel. While warm, score with a knife to mark where you will cut.

4. When the brittle is cool, gently cut into pieces. Store in a covered container for up to 4 days.

BEET CARAMEL

MAKES ¾ CUP

2 cups chopped peeled red beets
½ cup plus 2 tablespoons sugar

I serve this with Molten Beet Cake (page 210), but beets and chocolate ice cream are a rich, earthy combo. Also try it with vanilla ice cream, which highlights the taste of beets.

1. Juice the beets to yield ½ cup beet juice.

2. In a small pot over low heat, melt the sugar in the beet juice and cook until the temperature reaches 225°F, about 8 minutes. Do not stir until sugar is dissolved. It won't be very thick, but should stick to a spoon.

3. Remove from the heat and let cool to room temperature. Use now or cover and store in the fridge for up to 2 weeks. Reheat gently over very low heat when ready to serve.

CINNAMON CARAMEL

MAKES ½ CUP

½ cup sugar
½ cup heavy cream
¼ teaspoon vanilla extract
½ teaspoon ground cinnamon

This method of melting sugar is different from what I use in other recipes because this is a true caramel: darker, richer, and thicker than my other caramel recipes, which make something between a sauce and a syrup.

1. Dissolve the sugar and 3 tablespoons water in a small pot over low heat. Cover and cook for 6 minutes. Do not stir.

2. Turn the heat up to medium and remove the cover. Let the mixture boil until the sugar reaches 225°F, 5 to 7 minutes.

3. Remove the pan from the heat and slowly add the cream, vanilla, and cinnamon. Be careful of splattering. Cook over medium heat until the sauce is smooth and thick and the temperature is 210°F, 4 to 6 minutes.

4. Remove from the heat and let cool to room temperature. Use now or cover and store in the fridge for up to 2 weeks. Reheat over very low heat when ready to serve.

ZUCCHINI GINGER CAKE

WITH ZUCCHINI CREAM AND ZUCCHINI CANDY

| ZUCCHINI GINGER CAKE | ZUCCHINI CREAM | ZUCCHINI CANDY | CINNAMON CARAMEL (OPTIONAL) page 203 | CREAM CHEESE ICE CREAM (OPTIONAL) page 216 |

SERVES 8

ZUCCHINI CANDY

- 2 cups finely chopped seeded zucchini
- ¾ cup packed light brown sugar

ZUCCHINI GINGER CAKE

- 1 cup (2 sticks) unsalted butter
- 2 cups sugar
- 4 extra-large eggs
- 2½ cups plus 2 tablespoons unbleached all-purpose flour
- 6 tablespoons cornstarch
- 1 tablespoon baking powder
- 2 teaspoons ground ginger
- ½ teaspoon salt
- 1 cup whole milk
- 2 tablespoons grated peeled fresh ginger
- 1¼ teaspoons vanilla extract

ZUCCHINI CREAM

- 1 cup heavy cream
- 1 tablespoon sifted powdered sugar
- 1 teaspoon vanilla

1. To make the zucchini candy: Blanch the zucchini (page 19) until very soft, about 5 minutes. Drain.

2. In a small pot, combine the sugar and ¾ cup water and bring to a boil over medium heat. Turn the heat to low, add the zucchini, and cook for 15 minutes. Drain and place the zucchini on a baking tray lined with a Silpat liner.

3. Turn the oven to dehydrating temperature (page 21) and dehydrate the zucchini until there is no moisture left, about 4 hours. From here on out, check every 15 minutes until the zucchini is crunchy. This might take up to another hour. Remove from the oven and let cool completely.

4. Pulse the zucchini in a blender until broken up into pieces approximately the size of Nerds candy. Store in an airtight container in a cool, dry place for up to 2 weeks.

5. To make the cake: Preheat the oven to 350°F. Grease a 9 × 13-inch baking pan.

6. Beat the butter and sugar in a mixer with the paddle attachment on high speed until fluffy, about 5 minutes. Add the eggs one at a time, mixing well after each addition. This is the batter base.

7. Sift the flour, cornstarch, baking powder, ginger, and salt into a bowl. ***These are the dries.***

8. In a separate bowl, whisk the milk, grated ginger, and vanilla together. ***These are the wets.***

9. Add half the dries to the batter base. Beat for 10 seconds, starting on low speed and moving to high.

10. Add half the wets to the batter base and beat for 10 more seconds.

11. Using a spatula, turn over the mixture, making sure to scrape the bottom of the bowl.

12. Repeat steps 9 through 11, first with half of the remaining dry ingredients, and then with all the rest of the wet. Mix in the remaining dry ingredients.

13. Pour the batter into the prepared pan and bake until a toothpick or knife inserted in the center of the cake comes out clean, 25 to 35 minutes. Cool the cake in its pan for about 15 minutes. Turn the cake out of the pan and let cool completely.

14. *To make the zucchini cream:* In a mixer on high, beat the heavy cream for about 2 minutes, until it starts to thicken. Add the sugar and vanilla and beat until fluffy, about 1 minute.

15. Gently fold in ¼ cup of the zucchini candy.

FOR THIS STEP AND THE NEXT FEW STEPS, DO NOT OVERBEAT. YOU ARE NOT BEATING TO FULLY INCORPORATE THE INGREDIENTS, JUST TO GENTLY MIX THEM.

RECIPE CONTINUES ➡

16.

Using a 3-inch ring mold or a clean, open can, punch 8 rounds out of the sheet cake.

17.

Cut each round in half horizontally to make 2 layers. Spread 2 tablespoons cream on each of 8 bottom layers.

18. To serve:

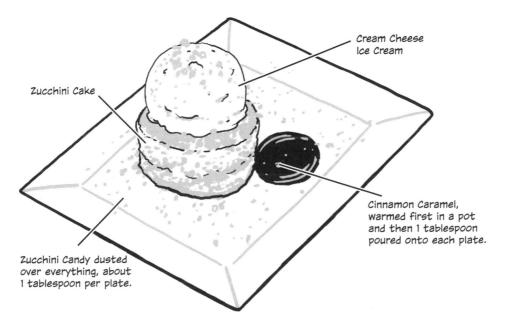

Cream Cheese Ice Cream

Zucchini Cake

Cinnamon Caramel, warmed first in a pot and then 1 tablespoon poured onto each plate.

Zucchini Candy dusted over everything, about 1 tablespoon per plate.

RED PEPPER VELVET CAKE
WITH PEANUT BRITTLE AND PEANUT ICE CREAM

 +  **+** **+**

| RED PEPPER VELVET CAKE | ¼ CUP RED PEPPER JAM page 42 | PEANUT BRITTLE (OPTIONAL) page 202 | PEANUT ICE CREAM (OPTIONAL) page 217 |

SERVES 10 TO 12

RED PEPPER VELVET CAKE

- **4 red bell peppers, seeded and cored**
- **¾ cups sugar**
- **½ cup (1 stick) unsalted butter**
- **2 extra-large eggs**
- **2 cups plus ½ tablespoon cake flour**
- **1½ teaspoons baking powder**
- **½ teaspoon baking soda**
- **¼ teaspoon salt**
- **½ cup plus 2 tablespoons buttermilk**
- **½ teaspoon vanilla extract**

ICING

- **3 cups white chocolate pieces**
- **1½ cups cream cheese (12 ounces), at room temperature**
- **1 cup unsalted butter (2 sticks), at room temperature**
- **Grated zest of 1 lemon**
- **1½ cups powdered sugar, sifted**

This is a play on red velvet cake and it's insanely flexible: you can make it with orange peppers, yellow peppers, or even beets.

1. To make the cake: Juice the red peppers in a juicer and refrigerate the juice. Spread the pulp on a baking sheet lined with a Silpat liner, turn the oven to dehydrating temperature (page 21), and dehydrate the pulp for 8 hours or until dry. Let cool.

2. Blend about half of the dehydrated pulp in a blender to make about 2 tablespoons powder. You need only 1 tablespoon for this recipe, but it's impossible to blend less; save the rest for the next time you make this cake. In a food processor, pulse the other half into flakes for use as a garnish. Set aside.

3. Measure the juice; you should have about 4 cups. In a pot over medium heat, reduce it to 1 cup, about 40 minutes.

4. Preheat the oven to 325°F. Line two 8-inch square baking pans with Silpat liners.

5. Beat the sugar, butter, and 1 tablespoon red pepper powder in a mixer with the paddle attachment on high until extremely fluffy, about 5 minutes. Add the eggs one at a time, beating well after each addition. This is the **batter base.**

6. In a bowl, sift the cake flour, and then mix in the baking powder, baking soda, and salt. These are the **dries.**

RECIPE CONTINUES →

7. In another bowl, whisk together the buttermilk, 6 tablespoons of the red pepper juice, and vanilla extract. These are the **wets.**

FOR STEPS 7 THROUGH 11, DO NOT OVERBEAT. YOU'RE BEATING TO GENTLY MIX THE INGREDIENTS, NOT TO FULLY INCORPORATE THEM.

8. Add half the dry ingredients to the batter base. Beat for 10 seconds, starting on low speed and moving to high.

9. Add half the wet ingredients to the batter base and beat for 10 more seconds.

10. Using a spatula, turn over the mixture, making sure to scrape the bottom of the bowl.

11. Repeat steps 8 through 10, first with half of the remaining dry ingredients and then with all the rest of the wet. Mix in the remaining dry ingredients.

12. Pour the batter into the prepared pans and bake until a toothpick or knife inserted in the center of the cake comes out clean, 25 to 35 minutes. Cool the cake in the pan for about 15 minutes. Turn the cake out of the pan and let cool completely.

13. ────────────────

To make the icing: Bring a small pot of water to a simmer and place a heat resistant bowl over it so that its bottom doesn't touch the water (or use a double boiler).

14. ────────────────

In the bowl, melt the white chocolate and let cool to room temperature.

15. In a mixer, beat the cream cheese until fluffy, about 1 minute. Add the butter and beat until fully incorporated, about 2 minutes. Add the lemon zest and powdered sugar and beat until fully incorporated, about 1 minute.

16. Turn the mixer to low and slowly stream in the melted chocolate. Gradually increase the speed to high and beat until fluffy.

17. Spread the ¼ cup Red Pepper Jam on the bottom layer (this helps to keep it moist). Refrigerate for 10 minutes. Spread half of the icing on top of the jam. Refrigerate for 30 minutes.

18. —

Gently place the top layer of the cake on top of the iced bottom layer. Spread the remaining icing on the top layer and sides of the cake.

Garnish with the red pepper flakes...

...and cut into individual portions.

19. To serve:

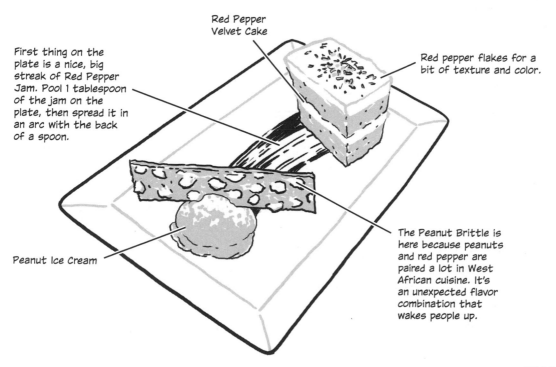

Red Pepper Velvet Cake

First thing on the plate is a nice, big streak of Red Pepper Jam. Pool 1 tablespoon of the jam on the plate, then spread it in an arc with the back of a spoon.

Red pepper flakes for a bit of texture and color.

Peanut Ice Cream

The Peanut Brittle is here because peanuts and red pepper are paired a lot in West African cuisine. It's an unexpected flavor combination that wakes people up.

MOLTEN BEET CAKE

WITH ROASTED PEAR SORBET AND PEAR AND BEET LEATHER

 +  **+** **+**

MOLTEN BEET CAKE	PEAR AND BEET LEATHER (OPTIONAL) page 105	ROASTED PEAR SORBET (OPTIONAL) page 216	BEET CARAMEL (OPTIONAL) page 203

SERVES 4

- 1 medium beet
- Nonstick spray
- 6 tablespoons unsalted butter
- 3 ounces bittersweet chocolate, chopped (½ cup)
- 2 extra-large eggs
- 2 egg yolks
- ¼ cup sugar
- 2 teaspoons unbleached all-purpose flour

1. Preheat the oven to 375°F.

2. Roast the beet until fork-tender, about 1 hour. Peel, chop, and then puree in a blender until smooth. Reserve 2 ounces (2 tablespoons + 2 teaspoons) and save the rest for another use.

3. Turn the oven up to 400°F. Spray four 3½-ounce ramekins with nonstick spray. Have ready four 1 to 1½-inch ring molds and spray them, too.

4. Bring a medium pot of water to a simmer and place a heat-resistant bowl over it so that its bottom doesn't touch the water (or use a double boiler; see page 208). Melt the butter and chocolate in the bowl and stir until they are incorporated. Let cool to room temperature.

5. Beat together the eggs, yolks, and sugar in a mixer with the paddle attachment until thick and creamy, about 2 minutes. Remove 1½ ounces (½ cup) and mix with the reserved pureed beet. Transfer this beet filling to a pastry bag with an ⅛-inch round tip or a resealable bag with one corner cut off; set aside.

6. Add the melted chocolate to the remaining egg-and-sugar mixture and beat in the flour until combined. ***Do not overmix.*** Put this cake batter in a separate pastry bag.

7. Cover the bottom of the ramekins with a thin layer of the cake batter. Place a ring mold in the middle of each ramekin and fill the rings halfway up with the beet filling (about 1 tablespoon per ring).

8. Fill the ramekins around the outside of the rings three quarters full with the cake batter, and then fill up the rings another quarter with cake batter. The level of the batter in the rings should be the same as the level of the batter in the ramekins. Pull out the rings. Refrigerate until ready to bake and serve.

9. Bake until the sides are set but the centers are quite soft, 5 to 6 minutes. Gently invert each cake onto one of four small plates; be careful not to tip it sideways or the filling will fall out.

10. To serve:

Molten Beet Cake

Roasted Pear Sorbet

Pear and Beet Fruit Leather cut into circles, strips, or folded swanky.

Dot 1½ teaspoons of Beet Caramel on each plate. Or streak it. Or drizzle.

 *VARIATION*

VEGAN MOLTEN BEET CAKE

SERVES 4

- 1 **medium beet**
  Nonstick spray
- 1 **tablespoon cornstarch**
- ½ **cup plus 2 tablespoons soy milk**
- 6 **tablespoons canola oil**
- 4 **tablespoons maple syrup**
- ½ **teaspoon vanilla extract**
- ¾ **cup cake flour**
- 6 **tablespoons Dutch-processed unsweetened cocoa powder**
- 6 **tablespoons sugar**
- ¾ **teaspoon baking powder**
  Pinch of salt

1. Follow steps 1 through 3, opposite, reserving ⅓ cup of the beet puree.

2. In a bowl, mix together the beet puree, cornstarch, and 2 tablespoons of the soy milk. Transfer this beet filling to a pastry bag and set aside.

3. In a bowl, mix together the oil, maple syrup, remaining ½ cup soy milk, and the vanilla.

4. In a separate, large bowl, sift together the cake flour, cocoa, sugar, baking powder, and salt.

5. Fold the oil mixture into the flour mixture. Transfer this cake batter to a pastry bag.

6. Follow steps 7 through 9 above to fill the molds.

7. Bake for 6 to 8 minutes.

FENNEL FUNNEL CAKES

WITH MANGO FENNEL AND CHOCOLATE SORBET

 **+**  **+** **+**

FENNEL FUNNEL CAKES | MANGO-FENNEL SALAD (OPTIONAL) | MANGO-FENNEL SORBET (OPTIONAL) page 215 | CHOCOLATE SORBET (OPTIONAL) page 215

SERVES 4

FENNEL FUNNEL CAKES

- 2 tablespoons anise seeds
- 1 extra-large egg
- ⅓ cup whole milk
- 2 tablespoons granulated sugar
- ¾ cup plus 2 tablespoons unbleached all-purpose flour
- ¼ teaspoon salt
- 1 teaspoon baking powder
- 2 cups canola oil
- ¼ cup powdered sugar

MANGO-FENNEL SALAD

- 1 cup small-diced mango
- 1 cup small-diced fennel
- ¼ cup unsalted butter
- ¼ cup sugar
- 2 teaspoons dark rum

 TO MAKE IT VEGAN

For funnel cakes, replace the milk with 1 cup unflavored soy milk and leave out the egg. For the mango-fennel salad, replace the butter with Earth Balance.

---

1. *To make the funnel cakes:* In a dry pan over medium heat, toast the anise seeds until lightly browned, about 4 minutes. Set aside.

2. In a bowl, beat the egg and milk together. These are the **wets.**

3. In another bowl, whisk together the granulated sugar, flour, salt, baking powder, and anise seeds. These are the **dries.**

4. Add the wets to the dries and gently beat by hand until smooth.

5.

Put this batter in a pastry bag with an ⅛-inch round tip. Or put it in a ziplock bag with one corner cut off.

6. In a large pot, heat the oil to 375°F.

7.

Squeeze the batter into the hot oil, making shapes as you go.

It should look like a cross between a carpet beater and a pile of noodles.

This dessert is my ode to carnival food, the new American food trend. Most TV food is carnival food. Fried Twinkies! Giant burritos! Doughnut burgers!

Funnel cakes are the easiest doughnuts on earth: Batter + Hot Oil = Funnel Cakes.

8. Fry for 30 seconds and then flip and fry for another 30 seconds. The cakes should be a *very* light golden brown. Dust with powdered sugar before serving.

9. *To make the mango-fennel salad:*
Combine the mango, fennel, and butter in a pan on medium heat and stir until softened but not quite cooked through, about 2 minutes. Add the sugar and cook, stirring, for about 1 minute. Add the rum and let it cook off, about 2 minutes. Remove from the heat and serve warm.

10. *To serve:*

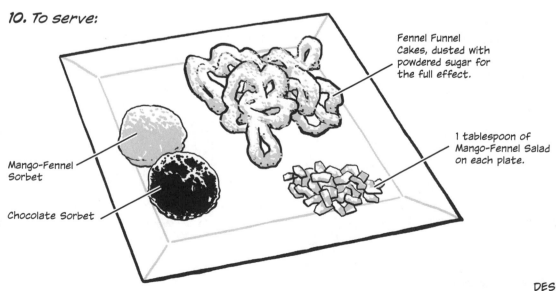

Fennel Funnel Cakes, dusted with powdered sugar for the full effect.

1 tablespoon of Mango-Fennel Salad on each plate.

Mango-Fennel Sorbet

Chocolate Sorbet

ALL DESSERTS SHOULD HAVE ICE CREAM IN THEM. I BELIEVE WITH ALL MY HEART IN THE CLASSIC FORMULA: CAKE + ICE CREAM = DESSERT.

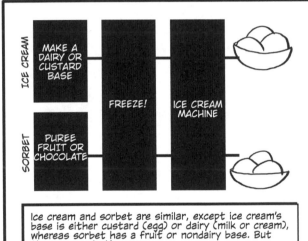

ICE CREAM

MAKE A DAIRY OR CUSTARD BASE

SORBET

PUREE FRUIT OR CHOCOLATE

FREEZE!

ICE CREAM MACHINE

Ice cream and sorbet are similar, except ice cream's base is either custard (egg) or dairy (milk or cream), whereas sorbet has a fruit or nondairy base. But the process is the same.

Whether it's hand-churned or costs $5,000, you need an ice cream machine to make ice cream and sorbet. It's basically a bladeless blender that spins the ice cream to fluff it with air while keeping it frozen.

THESE DESSERTS ARE *COMPLICATED*. SAVE YOURSELF THE HEARTACHE: USE YOUR FAVORITE STORE-BOUGHT ICE CREAM, SORBET, OR FROZEN YOGURT.

The last step is always "Freeze." Here's how:

Pour the base into pint containers, and put them in an ice bath until cool.

Put their lids on and put them in the fridge. You're cooling them slowly so ice chunks don't form.

Then into the freezer!

You're just getting it ready for your ice cream machine, so if it gives you different instructions here: *obey!*

CHOCOLATE SORBET

MAKES ABOUT 2½ CUPS

- ¾ cup Dutch-processed unsweetened cocoa powder
- ½ cup plus 3 tablespoons sugar
- 1½ tablespoons glucose powder
- ¼ teaspoon vanilla extract
- 6 ounces bittersweet chocolate, chopped (1 cup)

1. In a pot, whisk together the cocoa powder, sugar, glucose, vanilla, and 2 cups water. Bring to a boil over high heat, about 10 minutes.

2. Turn off the heat and add the chocolate. Stir until smooth.

3. Freeze in an ice cream machine according to the manufacturer's instructions.

Chocolate sorbet delivers a purer chocolate taste than chocolate ice cream, which muddies the flavor with dairy. This vegan sorbet was developed by Dirt Candy's first (and only) pastry chef, Debbie Lee.

MANGO-FENNEL SORBET

MAKES ABOUT 2½ CUPS

- 4 mangos
- 2 bulbs fennel
- 1¼ cups sugar
- 1 tablespoon fresh lemon juice
- 4 teaspoons rum
- Pinch of salt

1. Peel the mango and dice 2 cups (about 2 mangos). Juice the remaining mango to yield ⅔ cup juice.

2. Dice 1 cup of fennel (about 1 fennel bulb). Juice the remaining fennel to yield ⅓ cup juice.

3. Blend all the ingredients until smooth, about 5 minutes. Push the puree through a chinois to remove any remaining mango or fennel fibers.

4. Freeze in an ice cream machine according to the manufacturer's instructions.

Sorbets are lighter, fresher, and juicier than ice creams. Here the licorice taste of the fennel heightens and balances the sweetness of the mango.

BUY MANGO JUICE AT ANY JUICE BAR.

NO ONE SELLS FENNEL JUICE! MAKE IT YOURSELF!

BROCCOLI ICE CREAM

MAKES ABOUT 3 CUPS

> 1 head broccoli, stem removed, chopped
>
> 8 ounces cream cheese, room temperature
>
> 1 cup whole milk
>
> ¼ cup sugar
>
> ¼ cup sour cream
>
> Pinch of salt
>
> ½ cup heavy cream

VARIATION

CREAM CHEESE ICE CREAM

Proceed as for Broccoli Ice Cream, but omit the broccoli, add 1 teaspoon grated lemon zest, and increase the sugar to ½ cup.

1. Blanch and shock (page 19) the broccoli. Chop it very finely and puree it in a blender for 2 to 4 minutes, until smooth. If the puree is clumping, add a small amount of water to get it moving.

2. Add the cream cheese, milk, sugar, sour cream, and salt and blend until smooth, about 2 minutes.

3. Pour the contents of the blender into a large bowl and slowly fold in the heavy cream using a spatula. Push the mixture through a chinois (page 23) to remove any chunks.

4. Freeze in an ice cream machine according to the manufacturer's instructions.

ROASTED PEAR SORBET

THE DARK BROWN SUGAR MEASUREMENT MUST BE PRECISE OR THIS RECIPE WILL FAIL!

MAKES ABOUT 6 CUPS

> 7 pears
>
> 5.3 ounces dark brown sugar (see Note)
>
> 2½ teaspoons liquid glucose

This accompanies Molten Beet Cake (page 210) at the restaurant, but try it on its own with a garnish of Pear and Beet Leather (page 105).

1. Preheat the oven to 375°F.

2. Wrap the pears in foil, and roast for 45 minutes. Unwrap the pears and peel and chop them, discarding the seeds and core. Measure 4¾ cups of pear.

3. Put the pear in a blender with the brown sugar, liquid glucose, and 1 cup water. Puree until smooth, about 4 minutes. Push through a chinois.

4. Freeze in an ice cream machine according to the manufacturer's instructions.

PEANUT ICE CREAM

MAKES ABOUT 4 CUPS

- 1½ cups shelled peanuts
- 2 cups heavy cream
- ⅔ cup sugar
- Pinch of salt
- 5 large egg yolks
- 8 ounces white chocolate

1. Cover the peanuts with water and let them soak overnight in the fridge.

2. Strain the peanuts and then put them in a blender with 1½ cups fresh water. Blend until creamy, about 3 minutes. Push this peanut milk through a chinois (page 23) to remove chunks.

3. In a medium saucepan on low, heat the peanut milk, 1 cup heavy cream, the sugar, and the salt until the sugar is melted, about 2 minutes. Do not bring to a boil.

4. Beat the egg yolks in a medium-size bowl, then very, very slowly pour the peanut milk mixture into the bowl, stirring constantly. Pour the mixture back into the saucepan, and cook over medium heat, stirring constantly, until it reaches 165°F or coats the spatula, about 8 minutes.

5. Put the white chocolate in a bowl and pour the mixture through a strainer directly into the bowl. Stir until the chocolate has completely melted and the mixture is smooth. Stir in the remaining 1 cup heavy cream.

6. Freeze in an ice cream machine according to the manufacturer's instructions.

TO MAKE PEANUT ICE CREAM YOU NEED TO MAKE PEANUT MILK FIRST. I LIKE IT COMPLICATED!

USE A CANDY THERMOMETER FOR ALL TEMPERATURES! PRECISION!

SWEET PEA AND MINT ICE CREAM

MAKES ABOUT 3 CUPS

- 1 cup whole milk
- ½ cup plus 2 tablespoons sugar
- 1 cup fresh mint leaves
- 1 cup frozen peas, thawed
- 2 cups heavy cream
- 5 egg yolks
- Pinch of salt

This super-powered, intense mint ice cream is absolutely necessary for Nanaimo Bars (opposite).

1. Combine the milk, sugar, and mint leaves in a large saucepan and bring to a simmer over medium heat. As it simmers, stir until the milk starts to turn green, about 3 minutes. Turn off the heat, cover, and let sit for 1 hour.

2. Blanch and shock (page 19) the thawed peas.

3. Push the mint milk through a chinois (page 23). Pour into a blender, add the peas, and blend for 2 minutes. Push through a chinois to get rid of chunks.

4. Put the mixture in a pot on the stove and stir in 1 cup heavy cream. Over medium-low heat, warm the mixture, but make sure it doesn't boil.

5. Beat the egg yolks in a medium-size bowl, then very, very slowly pour the mixture into the bowl, stirring constantly. Pour the mixture back into the pot and add the salt. Cook over medium heat, stirring constantly, until the mixture reaches 165°F and coats the spatula, about 8 minutes. Immediately strain into a bowl containing the remaining 1 cup heavy cream. Stir to blend.

6. Freeze in an ice cream machine according to the manufacturer's instructions.

SWEET PEA AND MINT NANAIMO BAR

FOR CANADIANS LIKE ME, NOTHING SAYS HOME LIKE A NANAIMO (NAH-NIGH-MO) BAR. WHEN I REMEMBER MY CHILDHOOD, I REMEMBER NANAIMO.

NANAIMO BARS ARE JUST COOKIE BARS WITH CUSTARD FILLING, BUT IN CANADA THEY'RE AT EVERY BAKE SALE, BUFFET TABLE, AND BIRTHDAY PARTY.

I'M TRYING TO IMPROVE ON THE CLASSIC NANAIMO BAR BY FILLING IT WITH *ICE CREAM.*

COOKIE BASE + FILLING + CHOCOLATE TOPPING + SWEET PEA AND MINT ICE CREAM
opposite

SERVES 12 TO 16

COOKIE BASE

- ½ cup chopped, sliced almonds
- 2 cups graham cracker crumbs
- ¼ cup Dutch-processed unsweetened cocoa powder
- 1 extra-large egg, beaten
- 10 tablespoons unsalted butter
- 2 tablespoons sugar

1. *To make the cookie base:* Preheat the oven to 350°F and toast the sliced almonds until lightly browned, about 15 minutes. Set aside.

2. In a bowl, mix everything except the butter and sugar until well combined.

3. Put the butter and sugar in a pot over low heat; cook until the sugar is dissolved. Pour over beaten egg and heat until it reaches 165°F. Let cool until lukewarm, then pour into the cracker crumb mixture, and stir to combine until it forms a dough.

RECIPE CONTINUES ➡

4. Line a 9 × 13-inch baking pan with parchment paper. Using an offset spatula, press the dough firmly into the pan to make an even layer along the bottom. Freeze to harden, about 1 hour.

5. *To make the filling:* Combine all the ingredients and beat on medium-high speed in a mixer fitted with the paddle attachment until creamy and incorporated, about 4 minutes. It cannot be overmixed, but there comes a point when it won't incorporate any further.

6. Spread the filling evenly on the frozen cookie base. Put the pan back in the freezer and freeze until the filling is stiff, about 1 hour.

7. Take the ice cream out of the freezer and let it soften. Spread an even layer of ice cream on top of the filling. Return the pan to the freezer until the ice cream hardens, about 1 hour.

8. *To make the topping:* Bring a medium pot of water to a simmer and place a heat-resistant bowl over it so that its bottom doesn't touch the water (or use a double boiler, page 208). Melt the chocolate in the bowl. As it's melting, add the butter and stir to incorporate. Remove from the heat and stir in the cream.

9. Spread the chocolate in a thin layer over the top of the Nanaimo bars. It'll harden quickly so spread it very fast. Put it back in the freezer to firm up.

10. *To serve:* Turn the slab out of the pan by flipping it onto a cutting board chocolate-side up. Use a hot, wet knife to cut into bars. The top layer may crack while cutting, and the layers may separate but that's okay. Just hold it together as you cut.

FILLING

- ½ cup (1 stick) unsalted butter, at room temperature
- 6 tablespoons heavy cream
- ¼ cup vegan vanilla pudding powder
- 1 teaspoon vanilla extract
- 3 cups powdered sugar, sifted
- 3 cups Sweet Pea and Mint Ice Cream (page 218) or store-bought mint ice cream

CHOCOLATE TOPPING

- 2½ ounces bittersweet chocolate, chopped
- ½ teaspoon unsalted butter
- 2 tablespoons heavy cream, at room temperature

CHOCOLATE

ICE CREAM

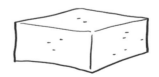

FILLING

COOKIE

MY 5-YEAR-OLD SELF WOULD HAVE THOUGHT IT WAS PRETTY COOL IF SHE'D KNOWN I'D GROW UP TO BE ABLE TO MAKE *NANAIMO BARS.*

YOU CAN MAKE NANAIMO BARS?!

YEP!

HOW'D YOU LEARN THAT?

IT TOOK A LOT OF *TIME,* AND A LOT OF *PEOPLE.*

CAN I HAVE ONE?

First and foremost, this book wouldn't have happened, and Dirt Candy wouldn't have survived, without you, our customers. So to each and every one of you who have eaten here, to all of you who have chosen to celebrate birthdays, anniversaries, graduations, and engagements at Dirt Candy—thank you from the bottom of my heart. It means more to me than you'll ever know.

I'd also like to thank my family, especially my parents, Judi and Mickey Cohen, but also Richard, Jessica, Jen, and Jill, as well as my extended family and my inlaws for all of their support. Glory Mongin taught me a lot of what I know and she and her dad, Stan, were there for me when building Dirt Candy got to be too much. I couldn't have opened without Jesus and Antonio, as well as Debbie Lee, my first pastry chef, and a big thank-you to Craig Kim, who designed Dirt Candy. My lawyers Barbara Kwon and Kevin Hirson have kept me out of trouble more times than I care to remember.

Danielle Ott, Diana Arnold, and Kristen Revier have been the heart and soul of Dirt Candy since it opened, and my thanks to Kristen, especially, who tested every single recipe in this book.

Thanks to my agent, Sharon Bowers, for getting this book sold, to my editor, Rica Allannic, and to Ashley Phillips, Ashley Tucker, Tricia Wygal, and the team at Clarkson Potter for making it happen.

Thanks to Justyna, William, Nin, Sherene, and Vincent, and all the interns who have kept Dirt Candy running over the years. And finally, a huge thank-you to Ryan Dunlavey, for making my lame jokes actually funny, and to Grady Hendrix, the panda to my monkey.

—Amanda Cohen

I would like to thank Amanda and Grady for inviting me along on this awesome project, for their bottomless support and trusting me to do things right; Fred Van Lente for his invaluable insight and friendship throughout this book's production, GB Tran and Monica Gallagher for their eleventh-hour art assist, and biggest thanks of all to Liza, Luke, and Pearl—for *everything.*

—Ryan Dunlavey

INDEX